SharePoint 2010 Consultant's Handbook

A Practical Field Guide

Chris McNulty

Harsha,
Thanks for coming!

Chris

SharePoint 2010 Consultant's Handbook – A Practical Field Guide

First Edition: December 2010
Second Edition: February 2011

ISBN: 1453839216
ISBN13: 978-1453839218

Cover Photo – Sabbaday Falls, New Hampshire, © 2010 Christopher F. McNulty

Contents

Welcome to the new edition of the SharePoint 2010 Consultant's Handbook.

I'm on my second decade with SharePoint now. In the late 1990s, I first heard about Microsoft's new knowledge management tool, code named *Tahoe*. At the time, we were working with Exchange public folders, but were looking to do something web based. I had a side project developing ASP.NET pages to show icons, document and properties from public folders to let users get to Exchange content in their browser. A friend hooked me up with a preview of what became SharePoint Portal Server 2001. That started a long love affair with the platform.

In 2009, when I first started working with SharePoint 2010, I immediately latched onto Managed Metadata Services ("MMS") as a fantastic new set of features for social collaboration and enterprise content management. MMS became one of my most frequently requested presentation topics at conferences and client briefings around the U.S. and online. That led to my first book, the *SharePoint 2010 Consultant's Handbook – A Practical Field Guide to Managed Metadata Services*.

I've gotten tremendous response and interest in the original book, but I had always hoped to pair my original content with comprehensive information about SharePoint. My ongoing writing on my KnowPoint blog (http://www.chrismcnulty.net/blog) and formerly the Microknowledge blog at http://blogs.kma-llc.net/microknowledge have shaped a lot of material. But there are blog posts that don't relate to this book. Most importantly, most of this book is all new – it's a lot more than the first book plus the blog. Plus, there's now an opportunity to include newer topics – such as Office 365, Service Pack 1 and SQL Server 2012 – that didn't exist at SharePoint 2010's launch.

Before I joined Quest Software, I ran the SharePoint practice at KMA – a Microsoft Gold Partner, based outside Boston, that focuses on Microsoft solutions using SQL Server, Office, Project Server, and, of course, SharePoint. KMA was always committed to ongoing staff development through internal training, writing, and collaboration. This book is your chance to share that internal training, and be your own consultant.

Essentially, this material began as a series of guides and blog posts to help our team understand how to design and develop client solutions based on SharePoint 2010. For experienced SharePoint consultants, 2010 offers new capabilities and interfaces. New team members need to absorb our standard base of knowledge quickly. It's helpful for our consultants.

So why should you read this book? In short, it's a great summary of the advice and counsel you might receive onsite from one of our consultants. The SharePoint community has a great commitment to sharing our knowledge and expertise on our websites, blogs, webinars, live events, and conference presentations around the world. This book is a natural extension of those efforts.

Since we were already sharing this information with the community, we wanted to make sure internal teams had the same content. (Besides, coworkers got tired of hearing me say "it's in the blog" over and over!)

So here it is – a much more comprehensive new edition. I'm really proud of it, and I hope you like it! Inside, in addition to everything in the first book, you'll find information about:

- Managing your SharePoint project
- IT Infrastructure, Architecture and Planning
- Installation and Upgrade
- Business Intelligence

- Communities and Social Networking
- Managed Metadata and Enterprise Content Management
- Collaboration
- Custom Development
- Customization and Administration
- Governance and Adoption

So what isn't in here? A lot. This book is not intended to be a comprehensive, soup to nuts compendium of everything that can be done with SharePoint 2010. For example, it's not a deep dive into end user topics, like adding columns to custom lists. Nor do I go too deeply into custom development.   I've left out Project Server, a subject near and dear to my heart. But it's a good road map, I think. In most cases, I'm presenting one or two walkthroughs of how to use a specific feature, module, or interface – but I'm not presenting an exhaustive range of sources for all possible configurations. But there's still a lot of uncharted terrain. I leave that to your exploration.

Anyway, I'm offering it in the hope that you may find it useful to understand SharePoint 2010 the same way as field consultants.

A final note. If you study my background, you'll see that I work for a SharePoint software publisher Quest Software. I've tried to keep my comments and suggestions as neutral as possible.

Many thanks to a large group of people who encouraged and supported me while I wrote this book.   It's a group too numerous to mention, but I must include many colleagues from KMA, especially Sara Clark, Adrian DuCille, Mike Gilronan, David Goldstein, Max Herve, Betsy Johnson, Vadim Maystrovsky, Jorge Rodriguez, Amy Talhouk, Rebecca Tellefsen, Yang Song, Julie Turner, and Sadie Van Buren.   In addition, I've received a lot of feedback and encouragement from a number of Microsoft staff, clients, vendors, and members of the worldwide SharePoint community, including Chris Bortlik, Christian Buckley, Clayton Cobb, Brian Culver, Christophe Fiessinger, Inna

Gordin, Jason Himmelstein, Jim Bob Howard, Michael Hinckley, Becky Isserman, Todd Klindt, Sean McDonough, Barrie Mirman, Michael Mukalian, Joel Oleson, David Rubinstein, Dux Raymond Sy, Erica Toelle, and Fabian Williams. Finally, many thanks to all the other users, conference attendees and online readers who have offered scenarios, questions, suggestions , examples, critiques and other influences on this material.

Finally, as ever, I can't say enough in gratitude for my loving, supportive, patient wife Hayley (and my kids Devin, Nate & Rachel!) They've endured many hours of watching me type away on my laptop or travel for yet another SharePoint event. Once again, Hayley pitched in as adjunct, part time editor and reviewer. I'm not sure that this book is great bedtime reading for preschoolers, but I'm humbled by my family's enthusiasm.

When I was growing up on Long Island, NY, one of my best friends showed me the new time sharing, line printer terminal at his local public library in Dix Hills. (It was the 1970s.) We learned to type BASIC programs, saved to punched tape, for games like Lemonade Stand. A few years later, I progressed to writing Presidential campaign simulation games on the Commodore PET in my 8th grade classroom – now, saved to cassette tape. After that, my brothers and I spent our weekends typing in machine code from magazines, and if we got it 100% correct, it would compile into video games for our Commodore 64. Or, if we were really lucky, one of my high school teachers would take out his Apple II and let us play the text game Adventure.

In that game, you sometime found yourself "in a twisty maze of passages, all alike". Insiders knew the magic word[1] that would sometimes rescue you from being lost. Hopefully, this book can also help get you out of SharePoint's twisty mazes.

---

[1] It was "xyzzy".

SharePoint 2010 Overview

Welcome to SharePoint. SharePoint 2010 is Microsoft's server solution for internal and external web sites, collaboration, data access – wait, that's already a lot! Microsoft groups SharePoint's functions into six major workloads[2]:

- Sites
- Content
- Communities
- Search
- Insights
- Composites

That doesn't begin to describe all the things SharePoint can do. It's the Swiss Army knife of Microsoft server solutions. On an intranet, an extranet, or the public Internet, SharePoint provides:

- Document collaboration with version management
- Content management, record management, information lifecycle management
- Standards-based Web page authoring and versioning
- Data sharing and web access in native lists and external databases
- Forms and workflow
- Business intelligence and reporting
- Lightweight project management
- Browser-hosted Office applications, such as Excel
- Social networking and personalization

It's probably necessary to set the stage by giving some historical context.

---

[2] Often shown in a marketing graphic called the "wheel" or the "pie".

SharePoint was originally released in 2001. The first version was a web-based, team document sharing tool, with some limited support for "web parts". In 2003, Microsoft released SharePoint Portal Server 2003, which was a far more robust, SQL-based platform that enabled more widespread customization of lists and applications. More recently, the release of Microsoft Office SharePoint Server 2007 (a/k/a "MOSS") brought new capabilities for metadata, content types and granular permissions to the platform.

On May 12, 2010, Microsoft finally released the long awaited successor to MOSS – SharePoint Server 2010. June 2011 saw the release of SharePoint Server 2010 Service Pack 1 ("SP1"), a key benchmark in platform stability for many large-scale deployments.

Here's a summary of some of Microsoft's key investments in the new platform:

Sites

SharePoint 2010 supports Internet Explorer 7.0 and 8.0 as expected – but also adds full support for Mozilla Firefox and Apple Safari browsers. And with the SP1 release, support is broadened for IE 9.0 and Google Chrome.

SharePoint 2010 now features an inline content editor that uses wiki syntax, along with a theme builder right in the browser. Multilingual support is greatly enhanced, and there's much better support for managing and serving digital media (audio/video) directly from SharePoint. In addition, "OWA" now means Office Web Applications – there's a browser based, server hosted version of almost all Office applications, including Word, Excel, PowerPoint, Visio, One Note, and Outlook. And they run equally well in Firefox!

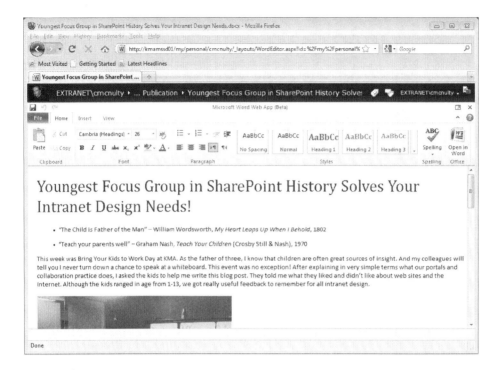

Figure 1 - Word Web Application

In addition, your SharePoint sites feature simpler-to-maintain web pages. Page edits are now made directly on the page, so you can see your changes on the fly. Using wiki syntax, you can also customize themes and brands from the browser without needing to understand HTML, XML or CSS.

Content

Document library support is improved – you can now host up to 50 million items in a library, and there's a new out-of-the-box Document Center template designed to offer an optimal experience for a larger (500,000) item document library. With all that scale, SharePoint is now well positioned as a high capacity ECM platform, making it a viable candidate to replace many large-scale enterprise systems. All that scale is accomplished by increasing power and sophistication in document information lifecycle management. Records management also gets a big overhaul – when you declare a document as a "record", you can now move it to a central Records Center site, and leave behind a "shortcut" link, or you can manage an official record **in place**.

But probably most exciting is the new Managed Metadata Service ("MMS"). MMS lets you define a central hierarchy of document tags and groups and share them across multiple web applications and site collections. There's also support for watching end user-defined tag trends ("folksonomy") and promoting commonly used tags to the enterprise term store.

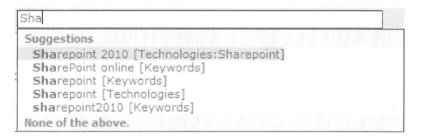

Figure 2 - Adding tags from the SharePoint 2010 MMS

MMS tags and ratings are also surfaced through the interface as navigational elements, both in document libraries and in search results. You can reach across content anywhere in your farm to find all documents tagged as "WSS 3.0", for example.

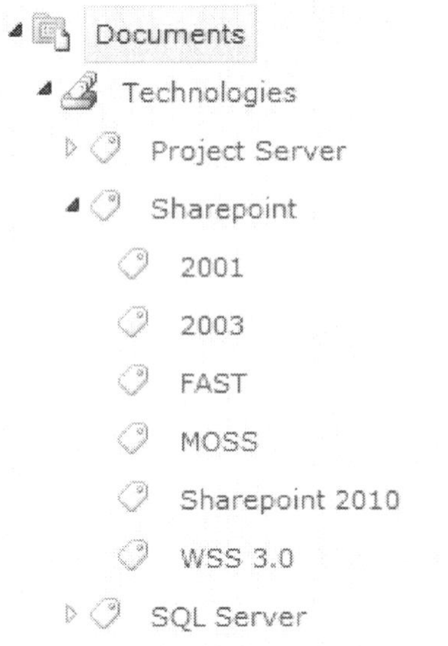

▲ 🗏 Documents
  ▲ 📚 Technologies
    ▷ 🏷 Project Server
    ▲ 🏷 Sharepoint
        🏷 2001
        🏷 2003
        🏷 FAST
        🏷 MOSS
        🏷 Sharepoint 2010
        🏷 WSS 3.0
    ▷ 🏷 SQL Server

Figure 3 - Metadata Navigation

SharePoint 2010 adds supports for audio and video as managed content types, along with a Silverlight client to stream audio and video to the browser UI.

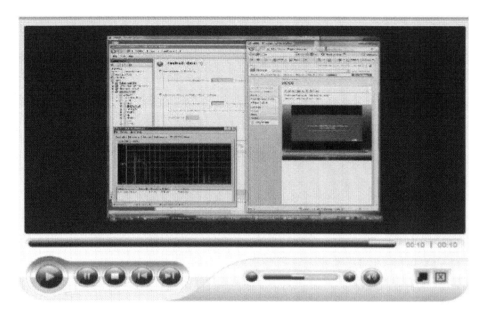

Figure 4 - Silverlight Video Content Viewer

Communities

Social networking – especially Facebook and Twitter – has exploded in the years since SharePoint 2007 was released. As a result, enterprise users have come to expect the same types of Web 2.0 interactions from their internal web platforms. SharePoint 2010 makes good on that promise by adding or extending contemporary social networking, including:

- Twitter style micro blogging
- LinkedIn style expertise finding
- Facebook-like wall posts
- Digg/Del.icio.us tagging
- User-driven ratings (1-5 stars, etc.)
- Wikis and blogs
- RSS feeds [not new]

In addition, there a fantastic new Silverlight-based org chart browser, which relies on your Active Directory information to generate a real-time navigational view of your enterprise hierarchy.

Figure 5 - SharePoint 2010 Communities/My Sites

SharePoint blogs also get an overhaul, with more graphic editing and better support for permalinks.

Search

Microsoft has made extensive improvements in the 2010 search platform. Relevance engines are refined to show more accurate results from the outset. User behavior automatically tunes search relevance, so usage, tagging, and ratings all influence search rankings. There's also better support for federated search (pulling in remote search engine results) and faceted search (drilling down through results by tags, dates, or other classifications.)

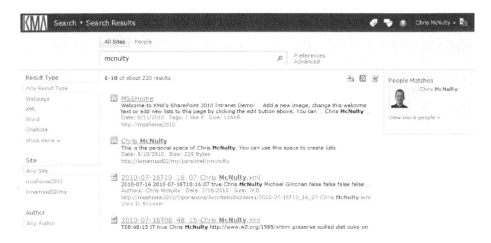

Figure 6 - SharePoint 2010 Search

Microsoft's integration of the FAST reporting engine extends these capabilities further. Let's suppose that you work in construction. A search for "Windows" is likely to mean different things to a glass designer than an IT professional. FAST allows you to customize results based on a user's role. And relevance of document can also be dynamic – so a document about Microsoft Windows would be ranked more highly for an IT user than for a manufacturing engineer.

FAST can also find and interpret metadata embedded in documents -- such as locations, dollar values, and dates – without users needing to add keywords. FAST results can show better previews and full results counts in refinement "facets" (the left hand navigators in *Figure 6 - SharePoint 2010 Search* above).

Finally, from an architecture level, search has been reengineered to allow you to scale for performance and redundancy by adding multiple indexing servers, instead of the single index role that was used in 2007.

Insights

Performance Point dashboards and Excel Services are well integrated in the new release, allowing much simpler deployment of interactive data modeling solutions. Dashboards may be Excel-oriented for working with very large data sets, using an optimized Excel interface (PowerPivot), and using new Excel 2010 features like Slicers and Sparklines. Slicers automatically add a series of toggle buttons to filter a data view. Sparklines are simple, single cell bar/line graphs. The Office Web Application support means users don't need a copy of Excel 2010 running locally to use these functions, either. Business processes can be monitored and exposed as diagrams using the hosted Visio Services.

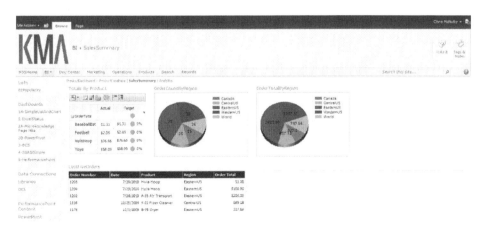

Figure 7 - SharePoint 2010 Business Intelligence Dashboards

There's also a powerful new Chart Web Part that can pull data from all these rich data sources. Dashboard charts can be extended using the "Decomposition Tree" to let you drill back, graphically, through a chart to find elements that contributed most or least significantly.

SharePoint Business Intelligence ("BI") is also significantly enhanced with the inclusion of SQL Server 2012 ("Denali"), released in March 2012. Denali adds powerful user self-service functions. Power View is a browser based end user report designer, and SQL Server Reporting Services ("SSRS") lets users subscribe to alerts based on data changes.

Composites

Microsoft uses the term "Composites" to describe hybrid applications assembled from custom code, in-the-box, tools, data access, forms and workflow. SharePoint 2010 is a stronger application platform than ever. Three key investments here:

- SharePoint provides more tightly integrated tools *s for bundling and applying changes to existing objects that have already been deployed to production.* All updates can now be easily packaged as WSP[3] packages in SharePoint Designer 2010 as well as Visual Studio 2010. You can now use Visio 2010 to design a simple workflow, extend it using Designer, and make detailed enhancements in Studio, all using a common interface to package the deployment.
- Visual Studio 2010 now intrinsically understands how to create SharePoint elements from templates for packing and

---

[3] .WSP is the file format used as the container for compiled code solutions for SharePoint = Web Solution Packages. They can be automatically generated from Visual Studio and SharePoint Designer 2010.

deployment from the Visual Studio Integrated Development Environment ("IDE").

- Business Connectivity Services ("BCS") replace the 2007 BDC (Business Data Connector). Most external data tables can now be presented as read-write lists, with customizable forms.

InfoPath is greatly enhanced as the non-developer interface for customizing list based forms. This is available in SharePoint Server, but is not extended uniformly down to the "free" version of SharePoint Foundation (f/k/a Windows SharePoint Services [WSS] 3.0).

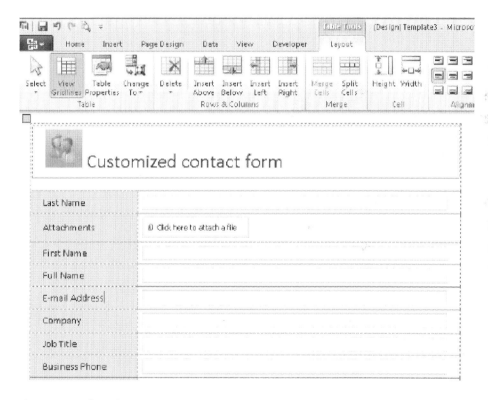

Figure 8 - InfoPath 2010

Infrastructure

SharePoint 2010 is a 64 bit only platform. Direct upgrades from 32 bit to 64 bit servers will require some advance preparation. The basic requirements:

- Windows Server 2008 or Windows Server 2008 R2 X64
- SQL Server 2005 x64 SP3 CU3
  - Or
- SQL Server 2008 x64 SP1 CU2
  - Or
- SQL Server 2008 R2 x64

Memory requirements are a little heavier – 4GB is an absolute minimum to get SharePoint 2010 to run at all, and for acceptable performance, 8GB is probably a good starting point. But don't worry about that yet – there's plenty of architectural detail to come.

Finally, there are some much-needed enhancements to the core server infrastructure:

- Services "a la carte" – rather than using one monolithic Shared Service Provider, you can mix and match among User Profiles, BCS, MMS, Excel Services, Visio Services, etc., to only deploy services you need.
- The code "sandbox", which runs untrusted end user code in a throttled environment and prevents runaway code from impacting the rest of your farm
- Elimination of the indexer as a single server, single point of failure in larger farm topologies

All in all, SharePoint 2010 provides rich business productivity combined with a robust, manageable platform. Let's turn first to understanding how to plan your SharePoint project.

Why Planning Matters

At KMA, I was heavily involved in SharePoint 2010 readiness and upgrade projects. Many of our most successful engagements began with a formalized deployment planning project – SharePoint Deployment Planning Services ("SDPS").

If you think about, it makes sense – we shouldn't start building systems before we understand our surroundings. For new engagements, planning almost always involves discovery. SharePoint planning usually includes the following elements:

- Functional education
- Systems/IT architectural briefing
- Development, testing, and business continuity plans
- Review of current usage patterns and content sources
- Overview of data center and IT Service Management processes
- Forecast of future user/data growth and business/technical initiatives
- Qualitative vision about branding and user experience

Typically, these sessions run for 3-5 days. At the end, we were able to formulate a clear roadmap and estimate for immediate rollout, design, and long-term expansion strategy.

Recently, a long standing client started an upgrade project. Since we had been engaged for the prior three years on the current platform, we anticipated a smooth transition into project execution. However we rapidly discovered some unanswered questions. (How do they want to handle disaster recovery now? How big will the content pool be in two years?) We reconvened to review topics we had assumed were better understood. It didn't take as long as a full SDPS project, but we answered our essential questions.

In the end, planning was essential not just because of discovery, but because everyone understood the rationale for our designed solution. Planning helps create stakeholder consensus at the outset of a project, instead of at the end.

Sometimes, clients tell us initially that they have about 50GB of data in eight sites – but when it's time for migration we learn it's really 400GB across two different databases. Or an estimate of 2TB of data turns out to be only 100MB after we design a large database system. Accurate planning is obviously crucial. Experienced consultants usually keep a few PowerShell scripts in their toolbox to capture information in a pinch. It's also helpful when the client already has an integrated management suite, like Axceler Control Point or Quest Site Admin, that generates comprehensive usage time, sizing, and security information. It saves time during planning, and it prevents false starts during implementation.

Project Lifecycles

In my experience with IT Project Management Offices ("PMOs") I've seen many different project governance frameworks. Some are traditional "waterfall" lifecycles, including those derived from the Project Managers' "Book of Knowledge" or PMBOK. More recently, software development has focused on Rational, Agile methodologies, using techniques like "Scrum" or "Rational Unified Process".

A project, by one definition, is a **temporary** endeavor to construct a good or service. The most important concept is that's its temporary – a project has a start date and, importantly, an end date.

There's no single framework that's perfect for SharePoint. The following table details a high level summary of project lifecycles that's common in the SharePoint world. Oftentimes, there's overlap between phases. Sometimes, in agile-oriented environments, there may be several iterations of plan-build-stabilize embedded in the overall project lifecycle.

SharePoint as a technology can lend itself to highly iterative, accelerated prototyping and rollout schedules. That's a good thing. However, Agile development is NOT an excuse to circumvent process, or documentation of requirements and design. Scrum, for example, is a controlled, disciplined approach to determining which functions are addressed in each iteration, or "sprint", and how those are implemented". Rapid development and prototyping shouldn't be an excuse for "we don't need to write things down"; "we don't need to test" or "we don't need change management".

Phase	Activities	Key deliverables	Goal	Typical duration
Envision	Kickoff, scheduling, negotiating	Summary statement of the project, schedule, purpose, stakeholders and budget, proposed solution hypothesis	Vision and scope approval	1-4uilu weeks
Plan	Gather and document requirements Formulate solution design	Detailed summary of solution, requirements and design, schedule Development and test environments	Detailed project plan is approved	2-6 weeks
Build	Construct custom solutions, code, and architecture, unit testing	Code, proposed final solution, test scripts	Scope complete	variable
Stabilize	User and integration testing, training, preparation for going live	User training and signoff that solution matches the scope	Release readiness approved	2-4 weeks
Deploy	Whatever you built – sites,	Production release of the solution;	Deployment complete	2-4 weeks

code, manuals,	final training and
etc. – to meet	documentation
the requirement	

In addition to project phases, all projects have certain "maintenance" functions. How are issues and risks defined, maintained, logged, and addressed? What's the best way to collaborate and store project documents? It's obvious to note that SharePoint sites, sometimes enhanced with Project Server, are an effective way to ensure effective project collaboration. A detailed proscription for using SharePoint to run your project is highly dependent on the overall business and technical culture.

Change/Release Management

Most well run data centers already have some form of change or release management. I recommend using at least three distinct server regions (development, test production) to govern the creation, acceptance, and deployment of solutions. Production regions should be optimized for maximum performance and reliability. In general, test or staging regions should match production as closely as is practical, in physical architecture, software configuration and security.

Also, I would strongly discourage the use of servers shared across the three major system regions for software development. Although SharePoint and SQL can support multiple instances on the same physical hardware, they also share access to some .NET code libraries (.e.g. the global assembly cache, or GAC), that make it impossible to release code to testing without also installing it into production. In many cases, virtualization can provide an appropriate federation layer without additional hardware expense.

Protecting the data and operations for production is paramount. Controlled testing and deployment of only approved solutions reduces the likelihood of incidents or other unplanned downtime in production. In addition, it helps to have standard, repeatable processes for installing releases in production. Among those standards, there should be a permissions barrier between development and production. Developers should not have direct access to production. Ideally, releases are performed by release engineers under traceable release accounts with temporarily elevated permissions ("firecall").

A typical set of guidelines for each of the three regions is outlined below.

Development	Staging/Test	Production
• often internal to the development team • problem reproduction that require advanced inspection tools (e.g. Visual Studio) are done here • permissions can be looser, may have multiple environments for multiple developers • sensitive data from production cannot be copied here without masking or customer sginoff • changes here can be deployed ad hoc	• no Visual Studio, no MS Office • match/mirror production as closely as possible; match hardware/system performance as closely as practical • security permissions match production • any sensitive data copied here stays under production-grade controls • test accounts should be created in a separate OU if possible • changes here can only be delivered and deployed from source control and according to production release methods	• optimized hardware configurations • highly secure • no use of user rotating password accounts as service accounts • changes here can only be delivered and deployed from source control and according to production release methods

Change management requires acceptance and advance approval of scheduled changes to production environments. All material changes MUST be documented and captured in a configuration master database and/or documentation.

In general, third parties should not directly access production environments without prior arrangement from an appropriate approver at the client.

Artifact management

Any development and release process for SharePoint can generate a lot of elements, or artifacts – compiled code, passwords, release notes, training materials, project documents and more. Here are some good practices.

Password control
User/service account passwords should be kept in standard locations on project team sites if those are being used.   Each site should have distinct permissions (no inheritance) so that user accounts don't gain unnecessary extra access to the password store. Each store should also be kept separately to avoid one central repository with access to all client passwords.

Although service accounts may have some common naming standards, don't use the same passwords for multiple accounts. At a minimum, adopt some level of password complexity.

Source control
All projects should be kept in Team Foundation Server, Visual Source Safe, or other source code management system. All changes need to be checked in. Code should be deployed from the checked in, published version and not from local workstation copies of these files.

Delivery packages
Release code, documentation, and the like for a delivery package, once ready should be permanently stored in an appropriate archive – file shares, SharePoint, or source code management systems may all play a role.

SharePoint Release Process

SharePoint intrinsically mixes workflows, lookup tables, list structures and other elements one might think of as "code" in the content database. As a result, deploying changes is never as simple as copying the content database from development forward to test and production environments. However, since production systems contain a "full" set of data, you may sometimes need to refresh test, or development systems with a recent snapshot of production content. Once this process has completed, the proposed release, with all changes, workflows, screens and the like can be deployed to test systems according to the documented release process. In that manner, the test system is a nearly complete copy of production. So long as that process is repeated identically in the production release, this provides a great simulation if what can be expected in a production release.

In some environments, however, production contains some data, such as salary or Social Security numbers, that are subject to strict permissions. Bringing this category of data into a comparatively "open" development system, with few controls on data access, may be inadvisable.

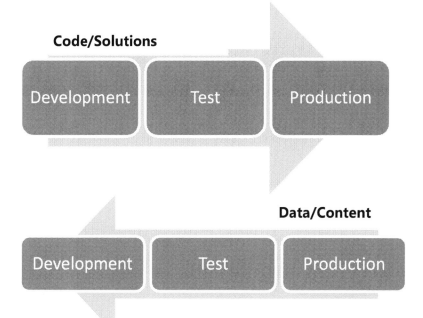

Design and Architecture

SharePoint 2010 is built from the same familiar elements as SharePoint 2007. Web front end servers (WFE) handle the http traffic to and from clients. Application servers supply common application tasks, such as search, user profiles or Excel calculation processing. Finally, database servers provide storage of web pages, documents and configuration settings.

There's no requirement that each of these run as separate physical or virtual servers, and in many smaller installations, WFE, application and database roles may even be combined on a single server. But let's review each of these in turn.

Web front end (WFE) servers

Web front end ("WFE") servers are the workhorses of any SharePoint installation. WFEs run Internet Information Server (IIS) 7.0 (or better). IIS receives inbound traffic requests, typically on ports 80 or 443, and directs the request to the appropriate SharePoint application or applications. In SharePoint, users usually think of these systems as "the" SharePoint server.

The other most common service for WFEs is queries. We haven't explained the search architecture yet. In conventional SharePoint searches[4], there are two major activities:

- **Crawling and indexing.** These servers scan and retrieve the full text of content to develop an index of terms and locations. This search index is stored in a database.

---

[4] By which I mean, not FAST Search Server.

- **Querying**. To answer user queries, these servers "syndicate" a copy of the index from the database to their local file system. When users search for a word, the server uses the index to returns a filtered list of results to the user.

It's fairly common for the WFE server to host the query role, at least for mid-sized architectures.   Index hash data is maintained in a dedicated database. Query servers receive a copy of the index hash tables from the database itself, not via file replication as in earlier versions. In addition, the query data itself can be partitioned (for performance optimization) and replicated among multiple servers, allowing for fault tolerance.

WFEs are easily scaled in a load balanced cluster, either using Microsoft's own software Network Load Balancing (NLB) or external hardware solutions, such as F5.   Also, when multiple WFE's are used, they need not share the same URL – you may have different URLs for internal and external users, for example.

The single most important thing you can do to optimize the performance of a SharePoint WFE is add RAM. 8GB is a minimum operational standard. If you even get SharePoint to run in less (even without SQL) you're lucky. 12GB is a better operational point for busier servers, and 16GB will help for the busiest conditions.   Your demand will vary by usage style as well. Document collaboration is a relatively less taxing operation but users with heavy usage of Office Web Apps or PowerPivot (especially if they open large PowerPivot models) add to the RAM demands.

Finally, disk space requirements are not extensive for a WFE, unless your server hosts the query role and your search corpus is relatively large. A basic WFE may only need 100-120GB of local storage. However, if you are crawling a large set of content, a WFE acting as query server needs more storage. Microsoft guidance on the topic is to reserve additional disk storage of 10-30% of the crawled content (the "corpus"). It's important to remember that this is based on the total crawled volume. If your site contains three content databases:

- 30GB Intranet Content Database
- 50GB Project Site Collection Content Database
- 20GB My Site Content Database

You might think you have a smaller site. But if you are also crawling a 900GB file share, you have 1TB of crawled content. In my experience, the 30% figure is overgenerous. Real world scenarios often only consume 2-3% of the total corpus size. Size also varies by the type of content; 1TB of video files aren't as "crawlable" as 1TB of text files, since there's more indexable text content in a text file. For our estimation, we usually reserve 10% - 5% of total searched content size in the search database, and 5% for the file system query partition. If you anticipate a growth rate of 20% and you are designing for at least three years future usage, that 1TB becomes a 1.728TB corpus – and you need an additional 86GB of disk space on the query server.

If you're virtualizing the servers, it's easier to resize the disk as you go. In Windows, virtual disks are more easily resized when they don't host a boot partition (a/k/a the C drive).[5] But keep in mind that the index has to occupy the same relative directory path on all servers, so the index files can't be on the C:\Program Files... default on one server and D:\SPINDEX on the next.

Finally, if you have "extra" disk space, it's a good practice to move IIS logs and other logs from the root C drive to another drive. Here's how to move the IIS Logs:

- Open up IIS Manager from Start Menu | Application Services. You don't need the IIS6 Manager; it provides SMTP admin services not found in the IIS7 admin tool.

---

[5] I know you can use DISKPART.EXE on Windows 2008 R2.

- Open up the list of **Sites** on the left hand panel. Select the site that corresponds to your SharePoint web application.
- In the center panel, select a new directory for the log files.

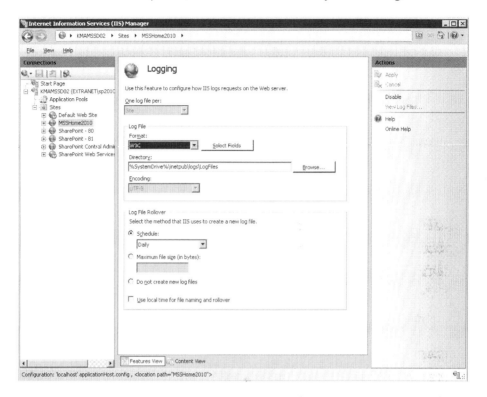

Figure 9 - Relocate IIS Logs

- Click Apply in the right hand panel to save changes.

Application Servers

Application servers ("app servers") provide the second layer of SharePoint services. These servers typically are used to run searches, provide user profiles, metadata services, or Excel calculations. (These services can be run directly on a WFE in a small installation).

Unlike in previous versions, most application services can be spread across multiple servers to provide greater scalability and fault tolerance. In particular, search indexing roles, and the hash table partitions, can be divided, duplicated and marked as failover copies to allow indexing and querying to continue even if one off the application servers is offline. Conversely, services that might consume a lot of server resources (e.g. PowerPivot models with large concurrent usage) can be moved to dedicated servers.

The most important server attribute to optimize performance is CPU – adding CPU cores and assign faster cores will help. Memory configurations are commonly 8-12GB RAM, with more for large environments with extensive application usage.

Database Servers

SharePoint 2010 uses databases. Lots and lots of them – more than ever before! A "standard" installation can use 20 or more. SharePoint databases are used for:

- Web content management
- Search data
- User profiles and tags
- Metadata
- Shared service configuration

In addition, SQL servers sometime provide business intelligence subsystems, such as Reporting Services or Analysis Services.

Database servers can be memory hungry. 8GB-24GB is the most common range of configuration. Even more memory can benefit SQL systems with content database sizes greater than 500GB or beyond 1TB. Further optimizing the performance of SQL requires thinking in two dimensions – both in the size of each content database and the number of databases.

In terms of raw capacity, you can always add disks. The nominal optimal maximum size for a content database is about 200GB. Around this limit, system managers can add additional databases. Or they can use External BLOB Storage (EBS) or Remote BLOB Storage

(RBS) to move content out of the content database and redu
size of the database. When the files move out to the BLOB S
may move to a file share, a directory, or a remote storage app
supported. (They are stored in serialized form – you won't see the
native files floating out there in BLOB land!)

The distinctions between EBS and RBS are not well understood. EBS
can offer slightly better performance in some benchmarks, and can be
implemented on SQL Standard Edition, but it requires a heavier
application footprint on the SharePoint servers. RBS is a more recent
technology, and runs almost exclusively on SQL. (SharePoint is mostly
blind to how SQL optimizes its file storage.) RBS offers better native
manageability, but it requires SQL Enterprise Edition. Both
approaches usually require some use of third party software, such as
Metalogix StoragePoint or Quest Storage Maximizer to maintain the
BLOB store. For example, you may want to set up rules to only move
contents into the RBS provider after 30 days, if they exceed a target
size, or other conditions.

200GB is a good benchmark for size limits. However, there can be
some real world scenarios where, the target number might be higher,
or even smaller, before adding additional databases. If you have
multiple content databases inside a web application, you might
consider a 100GB target for each. Conversely, you may have a web
application principally dedicated to archive storage or document
images. Archives usually are written once and then accessed
sporadically. For these scenarios, Microsoft guidance provides that
databases of 1TB or more can still provide adequate performance.

Service Pack 1 Storage Limits
In June 2011, Microsoft released the long awaited Service Pack 1 for
SharePoint 2010 (SP1), along with updated guidance on maximum
content database size and RBS. Instead of the traditional 200GB limit,

..osoft now recommends that the maximum can be anywhere from 200GB to 4TB, depending on disk performance.

"SharePoint can support up to 4 TB of data in all usage scenarios and has no imposed size limit for document archive scenarios."[6]

Wow. 4TB is a lot! But read the fine print – surpassing 200GB requires that your disk subsystem supplies performance of at least .25 IOPS per GB; 2 IOPS per GB is recommended for optimal performance. This guidance is based on real-world experience – it's not something that gets installed as part of SP1. Let's look at what this means for collaborative content databases.

So...what's an IOPS? IOPS stands for Input/output Operations Per Second – in short, how many read write transactions per second can be moved through the disk.

A traditional calculation is:

$$IOPS = \frac{1}{avgheadlatencytime + average(avgreadtime + avgewritetime)}$$

Essentially, if you know how long each disk transaction takes, you can determine how many of them you can get through in a second. So, if your database disks take .001 seconds to move the disk heads, .005 seconds average read time, and .013 seconds average write time, the math tells us that the average total time is .01 seconds, for an IOPS rating of 100.

How best to measure this? There are two decent techniques. The first uses Windows Performance Monitor. If you add the counter for **Windows | Logical Disk | Avg Disk Sec | Transfer**, you can get a good approximation of the average time for disk transactions. Make

---

[6] See http://sharepoint.microsoft.com/blog/Pages/BlogPost.aspx?pID=988

sure you run the test for a long enough time, and perform some disk operations, like database backup, that generate sufficient traffic for a fair stress test.

The more comprehensive technique is to download the free open source tool, IOMeter from www.iometer.org/doc/downloads.html. IOMeter was originally developed by Intel, and provides a way to stress test a disk system more comprehensively, under a variety of loads. Please note – IOMeter adds a large temporary file to the root directory of a target drive– so if you must test in production, I suggest finding a time of low utilization and little or no production usage. The scenarios we usually use are:

- Default
- 4k Write size, 75% read/write ratio, 50% random sequencing of disk locations.

I ran these tests against a production SQL system – a Dell PowerEdge 2950 with a local PERC5 based SCSI array. Here's our observed data and derived content DB maximums:

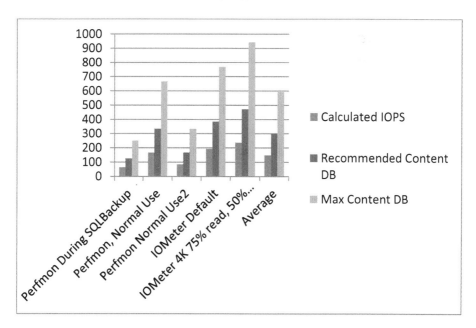

We observed calculated IOPS from 62.5 to 235.79 using a mix of Windows Performance Monitor and IOMeter tests. These predict a total maximum content database size of anywhere from 125GB to 471GB – however, 200GB is still the "floor" recommendation – using Microsoft's "optimal" recommendations. The theoretical support maximums are higher – 250GB up to 943GB. This is a broad range. My recommendations tend to favor IOMeter based metrics, and Microsoft's 2.0 IOPS per GB guidance – yielding a maximum content database size of 384-472GB.

There's another lovely bit of fine print in the SP1 guidance:

"The content database size includes both metadata and BLOBs regardless of where the BLOBs are located and use of RBS does not bypass or increase these limits."

This may come as a surprise to organizations that used RBS to get around traditional 200GB thresholds. What Microsoft is saying is that the performance of the disk still matters for BLOBs – there is no free lunch. There are many reasons to use RBS – including the use of lower cost disk for BLOB storage, and the reduction of core content database size to a point for efficient backup/restore operations. Small content DBs are also better candidates for solid state disk, etc. But RBS alone will not allow you to throw all your file content on a remote, slow file share without seeing degraded performance.

RBS is still really important in large SharePoint installations. But deploying it without planning may lead to disappointment.

Performance Optimization

Disk I/O

As has been noted elsewhere, disk input/output performance (I/O) is the single biggest constraint on database performance in the SharePoint world. Run SharePoint on an underpowered or poorly designed SQL server, and you will see slow performance throughout the farm.

It's obviously important to also make SQL databases are kept highly available. So some level of disk redundancy is usually factored into physical designs for database servers. Disk redundancy is often classified by RAID[7] levels. RAID technologies predate PCs and modern x86 server designs. A full exploration of all the possible RAID levels is beyond the scope of this book, but here are three of the most common:

RAID 1

RAID 1 consists of running mirrored pairs of disks. If one disk fails, the other has full copy of all the data and goes on operating. RAID 1 is a high performance technology, but requires purchasing 2GB of raw disk for every 1GB of effective capacity, since you need two of everything. So RAID 1 is a comparatively expensive "inexpensive" disk.

RAID 5

This technique uses groups of disks to create a larger synthetic unit. For example, five 150GB disks could be combined to create one hybrid 600GB storage pool.

Wait a minute, you say! I may not be great at math, but even I know that 150GB X 5 disks should equal 750GB, not 600GB. However, in RAID 5, one disk is dedicated to calculating a checksum, or "parity bit", every time data is written to the group. That way, if any of the single disks fail, the data can be redistributed to other disks by reversing the parity calculations. As a result, RAID 5 is highly efficient at optimizing the volume of data stored. It's also great at handling high volume read operations – more disks working together means more systems to read bits from a disk platter and fewer chances for bottlenecks. But

---

[7] Redundant Array of Inexpensive Disks

write operations are a different story. Since every write operation requires a calculation, high volume write operations are slower than they would be in a traditional disk system.   However, for SharePoint, that's not always the worst thing, since SharePoint is a read-heavy database consumer.

RAID 10

Some people make distinctions between RAID 1+0 vs. RAID 0+1 – stripes across mirrors, or mirrors of stripes. These debates don't really matter for SharePoint design. RAID 10 is the most available, highly performing way to engineer a disk subsystem. It has a lot of moving spindles for maximum performance – but it's also fully redundant. So it "costs" twice as much in raw disk as it delivers in usable storage.

SQL databases are the largest consumer of disk space in the SharePoint world. So engineering your disks for maximum performance at the database layer is more critical than for any other level. Here are some general design considerations.

- It's usually a good idea to break up SQL databases into multiple logical drive letters. Database files, transaction logs, backup files, and temp database benefit from having multiple independent sets of disk spindles working. That way, when data is bring written to the database, since it's going into both the master database and the transaction log, adding more spindles spreads the load across multiple parallel operations.
- But if you're in a SAN or virtualized environment, make sure you understand where the different drive letters are mapped. If the D, E, and F drives all point back to separate LUNs[8] on your SAN, but those LUNs are all part of the same storage group and same set of physical disks, splitting those files into

---

[8] Logical Unit Number

multiple drive letters adds complexity without significant performance gains.

- Don't virtualize SQL if you can help it. SQL is already an integration platform. If you have to, try to limit SQL virtualization to test or development systems, but not production. SQL virtualization is supported, but raises the bar in disk engineering to get good performance. SQL databases stored in virtualized disk files are inherently slow compared to dedicated physical disk. If you need to virtualize SQL, use a SAN to provision dedicated physical storage.
- RAID10 is great – but you may not be able to justify it for all applications. For example, it may be overkill for backup files. Balancing disk performance and cost is a reasonable tradeoff. One possible design:
  - RAID1 on boot disks
  - RAID5 on data disks
  - RAID10 on log disks
  - No RAID, or RAID 5 on backup disks
- If you have large content databases, you can engineer even better performance by breaking each large database into multiple database files – each on a separate disk.

SQL databases can be set to automatically grow as needed – but this can lead to massive file fragmentation. Presizing the databases to sufficient size at the outset helps ensure contiguous file allocations.

Automatic database growth settings, when used, should be set to grow in 50-100MB clumps – not by percentage. Setting a 100GB database to grow in 10% clumps means the database essentially stops to add 10GB or more on each increment. Using a small size leads to more frequent, but smoother, steady state growth.

SQL Server's tempdb database is heavily used by SharePoint. Presize it to about 20% the size of the single largest content database.

Memory and page files

Somewhere between the amount of disk space and the raw memory, the page file sizes are poorly understood. I've restated Microsoft's guidance on page file sizes below. (I've left out there recommendations about servers with less than 1GB or RAM, since that should NEVER be happening in SharePoint,) It's fairly common for this file to be left on the server C drive, although it can be moved among alternate local drives as well.

In general, don't underestimate the need for local index files, crash dumps, and page files (f/k/a swap files).

TIP: *When sizing local drives also understand the size of your index files on any server that hold the index or query roles.*

System Memory Size (RAM)	Minimum Page File Size	Maximum Page File Size
Windows Server 2008, Windows 7 and Windows Server 2008 R2. >= 1GB	Large enough to hold a kernel-memory crash dump and is RAM plus 300MB or 1GB, whichever is larger	3 x RAM or 4GB, whichever is larger

Each category of server has its own memory needs. The actual amount needed will vary based on user load and the application mix – for example, a large pool of users access PowerPivot put greater demands on the memory used by those application services. 8GB is always the floor. However, contemporary virtualization environments, like HyperV or VMware, make it easy to dynamically add memory as needed. You could start small and grow.

- Web Front End (WFE): 8-16GB

- Application/search: 8-12GB
- SQL: 8-24GB

Some of the application services can require significantly larger memory sizes. For example, PowerPivot data cubes lives completely in memory. So if you have a large amount of larger PowerPivot models, the servers where that SSA runs will use a lot more memory.

If you are deploying a lot of independent application pools, each of those pools consumes about 800MB. And keep an eye on the performance counter for Available Memory – if it's consistently below 50%, you need more memory.

Speaking of performance counters, here are a few good ones to check. If you have a system that's consistently breaking these thresholds, you may have a problem that can be addressed through system engineering:

Processor/CPU utilization >60%. You may need to add servers or redistribute services to reduce the load.

Available memory <50%. Again, add RAM.

Disk average reads/writes >15ms. This translates loosely into about 66.67 IOPS as discussed above, and is most common on virtualized SQL servers. That's slow, and predicts reduced performance even for smaller content databases on a SQL server. This isn't usually a problem with a physical disk though – it's more common in a virtual disk that itself is shared on a common SAN pool or local disk. If you can, move the volume to dedicated storage.

Sustained network bandwidth higher than 25%. Network latency output queue >0. This means the network can't keep up with users or the server. This may be resolved by adding physical switched Ethernet ports, adding server to divide the load. It can also happen on highly overloaded virtual machine hosts – in which case you may want to move the guest server to a new host.

SQL Server 2012 'Denali"

SQL Server 2012, scheduled for release in March 2012, provides a broad range of business intelligence and infrastructure enhancements. In this book, our review is based on the Community Technology Preview 3 ("CTP3"), and as always, features will change between CTP3 and the final release. For the most up to date information, check Microsoft's site at http://www.microsoft.com/sqlserver/en/us/future-editions.aspx.

We're going to take a look at the BI capabilities – SSRS Alerts and Power View – in the chapter on Business Intelligence. Here, we'll look at the two new features most relevant to infrastructure planning - scalability and upgrades.

Always On can be best thought of as an extension to clustering, log shipping and mirroring that allows for nearly continuous availability of SQL servers and/or individual databases in local and geographically dispersed configurations.

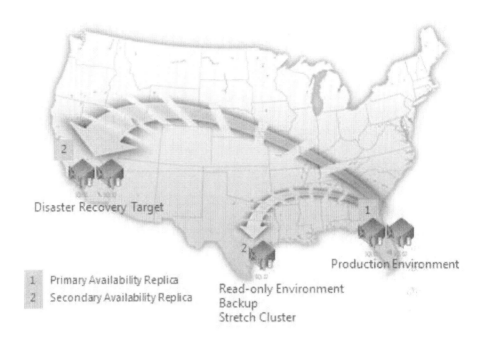

Disaster Recovery Target

Production Environment

1 Primary Availability Replica
2 Secondary Availability Replica

Read-only Environment
Backup
Stretch Cluster

Figure 10 - Always On replication - source Microsoft.com

Always On is beyond the general scope of our review here, and I would encourage you to explore Microsoft's online resources for more information. SharePoint has a few operating requirements that constrain some of the more exotic Always On configurations. First, SharePoint 2010 can't support clusters that stretch across broad geographies. Although SQL 2012 itself supports this technique, SharePoint requires 20ms of "first byte" and less than 1ms of subsequent latency, round trip, among servers and components in a farm. Few geographically dispersed clusters perform at that level. Secondly, although SQL 2012 supports asynchronous replication, its use is discouraged in SharePoint to ensure data integrity.

SQL Server 2012 can also support direct upgrades from prior versions of SQL. SharePoint 2007 upgrades often avoid in-place upgrades in favor of database attach or content migration, (see page 123 for a lot more on upgrades.) However, SQL Server can usually be upgraded in place to SQL 2012. Direct in place upgrades are supported from:

- SQL Server 2005 SP4
- SQL Server 2008 SP2
- SQL Server 2008 R2

So you don't have to flip back to earlier in the book, the officially supported versions of SQL for SharePoint 2010 are:

- SQL Server 2005 x64 SP3 CU3
- SQL Server 2008 x64 SP1 CU2
- SQL Server 2008 R2 x64

For planning, then, so long as your SQL Server has been kept current with the most recent SQL Service Packs, you should have no problem performing an in place upgrade for the SQL Database Engine.

Extranet Topologies

Sooner or later, you're going to be asked to open SharePoint up to the "outside". Why on earth might you want that? In fact, SharePoint has been deployed very successfully for a number of business scenarios.

- Remote employees want to login remotely without having a VPN connection in place. Some of these are truly working from mobile locations, such as field sales forces. Or you might have employees working from home (temporarily or full time) or remote customer sites. Increasingly, geographically dispersed virtual teams are a rising form of project staffing.
- External partners, customers, or clients want to access a document library either as a reader stakeholder or an active contributor. These are always "named users" in a controlled scenario (a/k/a the "walled garden".)

- SharePoint is also available to be licensed as a Web and Web Content Management platform. Although you may have logins, anonymous access to a "www" site is essential. This lets you reuse internal admin skills and deploy relevant functions like Audience targeting. Sometimes, the web site is published, but static – outside users don't modify anything on it.
- Lastly, the explosion of smartphones and tablets creates a network challenge, since traditional VPN clients aren't universally available for mobile devices. There's a mobile friendly view available – see the Mobile support section on page 350 for more information.

Microsoft makes two unlimited user licenses available for SharePoint Server. Each of these allows for an unlimited number of non-employee users. They are more expensive than the corporate licenses – but again, they allow a large pool of outside users. SharePoint Server 2010 For Internet Sites – Standard ("FIS-S") corresponds to SharePoint Server 2010 Standard functions, whereas "FIS-E" provides Enterprise-class functions and access to use FAST Search.

Let's look at the three basic topologies used to host SharePoint for external access. The three variations place the whole farm inside the firewall, outside the firewall, or both inside and outside. In each topology, pay special attention to the location of the WFEs, since they comprise the connection point for external users.

Edge Firewall

This configuration is the simplest, most traditional way to open up a SharePoint farm to the outside. This design publishes an external DNS entry to an address that points to the external side of the firewall, which screens the traffic and routes the request to the appropriate internal WFE server. The external DNS entry must be entered as a mapping in SharePoint Central Admin under Alternate Access Mappings (AAM).

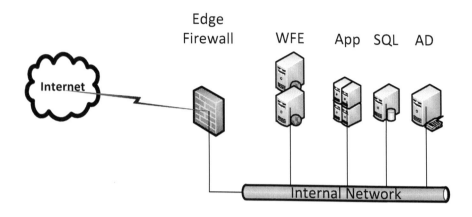

Figure 11 - Edge Firewall

Edge firewall topologies are relatively simple. The entire farm lives inside a private network, so no process or service communications between servers (like search indexing) have to run across a firewall. Similarly, internal web browsing isn't slowed down by a firewall. All data is stored in one trusted place – meaning external and internal users view the same content.

However, the simplicity carries a security risk. In this design, external users have to traverse **only one** border device – the firewall – before they access the internal network. Many consider this technique less secure, and prefer to redirect external web traffic to a connection point outside a private, internal network.

Back-to-back perimeter

Back-to-back perimeter topologies do just that – keep the outside traffic away from the internal network. In this configuration, the entire server farm lives in the perimeter network. In the most complex topologies, routers or firewall can be inserted between service layers to provide additional security. Internal network users can be routed through either the internal-facing firewall or to the public interface of the edge firewall.

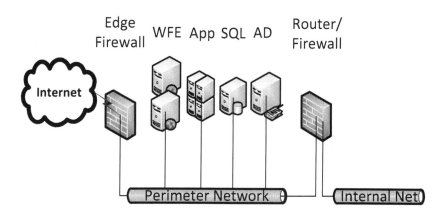

As before, content is kept in a single network, simplifying synchronization and publication processes. Since external usage is isolated to a perimeter network, security breaches for the farm are kept away from the internal network.

However, this is a more complex network design. It adds extra firewall devices and routers compared to the single edge firewall approach. It also adds an extra set of Active Directory servers.[9] Backup agents and devices also need to be configured to extend to the perimeter network or provisioned to run directly in that zone.

---

[9] In edge firewall topologies, the AD servers are usually preexisting domain servers.

Split back-to-back

This design splits the farm between internal and edge networks. WFEs are located in the perimeter network, while application and database systems are located inside the corporate network, along with Active Directory servers. (Sometimes, application and/or domain servers may be sited in the perimeter network.)

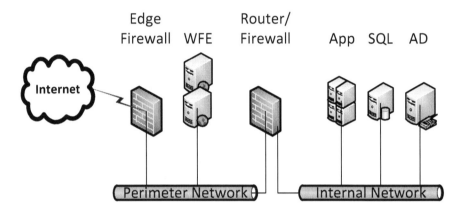

Figure 13 - Split back-to-back topology

If the perimeter network uses a different AD domain than the corporate network, a trust is required, and the "outside" perimeter domain must trust accounts and resources coming from the "inside" corporate domain. You can only avoid multidomain trusts if the WFE and app servers all live in the perimeter, and only SQL authentication is used back to the databases.

TIP: *During setup, you can't use the Product and Technologies "Gray" Wizard – instead you'll use PSCONFIG to specify a SQL-based database* *access account. See SharePoint Products Configuration Wizard on page 94 for more.*

To optimize search performance, keep the application servers inside the firewall, as shown, and add a web server/SharePoint Foundation role to this server solely for crawling content. This way, all the search indexing, crawling, and database access happens without traversing a firewall.

Split back to back topologies have many advantages. SQL database servers are kept in the most protected of locations – an internal network. Potentially, additional internal WFE servers can be added to provide a wholly internal web URL, and these internal farm components can use the same content databases. Since all content is also kept within a single farm, there is no need to adopt synchronization or publication processes.

On the other hand, the split back to back technique is more complex, especially when configuring firewall rules for the device between the perimeter and internal network.   In addition, a security breach of the perimeter WFE server raises the possibility of access to all the data on the internal SQL servers. Some inter-server communication is running across a firewall, which can add more latency.

Content publishing and cross farm services

Both perimeter networks and split back-to-back can be enhanced with content publishing. The content publishing engine allows you to create one way synchronization between an internal site collection and a public site collection. Only approved content is synchronized out to the subscribing site collection. Content is published on a schedule, or on demand (either for a single page or for the whole collection.)

This technique presumes that you have a separate internal farm to use as the basis for publishing content., However, understand that content publishing is a one-way trip – content added or created directly to the outside doesn't get synchronized back inside.

An advantage of this technique is that any security breach of the "outside" farm is isolated away from the internal network. When used with split back-to-back topology, since the content publication stream runs between the Central Administration sites of each farm, the communications can be kept securely on an internal network without traversing firewalls if servers are carefully sited. Search crawls can also be engineered to run across servers hosted inside the firewall.

However, content publishing adds additional servers, farms, and complexity to the environment, and is limited to one-way content delivery to the outside network. As a result, content publishing is the wrong choice for extranet collaboration sites.

Finally, multifarm design can also gain greater efficiency by using cross farm shared service applications. Search and managed metadata, for example, can be delivered from an internal enterprise farms and consumed by the "outside" farm, again, reducing the footprint of your public facing farm. A few caveats – multifarm SSAs often require two way domain trusts. And not all SSAs can be shared – for example, Project Server 2010 doesn't support cross farm services.

Firewalls and Forefront UAG

Microsoft has a related Internet "border" technology, Forefront Unified Access Gateway (Forefront UAG). Forefront UAG allows you to publish selected internal SharePoint sites to a unified external facing portal. Users can be authenticated securely and use encrypted connections to reach internal SharePoint sites seamlessly. UAG also provides protection against viruses and malware. It can enforce security standards on remote clients and devices, and cleanup client files (e.g. cookies, cache) as needed. UAG runs outside the confines of a traditional VPN.

Forefront UAG is the latest in range of prior Internet security products from Microsoft – including TMG (Threat Management Gateway), IAG (Internet Access Gateway), and ISA Server (Internet Security and Acceleration). Microsoft has more information available online at http://www.microsoft.com/en-us/server-cloud/forefront/unified-access-gateway.aspx Obviously, SharePoint doesn't require a Microsoft-based edge security device, and can work with many standard network security systems, including those from Cisco, F5, Check Point and others.

Farm Sizing

So how many of these things are you going to need? A few.

Single Server

SharePoint can always be installed on a single server, with SQL on the same machine. This is most commonly used for smaller teams and smaller sets of content – usually a few dozen users and several thousand documents. Although we've designed and supported extremely large single server builds with hundreds of users and 50-100GB of content, it's more common to see these builds used for proofs-of-concept or testing.

As a single server system, fault tolerance and search speed are usually not a principal concern. SQL Server and SharePoint live on the same server, which increases performance needs. Search is usually not a prime function for single server builds.

TIP: *Even if you are 100% certain you will never need more than one server, you should almost never install SharePoint in "Standalone" mode (see below at page 88). "Standalone" forces a limited version of SQL Express onto the server, and prevents you from ever growing the system to add a second server. "Complete" installations can be single server installs, but you retain the flexibility to add systems in the future.*

On the other hand, there's a global manufacturer based in the Midwestern U.S. Their external cloud-based server hosting gives them a great price on a per-server basis. As a result, they've had tremendous success running SharePoint 2010 on a single server with 16GB of RAM and almost 1TB of local storage for a pool of 500-1000 users. However, this is a special case.

Medium Farm

The vast majority of SharePoint installations qualify as "medium farms" – technically, a SharePoint farm with 2-6 servers:

- One or two web front end servers (WFEs) with load balancing between them if there are multiples
- One or two application and or indexing servers
- A single database server or some type of high availability configuration (clustering, mirroring, log shipping, or SQL 2012 Always On).

Figure 14 - Medium Farm

Medium farms are typically used in environments between 100 and 10,000 users. Usage scenarios run the gamut from simple document storage and search to enterprise portals and full custom application scenarios. Common content sizes run from 10,000-1 million documents, although this is the loosest of guidelines.

The number of servers used in each role varies by load, fault tolerance and budget. These are easily virtualized.

Each WFE server can handle up to 500 simultaneous users under the most common collaboration workloads. Microsoft guidance has indicated this number can actually approach 1000 simultaneous users, but I've found 500 to be a more realistic number as usage proceeds beyond simple document storage to more intense usage. The number of simultaneous users on your system can vary based on work schedule and usage patterns. For example, if you have 1000 users, each using SharePoint for 30 minutes a day, and an eight hour work day, you have:

$$\frac{1000\ users\ \times\ 30\ minutes}{8\ hours\ \times\ 60\ minutes} = 62.5\ average\ users$$

And 30 minutes is actually a lot of usage. If all your users are doing is saving a document, readiness a few, running a search and browsing a few pages, the actual load time is much less. This math also assumes that usage is normally distributed throughout the workday. It's not, though – 9-10am is usually a peak time, even more so if user browsers have the SharePoint home page as their default start page.

However, if you have different application loads, that 30 minutes of usage time can go up. For example, heavy use of Office Web Applications as a trial or total desktop replacement, workflow-oriented applications, or PowerPivot centric data modeling, these average usage times actually can go up. Still, a single WFE will usually suffice for most common medium workloads.

Yet there are two strong reasons for having multiple WFEs. One is fault tolerance. Obviously, a single server is a single point of failure.

Adding a second server provides much greater resilience. The other reason has to do with security.

Usually, web applications are equally provisioned across all front end servers in a farm. However, in complex, multi instance farms, you can achieve greater security isolation by restricting the web applications that run on certain front end servers. In the model below, there are two web front end servers – only one of which is exposed to the outside Internet (assume it's a variation on split back-to-back topology.) As you can see, highly secure web applications can be turned off in IIS on the external server, minimizing the security profile and exposure. The intranet is accessible internally and externally for employee convenience. The customer portal is available on both, although principally used externally. However finance and HR web applications are turned off on the external facing web server.

Web Application	Internal WFE	External WFE
Intranet	√	√
Customer Portal	√	√
Finance Web	√	X
HR Web	√	X

Application servers are also highly virtualizable. The number needed is, again, highly based on the application mix. Search services – especially the indexing role – are the mostly resource intensive. Services like MMS, BDC or Excel calculation services can also add to the need for more servers. Server services can be balanced across multiple servers by SharePoint – it doesn't require OS-level clustering. Again, redundancy and fault tolerance are the most common reasons for having two servers. In addition, for high volume environments, having a pair of servers for search services and a pair for everything else provides smoother application services, especially during "bursty" search activities like crawling.

Finally, we consider the SQL server. Your high availability designs should be consistent with the rest of your mission critical SQL enterprise applications. If you use log shipping, or SQL clustering, that technique is most easily supported for SharePoint's use of SQL, since it's probably the one you know best.

In addition, although SQL virtualization is supported by Microsoft, it requires great care. Usually, although the CPU and C drive are virtualized, the actual physical disks are dedicated. In general, I discourage virtualizing production SQL environments. (See further discussion above in the section on Disk I/O on page 40.)

Finally, assuming you have a well-engineered properly performing highly available instance of SQL to support SharePoint, try to avoid reusing it for other, non-SharePoint usage. It can become fairly common for different line of business systems (e.g. Client Relationship Management (CRM)) to grow rapidly. Runaway growth of "other" databases is the most common root cause of inadequate disk space on SQL systems that were originally engineered for the SharePoint workload alone.

In general, to sum up, the most common layout of medium farms are 1-1-1 (one WFE, one app, single SQL server) or 2-2-2 (two of each). As noted above, the most common reason to have multiple servers is fault tolerance, and once you've made the plunge to add redundancy at one level, you might as well make all levels redundant. Keep in mind, however, that you can add additional servers over time with minimal impact to an existing farm, especially for WFEs and app servers. Deferring redundancy may be a reasonable decision for budget constrained environments.

Large Farm

Finally, it's possible to need even more servers in highly available, highly secure environments with large user populations (typically over

10,000 users). There are few "one size fits all" rules for these –
distributed data centers and geo-replication are sometime part of
these designs. Four or more WFEs, with multiple application servers
and a larger number of index servers are not unknown. For example,
internally at Microsoft, a group of over 30 servers provides highly
available, common Search SSA services to other SharePoint farms on
the Microsoft intranet.

Some analysts would extend the number of servers in a "medium"
farm to seven or more; the distinction is fuzzy at best. A fair case can
be made that having two front end servers, four application servers
and a SQL cluster is a large farm.

Logical structure and Information Architecture

Information architecture ("IA") is the discipline for designing and
building logical systems to structure information supported by
physical systems. In SharePoint, IA is a discussion about web
application, sites, and libraries, among other things. SharePoint farms
have a hierarchical logical architecture that runs on the infrastructure
foundation supplied by WFEs, application servers and databases.

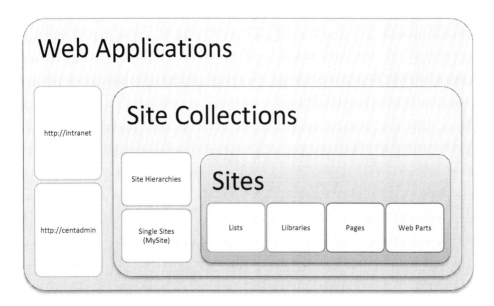

SharePoint farms contain a hierarchy of separate web applications. Each web application can contain one or multiple "site collections", and each site collection can contain one or multiple sites.

Web Applications

Each farm contains at least two web applications. Out of the box, SharePoint will install one web application for the Central Administration site and one (usually) for the initial user content web site. In the diagram above, you can see a reference to:

- http://intranet
- http://centadmin

In practice, you may provision multiple additional web applications – each with an independent top level URL. The URLs may each use DNS aliases, or the machine's physical host name. Each web application can also run on separate IP ports – not just port 80. So you might have a series of web applications for user content:

- http://server
- http://server:81
- http://server:90

And so forth. SharePoint also lets you share multiple aliases that point to the same SharePoint web application – so http://WFE1 http://WFE2 and http://intranet can all point to the same SharePoint web app. Each web application has its own set of features, and its own mapping to shared service applications (they can all share the same SSAs too). Also, each web application can use its own IIS application pool and execution credentials if desired. This requires some planning – each IIS pool consumes about 800MB of RAM, as previously noted, so you may not need a separate IIS process for each web application if there are many on your farm.

Finally, all the web application provisioning, name mapping and configuration happens entirely on the SharePoint site. SharePoint will add the correct IIS sites, application pools, and name/port binding to IIS on all servers in the farm as part of IIS provisioning process. We'll see this later during the section on installation – but that's why you are sometimes advised to run **IISReset** on each web server after certain configuration operations.

Site Collections

Site Collections are a really important container in SharePoint. Each site collection lives in one and only one content database. Although a content database can house multiple site collections, a site collection can't span multiple databases.

Each site collection also acts as a security, navigation, and branding frontier. There are many SharePoint native elements, such as security groups, global navigation bars and web part galleries that can be shared and visible anywhere inside a single site collection. However, running common navigation, security or branding across multiple site collections takes some manual synchronization or custom coding.

A site collection contains a top-level navigation bar – "Global Navigation". By default, the global navigation bar can automatically add links to subsites as they are created. Global navigation can also contain links to other site collections. Each of those site collections has an independent set of global navigation bars. So all site collections in the farm can use the same top navigation but it will be up to you to create the same menu bar across all those site collections. (See page 348 for more on navigation.)

Site collections also contain a very important security group – the site collection administrators. During setup, you're required to name at least one primary administrator and an optional backup. These administrators have permission to see and do virtually anything on the sites attached to that collection.

Site collections begin with a "root" level site at each web application. Each site collection may contain a hierarchy of subsites – which can all share and inherit the same branding, master pages and security, and live in the same database. Or a web application may contain multiple site collections, each with a separate group of subsites. The following hierarchy shows three site collections – one at the root and two attached separate collections attached to a "managed path".[10] In this example, each site collection has its own content database – although they could all share a common database as well.

Site Collection	Sites	Database
"Root"	http://intranet http://intranet/hr http://intranet/finance	WSSContent_Intranet
"PMO"	http://intranet/sites/PMO http://intranet/sites/PMO/project1 http://intranet/sites/PMO/project2	WSSContent_PMO
"Mktg"	http://intranet/sites/mktg http://intranet/sites/mktg/data http://intranet/sites/mktg/art	WSS_Content_Mktg

By default, you are likely to see two completely different approaches to site collection structure in a default SharePoint farm. For example, it's a best practice to have My Sites grouped in a common web application with at least one shared content database. But each individual My Site runs as a separate site collection – each with

---

[10] We'll get to this in depth later – but managed paths are defined in Central Administration | Web Applications and selecting **Managed Paths** on the Ribbon. By default, each web application has a managed path called "/sites". You can add new site collections under as http://intranet/sites/newsite - but http://intranet/sites itself **isn't** a site you can use.

independent navigation and security, a; attached under a managed path named "personal" (default setting):

http://mysiteapp/personal/cmcnulty

On the other hand, the principal content web applications are often comprised of a single site collection and a hierarchy of sites.   The example below illustrates a simple intranet hierarchy of one web application, with a root sites and four departmental subsites. Each subsite has its own document library, and, presumably other SharePoint elements, such as task lists, contacts, custom data and web pages.

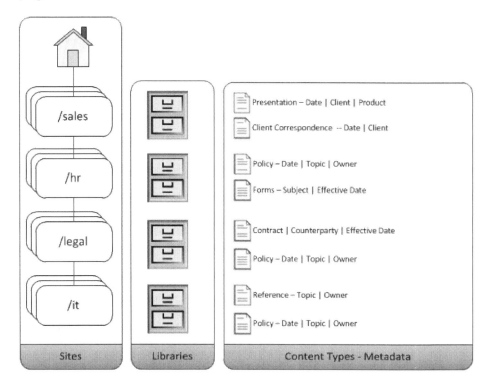

Figure 15 - Intranet Logical Structure

Sites

Sites are the principal container to house lists, libraries, and web pages. In the example above, each department site has its own document library to house files. All the sites can share a common set of themes, master pages, navigation and security, although security can be easily overridden and adjusted. For example, you might "break" security inheritance and restrict user access to the HR or Legal sites above. Sites gather related SharePoint containers (lists, libraries and pages) into a common interface. For example, sites may be used for each department, for a project, or to organize a temporary event.

Architecture Constraints

All those powers and capabilities aren't completely unlimited. Some performance caps and guidelines worth keeping in mind are noted below. Many of these are hard to exceed in real world usage. A complete list can be found online at http://technet.microsoft.com/en-us/library/cc262787.aspx

- 250,000 sites per site collection
- 5,000 site collections per content databases
- 300 Content databases per web application
- 30 million documents/library

200GB is the recommended maximum content database size if you have only one content database in the web application. For multiple content databases, none of them should grow larger than 100GB. These are optimal performance guidelines – the system doesn't crash or shutdown at 201GB. However larger content databases introduce inefficiencies for large queries, backups, and other resource intensive operations. In June 2011, Microsoft issued revised guidance about going beyond 200GB limits for databases on high performance disk or for archives. (For more detail, please see the section Service Pack 1 Storage Limits on page 37.)

The default maximum size for any file uploaded to SharePoint is 50MB. This can be increased if needed to 2GB (2047MB), as discussed below in the section Large File Upload Support on page 111.

Increasing the upload size increases the performance requirements, especially for RAM, but it's not a hard process. However, 2GB is an absolute maximum – it's the largest file size supported by SQL and by the SharePoint server object model.

Information Architecture Planning

In information architecture no two users are identical. There are many distinct usage styles. Users can be divided into at least four classes as they interact with any web site:

- Mailers
- Mappers
- Searchers
- Browsers

A fairly common technique in web site requirements and design has been dubbed "OTS" – over the shoulder. Basically, just by watching users interact with a web site you learn a lot about its organizational and navigation architecture. Some users jump right in and start clicking on things. Others use guidance from search or maps, or seek advice from other users. There's no right or wrong way to use any site – but you need to be able to accommodate all of these usage patterns.

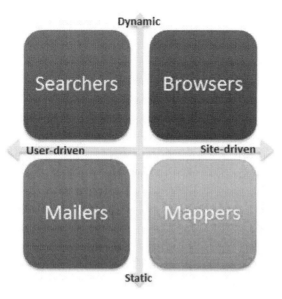

Figure 16 - User Types

I've grouped them along two axes:

- *Static vs. dynamic* – is the navigation changing in real-time as the site itself changes, or is it relying on preconfigured or remembered signposts?
- *User vs. site* – do users get guidance from the site itself or from something that's directly user generated.

Here are the four types:

Mailers – Historically, these users don't actually use a web site, just its contents. Rather than browse or search they ask friends, colleagues or administrators to "just email" links to them. Although this seems like the least sophisticated way to use a site, modern web trends have greatly expanded this technique. Instead of solely relying on email, users increasingly look to crowd-sourced innovations, like microblog status updates, personal sites, or wallboard posts to get and use the links they need.

Mappers – My dad would always look at the table of contents in a reference book first. Some users are the same way – rather than search, they look to a static site map to find the section they need.

Searchers – Instead of flipping to the front of the book for the table of contents, other readers start at the back – for the index. (Or else they're used to reading the Forward[11])   Similarly, some users search to find what they need. These users need to be accommodated by metadata crawling, faceted searches, refinements, and usage-oriented results ranking. Quality of search results, keyword management, and best bets are critical.   These users can teach you a lot about site IA – top search terms are usually good candidates for home page links. If the most frequently searched for term is "holidays", you should probably have a holiday list link on the intranet home page.

Browsers – Browsers just use the navigation links on the site to get what they need. You might think of them as "traditional" users, but they require a lot of care and planning. If the user interface and navigational structure aren't intuitive, they get frustrated and try another technique (search) or give up. A good example is a company travel policy. It may be obvious to Finance that Finance is the home of the travel policy, but if a user expects it in HR, how would they know to visit another internal area of an intranet?

We used to view this as evolutionary – meaning, how you get users to stop emailing each other for advice and build a self-navigating web site? In this view, users began by asking other users where to find things, then progressed to search, and finally "matured" to self-navigating site taxonomy.

---

[11] A Yiddish-language newspaper – and like all Hebrew-based languages, it reads in what I would call back-to-front.

It doesn't work that way anymore. The rise of search oriented user interfaces like FAST and social networking has changed this paradigm. I don't think you can expect a progressive evolution from Mailers to Browsers anymore. Instead, all usage styles can be expected at any point in a site's evolution. De-emphasizing search or overlooking social networking may disregard a permanent part of your user population. Remember, no two people – including you – use a site the same way.

Knowledge Management

Knowledge management should be a high level design goal for any information system architecture. Information warehousing is crucial for recordkeeping, but turning a trove of facts and details into meaningful information is the end result of proper IA design. "Knowledge" itself provides meaning and context. For example:

- *Information* - "I gave my daughter a calendar for her birthday this year. It was purchased at 50 Main Street for $12.95."
- *Knowledge* – "I've given her a calendar for her birthday for three years – she hasn't used the last one since she keeps her schedule on her phone".

The knowledge about the calendar allows me to make decisions and take actions – for example, asking her if she'd like something else, or picking a different gift.

Decision making is the probably the most important reason to develop knowledge management systems. Few organizations have disciplined processes for decision making, or for capturing the reasons for a decision as part of a self-learning process. For evidence, we need look no further than a litany of bad decisions – the global financial crisis of 2007-2008 was rife with poor decisions, such as the deal making around Lehman Brothers and Bear Stearns. Decision making requires good information and great knowledge. Getting to knowledge is hard.

 But there are also many clear examples of properly designed decision systems – such as insurance underwriting, package routing, or medical scheduling. It's not impossible! As a result, information architects (and business intelligence designers) should ask themselves if they understand the kinds of decision, or decision processes that will use their designs. Without knowing this, it's very easy to build something that answers the "wrong" questions.

Many organization cultures rely too heavily on "hero" decisions. In the 1990's one consulting firm dubbed this technique "BOGSAT" – for "Bunch Of Guys Sit Around Talking."

Unstructured decision processes might make sense for decisions with little impact, or when the "decider" has a high level of expertise and familiarity with evaluating intangibles.   But there are many other cases. SO, with that in mind, here are some key attributes of efficient decision making include:

- An inventory of important decisions
- Classification schemes
- Group of experts make the decision instead of a single person
- Decision are measureable and outcomes are evaluated
- Decisions are governed by systemic processes.
- Decision processes allow for selections of "how to decide"

So here are some key attributes of any knowledge system:

Purposeful and relevant
Records management is sometimes about preserving or "freezing" data/information until it can be applied in the future to create new knowledge, but recordkeeping for record keeping's sake is NOT knowledge management. For example, I could record the weight of

each calendar gift I've given – but since I'm not shipping it, no one probably will ever need that information again. It doesn't add to our knowledge.

Relevant means more than someone caring about the data at creation – that information should have a clear owner throughout its life. And its lifecycle should reflect is purpose. Separating the "wheat" of knowledge from the "chaff" of data isn't simple – but that information lifecycle should allow you to permanently exclude information that will never be needed again. It obscures,

Recoverable

We need to be able to get knowledge back upon demand. In part, we need to recreate the original context of the information – for example, how was it established that she doesn't use her calendar – observation, hearsay, or her direct statement. Second, as information is analyzed and compared with other information, we need to be able to recreate the context for re-analysis. That means understanding why I was looking at gift purchases. Was it for family budgeting, or to give her godmother a new gift suggestion?

Transferable and impersonal

I'm not suggesting that information need not have security. But knowledge can move among multiple **appropriate** stakeholders, originators, consumers without obstacle.

And it needs to be persistent without my sustained involvement. If the information as recorded says "Cal Dev BDay Wal 11/1", it may be obvious to me that I bought a calendar for Devin's birthday at Walgreen's on 1 November. But anyone else might need to ask me what I meant. That's not usable knowledge. Someone needs to be able to work with my information without my involvement. For knowledge management, information needs to be able to be moved from originators or holders without significant changes that require personal interpretation.

Recontextable

New knowledge is created is we can take granular information and rearrange for new meanings, or apply those facts in new contexts. Information shouldn't only make sense in its original context. For example, "95 degrees" requires additional information (it was at midnight on December 25 in Boston, MA) to make it equally relevant in a list of Christmas weather anomalies and all-time daily high temperatures.

Recreateable

Not all information is created equal. Some information is more accurate than others. Also, the perceived usefulness of information may change over time. That's why it's important to know the source of any single piece of information.

Translatable

In case I haven't been clear, knowledge is a higher abstraction than a series of recorded facts. In order to sustain that high level, the underlying information needs to be able to change storage, formats, and frameworks without necessarily changing the underlying knowledge. The knowledge that John Adams had a more contentious U.S. Presidency (1797-1801) than his predecessor George Washington persists whether or not the underlying sources include the print encyclopedias, Wikipedia, or a series of Twitter posts.

Services and Features Planning

Shared Service Applications (SSA)

In SharePoint 2007, the Shared Service Provider ("SSP") was a single application that governed user profiles, search, business data, etc. Having privileges to administer the SSP gave you rights to administer all the shared services, so the SSP was usually kept in the control of IT administrators.

In SharePoint 2010, the 2007 SSP has been "disbanded". Each of its elements is now a "Shared Service Application". You can mix and match them singly or in groups, as needed, to match your farm's actual needs. So there's no need to deploy Visio Services, or PowerPivot, for example, if you don't use them. You can also allow selected business users to administer the service without giving them broad privileges. For example, record managers can control metadata taxonomies, and HR may want to oversee additions to user profiles.

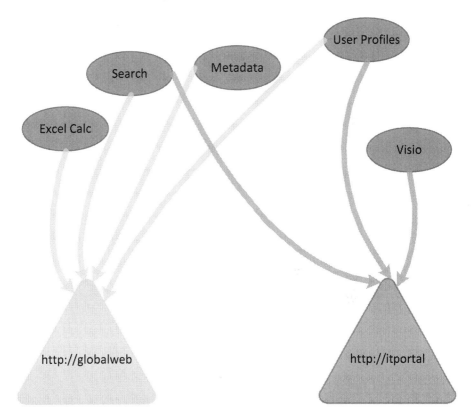

Figure 17 - Shared Service Application Architecture

Also in 2010, many of these SSAs can be shared across the enterprise to other farms – although not all SSAs. SSAs that can be published from an enterprise services farm to other farms include:

- Access Services
- BDC
- Lotus Notes Connector
- Managed Metadata
- Performance Point
- Search
- Secure Store
- SQL Server Analysis Services
- PowerPivot
- User Profile Service
- Visio Graphics
- Web Analytics
- Word Viewing Service

SSAs that cannot be published cross farm include:

- PowerPoint Service
- Project Server Service
- Word Automation Service

Site Subscriptions

Site subscriptions are a new element. Site subscriptions are groups of site collections, and you can delegate administrative control over a range of sites as a result. Although this was designed for shared hosting providers in a multitenant environment, this could also prove useful in large decentralized enterprises or large IT service centers that provide SharePoint service to independent business units.

Each separate customer, or tenant, can be assigned its own pool of site collections, known as "subscriptions". Features can be deployed across all site collections in a subscription, and tenants can be given the right to administer aspects of their site collections without impact to other subscriptions. Multitenant subscriptions, although powerful, are not common.

Server Services

Closely related to SSAs, server level services deliver essential SharePoint functions for the farm. You don't need to turn everything on everywhere. The following table, derived from dozens of field installations, represents a balanced approach to needed services mixed with disabling unused or unneeded services. Some of these services, such as Project Server or PowerPivot, may not actually be used anywhere in your farm. Again, your actual needs may vary, especially for larger, externally facing or complex farms.

Server Service	App Servers	Web Servers
Access Database Service	Y	N
Application Registry Service	Y	Y
Business Data Connectivity Service	Y	N
Central Administration	Y	N
Claims to Windows Token Service	Y	N
Document Conversions Launcher Service	N	N
Document Conversions Load Balancer Service	N	N
Excel Calculation Services	Y	N
Lotus Notes Connector	N	N
Managed Metadata Web Service	Y	N
Microsoft SharePoint Foundation Incoming E-Mail	Y	Y
Microsoft SharePoint Foundation Sandboxed Code Service	N	N
Microsoft SharePoint Foundation Subscription Settings Service	N	N
Microsoft SharePoint Foundation Web Application	Y	Y
Microsoft SharePoint Foundation Workflow Timer Service	Y	Y
PerformancePoint Service	Y	N
PowerPoint Service	Y	N
Project Application Service	Y	Y
Search Query and Site Settings Service	Y	Y
Secure Store Service	Y	N
SharePoint Foundation Search	N	N
SharePoint Server Search	Y	N

SQL Server PowerPivot Service	Y	N
User Profile Service	Y	N
User Profile Synchronization Service	Y	N
Visio Graphics Service	Y	N
Web Analytics Data Processing Service	Y	Y
Web Analytics Web Service	Y	Y
Word Automation Services	Y	N
Word Viewing Service	Y	N

Features

SharePoint also groups its functions into configurable, installable features at the farm, site collection, site, and web application levels. Here's the breakdown of how I've most commonly installed them. SharePoint provides actual descriptions of each inside the administrative interface if you need them. Again, actual mileage may vary. For these charts, the farm level and web application features rarely vary.

Farm Level Features	On	Off
"Connect to Office" Ribbon Controls	√	
Access Services Farm Feature	√	
Data Connection Library	√	
Excel Services Application Edit Farm Feature	√	
Excel Services Application View Farm Feature	√	
Excel Services Application Web Part Farm Feature	√	
FAST Search Server 2010 for SharePoint Master Job Provisioning	√	
Global Web Parts	√	
Office.com Entry Points from SharePoint	√	
Offline Synchronization for External Lists	√	
PowerPivot Integration Feature	√	
Social Tags and Note Board Ribbon Controls	√	
Spell Checking	√	
Visio Process Repository	√	
Visio Web Access	√	

Web Application Level Features	On	Off
Document Sets metadata synchronization	√	
SharePoint Server Enterprise Search	√	
SharePoint Server Enterprise Web application features	√	
SharePoint Server Site Search	√	
SharePoint Server Standard Web application features	√	

Site collection and site features will often vary significantly from the starting values noted below; these charts indicate common values for root-level sites and site collections for user content. For example, Office Web Apps might not be used in your environment. On the other hand, the Publishing feature requires the Enterprise license. Although not strictly necessary for collaboration, it's commonly used to support more sophisticated page designs, custom page layouts, and in-place editing techniques.

Site Collection Level Features	On	Off
Advanced Web Analytics	√	
Content Type Syndication Hub		X
Custom Site Collection Help		X
Disposition Approval Workflow	√	
Document ID Service	√	
Document Sets	√	
In Place Records Management	√	
Library and Folder Based Retention	√	
Office Web Apps	√	
Open Documents in Client Applications by Default		X
PerformancePoint Services Site Collection Features	√	
PowerPivot Feature Integration for Site Collections	√	
Publishing Approval Workflow		X
Report Server Integration Feature	√	
Reporting	√	
Search Server Web Parts		X
SharePoint 2007 Workflows		X
SharePoint Server Enterprise Site Collection features	√	
SharePoint Server Publishing Infrastructure	√	

	√
SharePoint Server Standard Site Collection features	√
Three-state workflow	√
Workflows	√

Site Level Features	On	Off
Content Organizer	√	
E-mail Integration with Content Organizer		X
Group Work Lists		X
Hold and eDiscovery		X
Metadata Navigation and Filtering	√	
Offline Synchronization for External Lists	√	
PerformancePoint Services Site Features		X
Report Server File Sync		X
SharePoint Server Enterprise Site features	√	
SharePoint Server Publishing		X
SharePoint Server Standard Site features	√	
Team Collaboration Lists	√	
Wiki Page Home Page	√	

Authentication Architecture

SharePoint 2010 continues to support **classic** authentication architecture. In classic mode, each web application is mapped to 1-5 alternate access mappings – essentially, URL aliases. (Default, Extranet, Internet, Intranet, and Custom) IIS "listens" for traffic on any of the possible alias "host headers", and each host header is linked to a specific authentication scheme. Authentication schemes supported by default are integrated Windows (NTLM or Kerberos), although other common authentication schemes include customized logins against anode server or a custom SQL table. In Classic mode, each class of authentication generates a separate NT Token on the server.

Custom authentication requires registering additional "membership providers" and "role providers" in the web.config files for Central Admin, the web application, and the Security Token Service web application. Assuming you have already written and developed a custom set of providers (you could also use the LDAP provider):

Add a Safe Control line to the SafeControls section of web.config:

```
<SafeControl Assembly="My.Intranet.CustomSecurityProviders,
Version=1.0.0.0, Culture=neutral,
PublicKeyToken=fb6e52c28c5170fe" Namespace="My.Intranet"
TypeName="*" Safe="True" />
```

Update the Role Manager and Membership sections:

```
    <roleManager defaultProvider="IntranetADAMRoleProvider">
      <providers>
            <add name="IntranetADAMRoleProvider"
type="My.Intranet.CustomADAMRoleProvider,
My.Intranet.CustomSecurityProviders, Version=1.0.0.0,
Culture=neutral, PublicKeyToken=fb6e52c28c5170fe"
server="SERVERNAME:389"
groupContainer="OU=groups,DC=DOMAIN,DC=com"
userNameProperty="mail"/>
      </providers>
    </roleManager>

    <membership defaultProvider="IntranetADAMMembershipProvider">
        <providers>
            <add name="IntranetADAMMembershipProvider"
type="My.Intranet.CustomADAMMembershipProvider,
My.Intranet.CustomSecurityProviders, Version=1.0.0.0,
Culture=neutral, PublicKeyToken=fb6e52c28c5170fe"
server="SERVER:389" userContainer="OU=users,DC=DOMAIN,DC=com" />
        </providers>
    </membership>
```

Then you can optionally extend the primary web application to a new URL, and use the new authentication scheme for that, or just use it with the AAM alias. In the diagram below, assume we have two separate URLs for the same core content application – external users are using one URL, internal users use another.

Mixed Authentication/Classic

AD Users	External Users
http://intranet .site.com [NTLM Web App]	https://site.domain.com [FBA Web App]

Content Database

Multi-Authentication/Claims

In SharePoint 2010, you can now support claims authentication running in **multiprovider** mode. Conceptually, you have only a single web application and a single access mapping, so the logical design is simpler. Inside that web application, you can activate multiple authentication schemes – say NTLM and Forms Based Authentication ("FBA"). When any user connects to the site, they're asked if they want to login with their Windows login or a user name and password. This unifies all users under a single URL, and avoids user disconnects when links are forwarded between users belonging to different login zones – i.e. if an internal user forwards an http://intranet/Quote.docx link to an external users, since everyone gets the same URL no one gets a "link not found" error because for them, they use a different URL and the links should be https://site.domain.com/Quote.docx . In Claims, all categories of authentication generate a SAML token.

What's a claim? Well, a claim can be anything we decide is OK to authenticate a user. Windows logins are a good one. User ID and password are another "claim".   Users with a key fob code, users in the email system, membership in a different single sign on system (e.g. SalesForce.com) users who click a box to continue – each of these, or combinations thereof, may be defined as "claims". In the end, you can support architecture like this:

AD Users	External Users

https://site.domain.com [Claims (NTLM/FBA) Web App]

Content Database

Office 365

There's a completely different architecture that's available "in the cloud". Third party providers like Amazon, Rackspace and FPWeb, among others, have made great strides in delivering cloud based implementation of SharePoint servers and services. However, the most critical provider of all is Microsoft, with SharePoint Online as one of the key components of Office 365, launched in 2011.

Office 365 ("O365") is comprised of four major elements:

- Exchange Online (email)
- Lync Online (voice and instant messaging)
- Office Web Applications (client productivity in a browser – Word, Excel, etcetera)

- SharePoint Online

Selecting an Office 365-based implementation of SharePoint introduces a completely different set of architectural constraints. Remember all our discussion about disk architecture, server counts and sizes, and extranet topologies. That all goes away in Office 365. Instead of running SharePoint on servers you own as a capital expense, Office 365 allows you to pay for the services and storage you need on a per-user basis, monthly.

Functionally, SharePoint Online strikes a balance between the functionality of SharePoint Foundation and SharePoint 2010 Server Enterprise. Office 365 usually runs in a multitenant, distributed architecture where SharePoint services are supplied from a range of servers in distributed across Microsoft' global data centers. So this requires a few tradeoffs in functions. In almost all cases[12], this restricts a few of the most complex functions in SharePoint Enterprise. Although there are a few tiers of service options, in general, SharePoint Online does not allow:

- Custom solutions that require direct access to the server, such as Visual Web Parts. Sandboxed solutions are supported, however.
- PowerPivot
- SQL Server Reporting Service Integration
- Business Connectivity Services (originally this was a blanket restriction, but a slipstream release in 2011 added support for access to web services-based remote data in O365 BCS.)
- FAST Search Server Integration
- Web Analytics

---

[12] Microsoft also offers a dedicated server option for extremely large SharePoint installations. SharePoint Online Dedicated removes constraints on storage size and custom solutions.

- Site collections greater than 100GB

For these reasons, O365 is seldom used to replatform mature, highly customized enterprise installations of "on-premises"[13] SharePoint. However, it is a good choice for getting SharePoint running quickly, and for growing into its functions, understanding some of the tradeoffs for getting a highly available, globally redundant, easily accessible managed environment. Early adopters have used O365 SharePoint for:

- Pilots and proofs-of-concept
- Test environments
- New implementations
- Field or remote access

And with the rise of third party tools, such as the Quest Migration Suite, that allow you to move content from on premises to the cloud and back, we're seeing a lot more "hybrid" scenarios – where part of SharePoint lives on premises and another part lives I the cloud.

Office 365 offers some compelling arguments for Exchange and Lync as well – especially where those environments are less likely to be customized than SharePoint. That said, many organizations use O365 for Exchange but leave SharePoint completely in their own data center.

So Microsoft offers two classes of SharePoint online. The "K" class, or kiosk, is designed for deskless workers with simple document storage and search needs. It provides user access to the standard O365 SharePoint content database (10GB, although extra storage can be

---

[13] Please don't call it "on premise"! Premise means a proposition based on an idea, and most data centers have stronger underpinnings than just a concept. This is a pet peeve of a long trusted colleague, and a grammatically correct one, at that.

purchased). Also, each user gets a 500MB mailbox through Exchange Online – but kiosk workers don't get individual My Sites and storage.

(Please note, all pricing was as-published Microsoft at press time, and is subject to change. Also, these tables don't detail all the non-SharePoint features of Office 365.)

Office 365 Kiosk Plans	K1	K2
Exchange Online	√	√
SharePoint Online	√	√
Office Web Apps	Read Only	√
Monthly cost per user	$4	$10

Most midsized business will need something more – that's where the Office 365 Enterprise plans come in.   There are four Enterprise plans. All of them provide:

- Administration and Active Directory integration
- 25GB Exchange mailbox storage with access from browser or Outlook
- Lync Online
- Forefront Antivirus for Exchange

And the high-end plan, E4, also includes Lync Online and On Premises for phone/PBX/voice messaging (that what the extra $3 difference between E3 and E4 gets you!)

But let's look further at SharePoint Online. All plans come with 10GB of SharePoint Online content storage, plus 1GB per user (500MB in the central pool and a 500MB quota-enforced My Site.

Office 365 Enterprise Plans	E1	E2	E3	E4
SharePoint Online	√	√	√	√
Office Web Apps		√	√	√
Local Copy of Office Professional 2010 Plus			√	√

Forms Services, Vision Services, Access Services		√	√
Monthly cost per user[14]	$10	$16	$24	$27[15]

In addition to the functional differences noted above, there are also a few details to remember for SharePoint Online:

- 10GB base storage plus 500MB for each enterprise user
- 500MB quota-limited My Site storage for each enterprise user
- No additional storage provided for "kiosk" or "partner" external users
- Additional storage available for $2.50/GB monthly
- 100GB maximum storage per site collection
- 300 non-My Site site collections maximum
- 5TB maximum storage (this factors in My Site usage on top of 300 100GB site collections)
- 250MB maximum single file size

All in all, Office 365 presents a completely different set of criteria for how to architect a SharePoint solution. Although there are some constraints, you also get rapid provisioning, backup, recovery, fault tolerance, and guaranteed uptime, and you are freed from the capital expenditure of a complex server farm. We'll cover highlights of Office 365 Administration later on at page 339.

Client Systems Overview

On the client side, Internet Explorer 7, 8, and 9; Mozilla Firefox, Google Chrome[16] and Apple Safari are all fully supported for portal

---

[14] Source: http://www.microsoft.com/download/en/details.aspx?id=13602
[15] Includes rights to Lync for on-premises voice usage.
[16] Chrome support was announced with Service Pack 1.

collaboration. However, Internet Explorer 6.0 is no longer supported, so don't defer that upgrade!

In the Office 2010 suite, Groove has been rebranded as SharePoint Workspace 2010. Groove began as a peer-to-peer collaboration tool, and in the 2007 release, Groove allowed users to synchronize local copies of a SharePoint document library. In 2010, Workspace gives offline, synchronized access to SharePoint forms and lists, in addition to the document library support already provided under Groove 2007.

SharePoint 2010 provides a server based version of most Office applications – Office Web Access, or "OWA". [It's going to be hard to stop thinking only of web access to Exchange as "OWA"!] In part, this enables simultaneous multiuser editing of Office documents:

- Excel in OWA, not client
- Word/PowerPoint on client if file saved in shared document library
- OneNote client or OWA

Installation and configuration of SharePoint 2010 merits an entire volume, particularly for complex architectures or requirements. That's not our goal here. This section will provide a walkthrough on setting up a single server reference implementation of SharePoint 2010. We'll also point out some of the most common best practices in an initial SharePoint configuration that aren't always used or even known. Here we go.

Prerequisites

There are a lot, but for this walkthrough, we're going to start on a single server, with Windows and SQL preinstalled:

- Windows 2008 R2 X64 Enterprise Edition
- SQL Server 2008 R2 x64

See http://technet.microsoft.com/en-us/library/ee662513.aspx for more on prerequisites.

Service Accounts

These are the domain accounts that are generally needed in a standard SharePoint installation. These accounts are shown with suggested names; names can be adjusted to confirm to any corporate naming standard for service accounts. For example, you may wish to designate ALL service accounts with a sv- or svc- prefix. Similarly, you may want to designate "regions" with a suffix, such as –dev, -tst, or –prd. Likewise, if you have already established SQL service account conventions, those accounts are fine as well.

- **spfarm** (Farm acct; local admin on the SharePoint servers and either sa or dbcreate, dbowner and security admin on the SQL server.)
- **svcsql** (SQL Server service acct)

- **sppool** (IIS pool acct)
- **spcrawl** (Search accts)
- **spadmin** Interactive admin (install account; local, site collection and farm admin privileges)

Installation

OK – we're ready to fire up the DVD or ISO – whatever installation media you have. The Setup program brings you to a screen where you can review production documentation ("Prepare") or Microsoft online information ("Other Information"). Let's plunge in!

As noted above, assuming you're using a range of accounts to configure and administer SharePoint, login to the server as the **spadmin** account, which should have local admin permissions.

Install Software Prerequisites

Installing prerequisites is an essential step, especially for first time installations. The prerequisite checker makes sure the system meets minimum requirements, and automatically installs and configures the following elements as needed:

- Application Server Role, Web Server (IIS) Role
- Microsoft SQL Server 2008 Native Client
- Hotfix for Microsoft Windows (KB976462)
- Windows Identity Foundation (KB974405)
- Microsoft Sync Framework Runtime v1.0 (x64)
- Microsoft Chart Controls for Microsoft .NET Framework 3.5
- Microsoft Filter Pack 2.0
- Microsoft SQL Server 2008 Analysis Services ADOMD.NET
- Microsoft Server Speech Platform Runtime (x64)
- Microsoft Server Speech Recognition Language - TELE(en-US)
- SQL 2008 R2 Reporting Services SharePoint 2010 Add-in

However, the prerequisite checker does not explicitly check to see if you have access to SQL Server. This is probably the most essential prerequisite. (Although there's a workaround later). In our reference, we already have SQL Server 2008 R2 running locally on the target machine. But for most installations, Medium Farm for example, the SQL Server will be on a remote machine – so the local prerequisite check wouldn't care.

TIP: *If you are actually installing a server farm, you'll run through this installation cycle on each WFE or App Server after the configuration database, Central Admin, and the farm have been established with the first server installation.*

Next you'll be prompted to enter the Product Key. This should have been supplied as part of your license. If you don't have one – sorry, can't help you here. The Product Key is a 25 character code that unlocks the installation process.

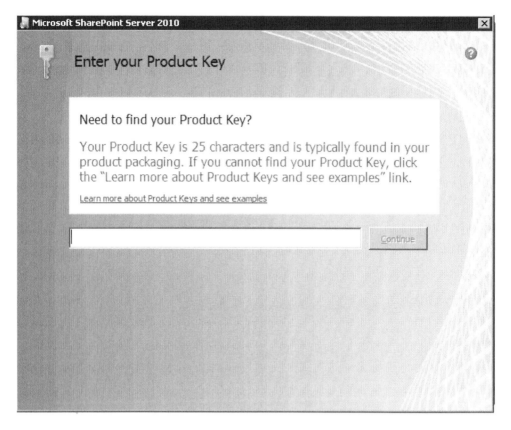

Figure 18 - Product Key

Now we come to our first big decision – the type of installation.   This
screen asks us to choose between:

- Standalone
- Server Farm

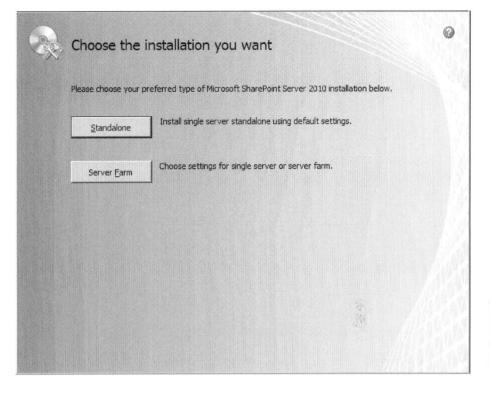

Choose the installation you want

Please choose your preferred type of Microsoft SharePoint Server 2010 installation below.

Standalone — Install single server standalone using default settings.

Server Farm — Choose settings for single server or server farm.

Figure 19 - Installation Type

Our reference build is a single server instance, so this should be a simple decision, right? Trick question! As Yogi Berra allegedly remarked, "when you come to a fork in the road, take it!" Truth is, there's only one decision here. Always, always, always select Server Farm. The Standalone option locks you into a single server configuration permanently – you can't add additional servers to the farm later. It also installs and forces you to use a local copy of SQL Server 2008 Express. That's great if you don't have a SQL Server sitting around (this is the workaround I just mentioned!). But the Standalone option doesn't look, or care, if you have a "better" version of SQL already installed locally- it just does its own thing.

You're still not safe from the accidental single server installation. Even if you choose **Server Farm**, the next screen asks you again which kind of Server Farm installation you want. Unless you really, really, really want an unexpandable farm that's limited to SQL Server 2008 Express Edition, choose **Complete**.

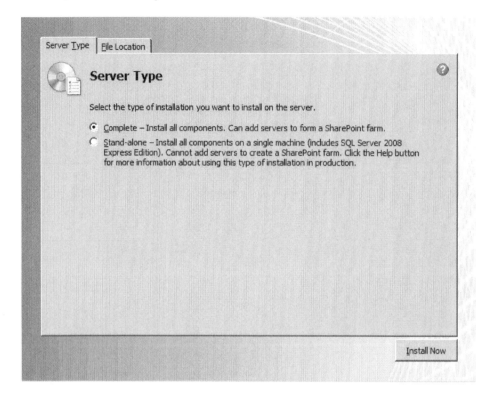

Figure 20 - Server Type

This screen also lets you specify alternate file locations and the initial location for local search index files. (The default is C:\Program Files\Microsoft Office Servers\14.0\Data) Those can be changed later. So let's click **Install Now**, and head out for coffee while the installer does its work.

At the end, you'll be asked if you want to run the SharePoint Products and Technologies Wizard – the so-called "gray wizard". Often this is OK, but for our example, we're also going to install the Office Web Applications. And we would need to run it again after the OWA installation. So, to save time, if you're installing OWA, you can uncheck the Run Now box and finish.

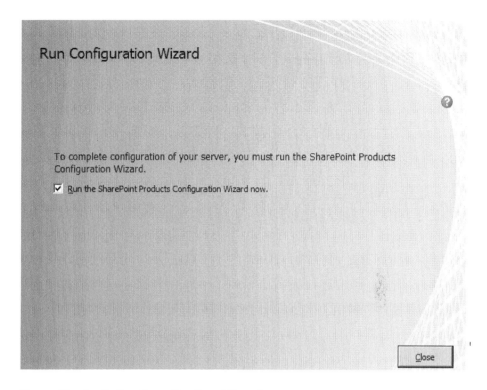

Run Configuration Wizard

To complete configuration of your server, you must run the SharePoint Products Configuration Wizard.

☑ Run the SharePoint Products Configuration Wizard now.

Close

Figure 21 - Invitation from the Gray Wizard

TIP: *Office Web Apps is a solid feature, and well accepted by most organizations. However, OWA is not an easily uninstalled feature – parts of it stay embedded in the farm and the UI. I've had one client decide after OWA was already in use to roll it back – they had decided to use the farm for public access, and the variability of opening documents in the browser or a mix of Office clients was hard to communicate. Bottom line – confirm that you want OWA before installation.*

Assuming you **are** installing OWA, run through the OWA default installation process. You need the license key, and usually accepting the default file locations is fine. At the end of that sequence, you will again be invited to Run Configuration Wizard. This time, it's OK.

SharePoint Products Configuration Wizard

The Products Configuration Wizard is also called the "gray wizard" – in part because its screens are principally gray, and in part to distinguish it from the Farm Configuration Wizard (the "white wizard") which shows up later. The gray wizard establishes SharePoint Central Administration and the configuration database. It will also get used again and again throughout the lifetime of SharePoint. For example, you'll use it to connect new servers to the farm, and to complete the deployment of Cumulative Update patches and Service Packs. We'll save that fun for another day...

The wizard starts. You'll be asked if it's OK to restart IIS during the process. (Yes.)

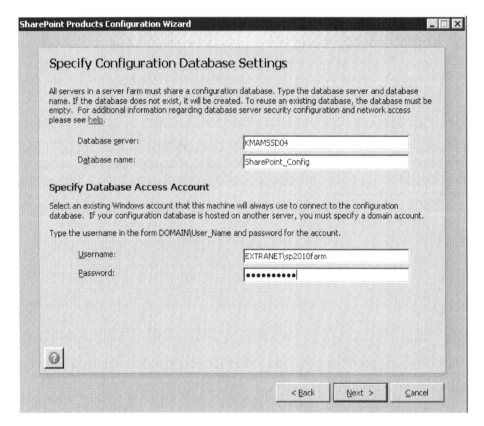

Figure 22 - Database Settings

Our first screen asks us to choose two critical elements.

Configuration Database Settings sets up the location of the SharePoint config database. The database server itself assumes that all servers have access to that database server, and that the database access account has a trusted login relationship with that server. Sometimes, especially in web-facing systems, there may not be a trust relationship. In that case, you're going to need to use the PSCONFIG command line tool to specify a SQL-server authenticated account for connecting to the database.

By default, the database name is **SharePoint_Config**. If you are only hosting one farm on your SQL instance, that's fine. If not, you should change the names to make clear which configuration databases are used with each farm.

TIP: *Although the configuration database can be moved once created, it's a more complex undertaking than just updating a dialog box. Try to place the configuration database in a persistent, permanent location.*

You also need to specify the database access account. Using the matrix of service accounts described earlier, this should be the **spfarm** account. Again, this is the most critical service account of all. As noted above, this is almost always a domain account.

Central Administration

SharePoint Central Administration is an independent web application that provides browser access to most key configuration settings for your farm. Central Admin usually runs on a port other than port 80, and the wizard will propose a random high port number. If you install SharePoint a lot, you may have your own preferences for standardizing the port – e.g. "55555" – because it's easy to remember. That's OK, but it's not ideal for external facing servers. Once someone figures out the port used for one installation, it's obvious to try the same port on other installations you may have performed.

TIP: *Don't use port 80 for Central Administration. It's too obvious and too accessible to external systems.*

Figure 23 - Central Administration Configuration

You'll also be asked to specify a farm "passphrase". The passphrase provides an additional level of security. The passphrase is needed to connect a new server to the farm. Having this requirement prevents security breaches from attaching "rogue" servers to established SharePoint farms.

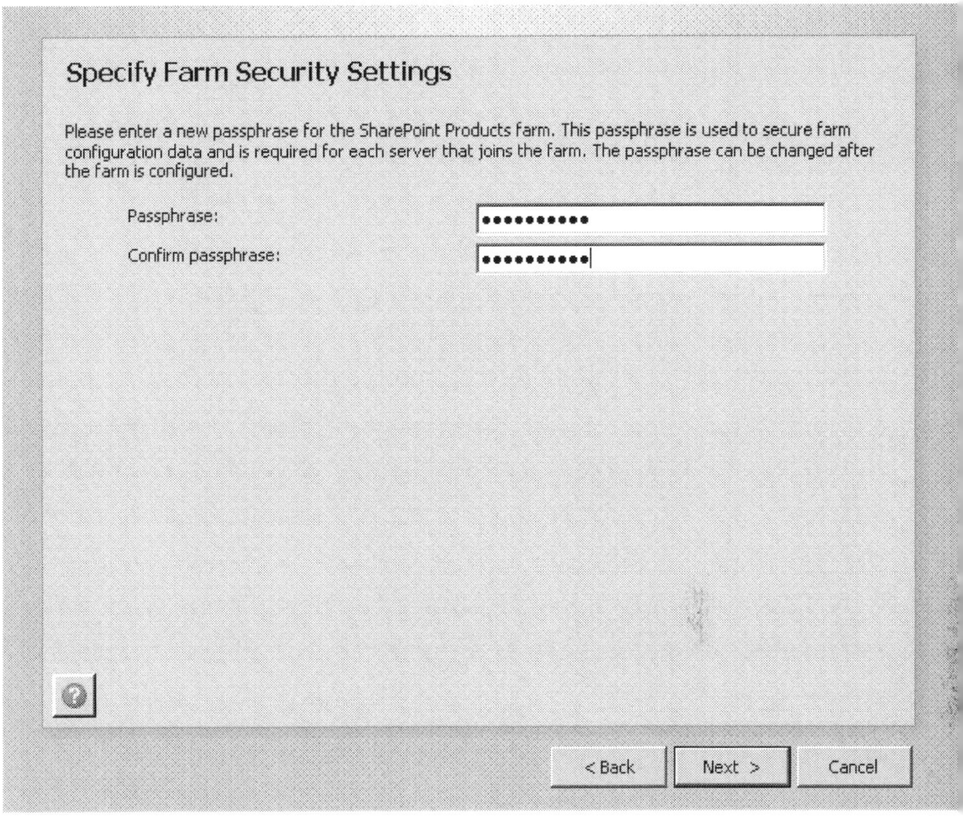

Specify Farm Security Settings

Please enter a new passphrase for the SharePoint Products farm. This passphrase is used to secure farm configuration data and is required for each server that joins the farm. The passphrase can be changed after the farm is configured.

Passphrase: ●●●●●●●●●●

Confirm passphrase: ●●●●●●●●●●

< Back   Next >   Cancel

Figure 24 - Farm Passphrase

Accept the final confirmation, and go get coffee (again!) The wizard take about 10-15 minutes to complete. During this time, the wizard creates the Central Administration web application, the configuration database, local registry security and IIS settings and deploys files into the local "SharePoint root".

If all goes well (and it should!) at the end of the process SharePoint Central Administration will launch in a new browser window. Congratulations, you are now the proud parent of an unconfigured SharePoint farm!

Farm Configuration Wizard

The SharePoint Farm Configuration Wizard offers to walk you through creating and configuring the farm SSA, My Sites, and the first user-facing site collection. As I said earlier, this process is sometimes called the "white wizard"[17]. This is to distinguish it from the "gray wizard" and to remind ourselves of our inescapable, inner Dungeons-and-Dragons style geekiness. The Farm Configuration Wizard will set up all required Shared Service Accounts using a specified service account. It's fast and easy, and it avoids the tedium of a command-line heavy, PowerShell-centric configuration of each separate SSA.

The downside of the white wizard is that it assumes too much. For starters, it sets up the My Sites site collection as part of the primary web application and content database, and most organization will prefer to run My Sites under an independent web application. (In short, if your farm is http://intranet, you are more likely to want your My Sites as http://mysites/personal/username than embedded as part of http://intranet/my/personal/username) In addition, all those SSAs will make presumptions about the database names, and those presumptions invariably add GUIDs as part of the name.

Servers don't care what the name of the database is – but DBAs certainly do. When it's time to work with the databases, the name

WSS_Content_Finance

Tells you a lot more than

WSS_Content_289b6979cc484ddfa176e693f382582e

It's a stylistic preference. If you haven't set up SharePoint before, and are unfamiliar with PowerShell, you're probably better off starting with the Wizard.

---

[17] First known usage by Todd Klindt at SharePoint 911.

SharePoint 2010 Central Administration ▸ Configure your SharePoint farm
This wizard will help you configure your SharePoint farm.

How do you want to configure your SharePoint farm?

This wizard will help with the initial configuration of your SharePoint farm. You can select the services to use in this farm and create your first site.

You can launch this wizard again from the Configuration Wizards page in the Central Administration site.

Yes, walk me through the configuration of my farm using this wizard.

[Start the Wizard]

No, I will configure everything myself.

[Cancel]

For our test case, let's set up the farm using the wizard. The first step allows us to define a "managed account". A managed account is an account credential that's registered to SharePoint and reusable from configuration screens. You can optionally choose to allow SharePoint itself to manage the service account passwords and automatically change and synchronize the passwords on a scheduled basis. For these service accounts, we want to use the sppool account. As noted earlier, we use sppool to run SharePoint services in a context different than that used for central admin and database access – so it doesn't expose the core services needlessly, and isolates the privileged access of Central Admin.

Service Account

Services require an account to operate. For security reasons, it is recommended that you use an account that's different from the farm admin account.

○ Use existing managed account

    EXTRANET\sp2010farm ▾

● Create new managed account

    User name

    EXTRANET\sp2010pool

    Password

    ●●●●●●●●●●

Earlier, we introduced the Shared Services Application ("SSA") architecture. The wizard asks you to select the initial group of SSAs. Default selections are:

- Access Services (important for Performance Point)
- Application Registry
- Business Data Connectivity (or "BDC". Used for BCS)
- Excel Services
- [off] Lotus Notes Connector
- Managed Metadata Service (essential for Communities)
- PerformancePoint
- PowerPoint
- Search
- Secure Store
- State Service (required for BDC)
- Usage and Health
- User Profiles
- Visio Graphics [sometimes off]
- Web Analytics

We'll keep those as selected and proceed. If there are any services to be disabled, just uncheck them.

Create Home Site

Finally, we're asked to choose a title, description, URL and template for the first site at the root of our web application. Technically, this is a "site collection", and not a "site". The title will be displayed on each page of the new site, and the description is optional.

The web site address, by default, will show you the "root" ("/") location on the server. Managed Paths are locations, such as "/sites", that provide logical, hierarchical places to set up new site collections. We don't need those yet.

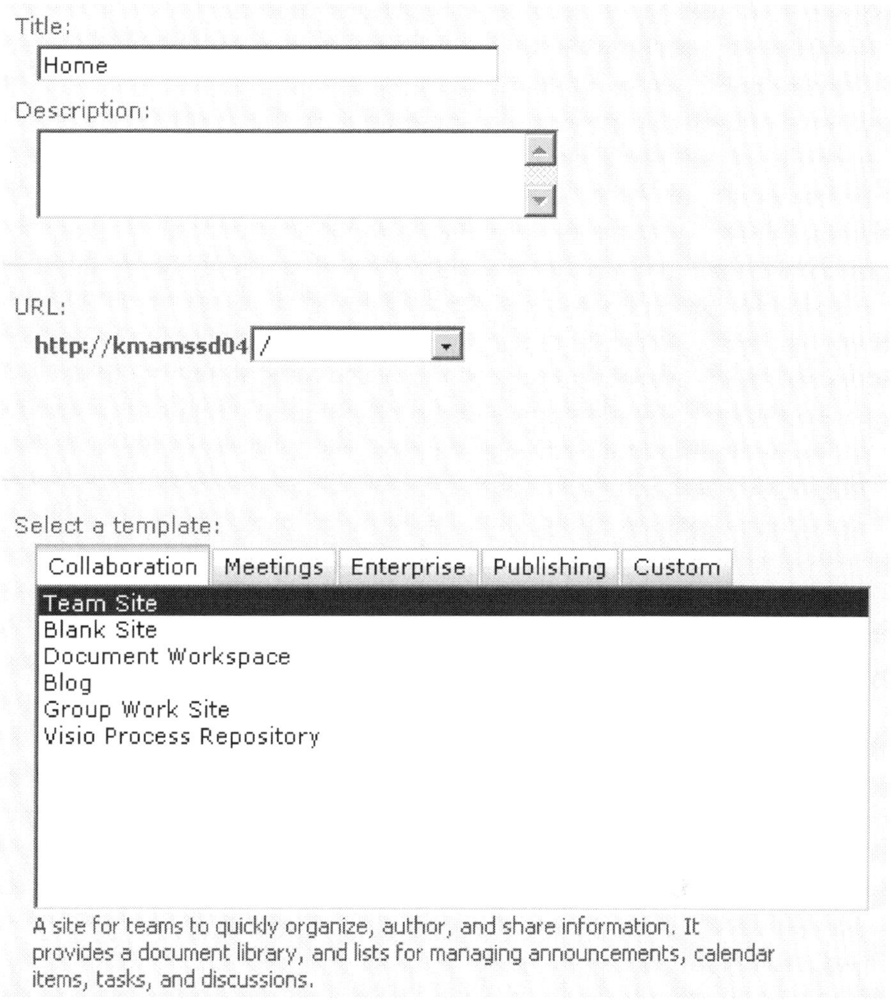

Title:

Home

Description:

URL:

http://kmamssd04 /

Select a template:

| Collaboration | Meetings | Enterprise | Publishing | Custom |

Team Site
Blank Site
Document Workspace
Blog
Group Work Site
Visio Process Repository

A site for teams to quickly organize, author, and share information. It provides a document library, and lists for managing announcements, calendar items, tasks, and discussions.

Figure 25 - Create Site Collection

Finally, the site template defines the base lists and features for the new site. Of all the types used "out of the box" the most common is the "Team Site", which includes a document library, announcements, calendar, tasks, and discussion forum. Although a site can be customized after its creation, you can't change the template after the initial selection. Not even with PowerShell.

And we're done! We now have a SharePoint 2010 farm running with a basic team site as the home page for our first user web application. Be default, the web application uses a content database named "WSS_Content", and its running on an IIS application pool using the sppool managed service account. Thank you, white wizard!

Skipping the Farm Configuration Wizard

Earlier, I referenced a series of PowerShell techniques that could be used to hand configure the services of a SharePoint farm. Although many of the SSAs and server services can be configured in Central Admin, other, such as the Secure Store Services, require PowerShell.

Ben Steginck has published an exhaustive inventory[18] of the steps involved in hand configuring a farm to completely eliminate all GUIDs from a farm build. For example, rather than using the Products and Technologies Configuration Wizard, or PSCONFIG.EXE, the basic PowerShell command for creating a new Central Admin site and a new configuration database is:

```
New-SPConfigurationDatabase -DatabaseName "SharePoint2010_Config"
-DatabaseServer "[ServerName]" -AdministrationContentDatabaseName
"WSS_Content_CentAdmin" -Passphrase (ConvertTo-SecureString
"[YourPassPhrase]" -AsPlaintext -Force) -FarmCredentials (Get-
Credential)
```

That gives you a sense of how it goes. In general, the sequence of events is:

- Set up Central Admin and Configuration Database
- Set Up User Profile Service
- Configure Search Services

---

[18] See http://www.sharepointben.com/blog/Lists/Posts/Post.aspx?ID=403 for more. This article also draws heavily on contributions from Spencer Harbar and Todd Klindt, among others.

- Usage Service
- State Service
- Secure Store Service
- Performance Point
- Cleanup

For more details, please visit Ben's blog.

Post Installation Best Practices

We've established the baseline SharePoint environment – but there's a lot more we can do to optimize our environment. I've summarized the most critical ones.

Adobe Acrobat

Adobe Acrobat PDF files are probably the most common file type in SharePoint, after the conventional Office document types. SO we need to make sure SharePoint knows how to retrieve and display PDF files.

PDF Icon Support

Word docs get cute little icons. So why not show a little 📄 instead of SharePoint's generic file icon?

- First, download the file from http://www.adobe.com/misc/linking.html and copy it to the SharePoint root[19], or "14Hive." Inside that location, the file

---

[19] We haven't talked about the "14 hive" yet. SharePoint establishes a root directory on all servers. By default, its C:\Program Files\Common Files\Microsoft Shared\web server extensions\14 on all SharePoint servers. Code, DLLs, standard web pages, configuration files and the like are all deployed somewhere below the SharePoint root. In SharePoint 2007, it was often called the "12 Hive", since SharePoint 2007 was part of the "Wave 12" of releases that were packaged with Office 2007, and that number shows in the file path. For unknown reasons, probably superstition, Microsoft skipped

goes in the TEMPLATE/IMAGES folder on all WFE servers.   And make sure to name the file pdf16.gif.

- Next, you'll need to edit the DOCICON.XML file. It's found in C:\Program Files\Common Files\Microsoft Shared\web server extensions\14\TEMPLATE\XML, or the TEMPLATE\XML folder under the SharePoint root if you've installed that on different path. Add the following line to the Mapping Keys section of the file and save it. You'll need to make this update on all WFE servers.

```
<Mapping Key="pdf" Value="pdf16.gif"/>
```

- Finally, perform an IISReset on all updated servers to force IIS to reload the icon maps.

File and Search Support

First, let's make sure the Acrobat PDF file type isn't blocked. SharePoint allows you to block file types within each web application.

- From SharePoint Central administration, choose Application Management | Web Applications
- Highlight the web application and select Blocked File Types on the Ribbon
- Make sure the pdf isn't a blocked file type.

Next, we need to make sure that the SharePoint search SSA knows how to index the full text of PDF documents. Industry standards define how to create an iFilter – an interpreter that provides the connection between the indexer and the particular file type. There are several iFilters available for Adobe PDF. Adobe itself publishes a free

---

13 and went right to "14" for SharePoint 2010. The next release is already known as "Wave 15".

iFilter at
http://www.adobe.com/support/downloads/detail.jsp?ftpID=4025

In addition, there are Independent Software Vendors ("ISVs"), such as FoxIt Software who produce high performance PDF iFilters.

- Install the iFilter on all SharePoint servers involved in crawling, indexing, or querying.
- Open up the Search SSA from Central Administration | Application Management | Service Applications.
- On the left hand Quick Launch, select File Types under Crawling.
- Make sure pdf is listed as a crawled file type. If it's not shown, click New File Type to tell the Search SSA to include PDFs in its crawls.
- Launch a full crawl to add PDF documents to the index.

Business Continuity and Backups

Most SharePoint systems aspire to mission criticality. To sustain this level of confidence, some level of system backup is essential.

Some of the basic techniques I'll note briefly:

- Use the Recycle Bin
- Backup SQL Server using SQL techniques. In part, SharePoint's intrinsic backup techniques become unwieldy on larger content pools (200-500GB).
- Use third party tools to provide granular backup and recovery.

That said, SharePoint provides some helpful tools to implement system backup and recovery.

SharePoint Backup

As a minimum, you can use a variation on the following batch file to run a nightly backup. The script will run a full farm backup and save it in the \\SERVER\SPBackup share, and will also cache the previous night's backup. The script can be scheduled to run on any web front end server using a local Windows Task Scheduler, or another scheduling tool. The share should be a location that can also be "seen" by the SQL server, since a SharePoint backup, essentially, tells SQL to run a full database diskdump and put those files in the share.

```
@echo off
echo =================================================
echo Backup the farm
echo =================================================
@SET stsadm="C:\Program Files\Common Files\Microsoft Shared\Web
Server Extensions\14\BIN\stsadm"
rmdir /S /Q "\\SERVER\spbackup\farmold"
ren "\\SERVER\spbackup\farm" "farmold"
md "\\SERVER\spbackup\farm"
%stsadm% -o backup -directory "\\SERVER\spbackup\farm" -
backupmethod full
echo complete
```

That's a traditional backup technique. This file is usually saved in a batch file named AUTOBACK.bat.

PowerShell Backup

But in SharePoint 2010, we can accomplish the same process using a PowerShell command file. The following lines are the same technique, translated to PowerShell. These commands can be saved to a PowerShell ps1 file and scheduled in similar fashion.

```
# NOT NEEDED write-output
write-host =================================================
write-host Backup the farm
write-host =================================================
Add-PSSnapIn Microsoft.SharePoint.Powershell
Remove-Item -Path "C:\PSBackup\farmold" -recurse
Rename-Item -Path "C:\PSBackup\farm" -NewName "farmold"
New-Item -type directory -path C:\PSBackup\farm
Backup-SPFarm -directory "C:\PSBackup\farm" -backupmethod full -
verbose -percentage 5
Write-host Backup complete
```

There will be more discussion of PowerShell in the section on Custom Development.

Unattached Recovery

SharePoint now supports granular restores from an unattached content database backup. Administrators can browse the backup and identify a list or library to pull out without attaching and mounting the entire database.

To use the technique, the SQL content database needs to be hosted somewhere – but that SQL server need not be connected to the SharePoint farm in any other way. It's unattached from SharePoint – not SQL (which makes it a little confusing.)

- From SharePoint Central Administration, under Backup and Restore, choose **Granular Backup | Recover data from an unattached content database.**
- Enter the database connection information. If you choose Windows authentication, the default database access/farm account needs rights to read the database.
- Choose browse to open up the content database.

- You can select a Site Collection, and after that, choose a sub site and an optional list or library. (That's as granular as we can get).

- Chose Export Site or List to export that element as a .CMP file.
- Use the PowerShell cmdlet Import-SPWeb to restore from that file to a target web application. For example:

```
Import-SPWeb http://msshome2010 -Path C:\ListRecovery.cmp
```

Recycle Bin Recovery

The SharePoint Recycle Bin has always provided a means for self-service recovery of deleted documents and items. With Service Pack 1, users (well, Site Collection Administrators) are now able to restore deleted sites from the Site Collection Recycle Bin. (You can get there from the Site Settings page under Site Collection administration). Deleted sites can be found in the option for "Items deleted from end-user Recycle Bin". Just click the site and select Restore.

Even whole site collections can be restored with SP1. SP1 adds two PowerShell commands for this.

- **Get-SPDeletedSite** – list deleted site collection sin the farm
- **Restore-SPDeletedSite** – returns the site collection to 'live' status

Disk-based BLOB Caching

With IIS7, Microsoft has introduced the ability to cache binary files locally on the web front end. For SharePoint, this can be a great accelerant for frequently used but non-dynamic content. For example, page graphics, video files, and PDFs, lend themselves well to caching. If you look around the "SharePoint Hive", the _layouts folder contains ASPX pages that are kept in the file system because it's faster than pulling them in and out of the database.

The same is true for files that are stored in a content database - audio/video files that are unlikely to change, graphic elements that are reused on a page, such as logos. Caching is time sensitive, so if you set it to cache PDF files, and someone changes the PDF file, the old version might be kept in the web server cache for 24 hours or whatever you set as the content expiration period.

Although it works on binary objects, it's completely different from Remote BLOB Storage (RBS), which is a database, backend technology. Disk BLOB Caching is something that runs on the front end. It also runs on client browsers – if a file is cached, it can be cached all the way down to IE8 or IE9. Cached BLOB files will be downloaded and saved in the local Temporary Internet Files folder on each browser.

The caching requires that your SharePoint sites have the publishing infrastructure active, and it's configured for each web application independently. Here's how.

- Edit web.config (C:\Inetpub\wwwroot\wss\virtualdirectories\...)
- Find the section noted below

```
<BlobCache location=""
path="\.(gif|jpg|jpeg|jpe|jfif|bmp|dib|tif|tiff|ico|png|wdp|hdp|c
ss|js|asf|avi|flv|m4v|mov|mp3|mp4|mpeg|mpg|rm|rmvb|wma|wmv)$"
maxSize="10" enabled="false" />
Location = Local Disk Location
maxSize = GB
```

- Set Enabled = true.
- Pick a local disk location (a folder that you create on each WFE
- Set the maximum size for the cache on GB
- Save and run an IISReset

You can adjust the file types to be cached by their file extension. Please, please don't add DOCX, XLSX, or other frequently changed file types!

Other Configurations

Outbound/inbound email

SharePoint likes to send alerts, site access requests, and other notices via email. You just need to direct it to the nearest SMTP server –

which could be a full email system like Exchange, or an SMTP relay. SharePoint can also receive emails, and automatically route messages or attachments to an appropriate library.

SMTP is usually a controlled environment – the machines that accept SMTP traffic in your organization may only accept traffic from a list of known good hosts – so make sure they accept your SharePoint servers too.

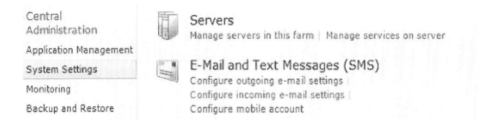

Figure 26 - E-Mail Settings

This is one of those settings you'll say – I remember it's out there – where is it? Central Administration | System Settings should do it. You'll see links to outgoing email, incoming email, and mobile settings.

For outbound email, you need to specify an SMTP host, as well as from and reply to addresses. The SMTP host should usually be an alias or a host name – don't use an IP address because if it changes, the setting also needs to be updated. The from/reply-to addresses should usually be something to indicate that a reply will not be seen – so donotreply@domain.com is a good answer.

It can also be a good idea to set up your own SMTP server – strictly for relay purposes – somewhere in your SharePoint-controlled environment. That server is configured to relay to and from the active mail systems in your company. Having a "nearby" SMTP server also helps in configuring inbound email, since SharePoint interfaces directly with it to retrieve messages – either directly from the SMTP drop folder or by automatic retrieval from a local SMTP host.

SharePoint can also be configured to automatically generate email addresses and distribution lists for email-enabled lists and libraries in an Exchange Global Address List (GAL).

In general, the remote email system uses emails like name@domain.com. The main mail system is then configured to route messages for a subdomain (e.g. library@sharepoint.domain.com) directly to SharePoint – which then handles the mapping and routing.

Finally, the same admin interface allows you to register with an external SMS text messaging service to send text messages instead of emails. These services can be a boon to a mobile workforce, but the SMS relay services usually require additional cost.

Path Support for the SharePoint Root
You're still going to need STSADM in SharePoint 2010. Why should you have to navigate to its directory every time? Add the BIN directory to the environment path variable, and you're all set. There are several ways to start:

- o From Control Panel | System & Security | System, chose Advanced System Settings.
- o Click the Environment Variables button
- o Under system variables, edit the path variable. At the end, add the path to STSADM.EXE. The default location is shown below [the semicolon matters!]:

```
;C:\Program Files\Common Files\Microsoft Shared\Web Server
Extensions\14\Bin\
```

Large File Upload Support
By default, SharePoint limits uploaded files to 50MB. However, if you need larger files, you can expand that support upwards, to a maximum of 2GB (which is a hard and fast SQL-based limit). It's not without

tradeoffs. Larger files take more memory resources during the process, etc. Anyway, here's how to configure SharePoint and IIS to support 600MB uploads.

- First, expand the maximum upload size in SharePoint Central Administration.
  - o From SharePoint Central administration, choose Application Management | Web Applications
  - o Highlight the web application and select General Settings | General Settings from the Ribbon.
  - o Scroll down to Maximum upload size. Update the value to 600MB and click OK.
- Since bigger files will take longer to upload, we should expand the IIS7 Connection Timeout:
  - o In IIS Manager, select the IIS Web Site for our SharePoint Web application and click Limits under Web Settings.
  - o Expand the Connection Timeout to 65536 seconds. (I mean, 18 hours should be enough!)
- Next, we'll need to update the web.config file for our web application.
  - o By convention, the web.config file will be in one of the folders under C:\inetpub\wwwroot\wss\virtualdirectories whose name corresponds to the web app. (Usually.)
  - o In that web.config file, change the httpRuntime node to read as below.
  - o `<httpRuntime maxRequestLength="2097151" executionTimeout="999999" />`
  - o In the 14Hive, under template\layouts, make the same edit as above to that version of web.config.
- Finally, as per http://support.microsoft.com/kb/944981/en-us we need to add a new section to allow 600MB content length (it's a new requirements in IIS7). The following lines need to

be added to web.config for each web application in the system.webserver section. The security section should go first inside the opening tag for system.webserver.

```
<system.webServer>
    <security>
        <requestFiltering>
            <requestLimits
        maxAllowedContentLength="629145600"/>
        </requestFiltering>
    </security>
    ...
```

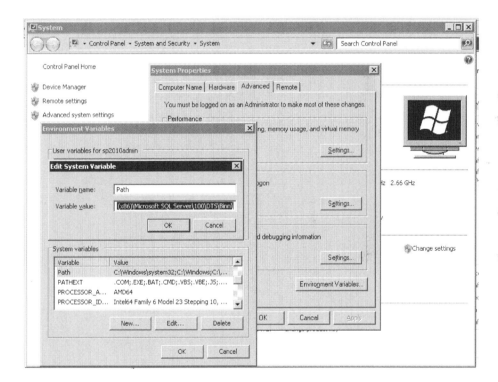

SharePoint root shortcut

Sometimes, it's helpful to be able to get right to the SharePoint root via Explorer, Run, or command line entry. Just as we updated PATH, I often set up "14Hive" as an environment variable to "C:\Program Files\Common Files\Microsoft Shared\Web Server Extensions\14" (the default location.) That way, by typing 14Hive% at a Run prompt, or cd

%14Hive% at a command prompt, you can shift directly to the SharePoint root.

Disable the loopback check

Several years ago, Microsoft introduced a security measure to prevent a process on one server from using http to reach port 80 for a web site on the same server under a different alias, since this is an attack profile for some malware. Unfortunately, this is also exactly what a search crawl looks like when a WFE retrieves content to index from a website that uses an aliased host header. If your search server won't crawl your content, this may be an issue, and you might consider disabling this measure – the loopback check. The following technique turns it off entirely. However, there are documented alternative techniques to exempt any specific host headers from the loopback check instead of removing the security functions entirely.

- Click Start, click Run, type regedit, and then click OK.
- In Registry Editor, locate and then click the following registry key:
  - HKEY_LOCAL_MACHINE\SYSTEM\CurrentControlSet\Control\Lsa
- Right-click Lsa, point to New, and then click DWORD Value.
- Type DisableLoopbackCheck, and then press ENTER.
- Right-click **DisableLoopbackCheck**, and then click Modify.
- In the Value data box, type 1, and then click OK.
- Quit Registry Editor, and then restart your computer.

SQL Maintenance Plans

As I think I've said many, many times before, SQL performance is essential to SharePoint performance. SQL makes it relatively easy for you to configure you own scheduled SQL maintenance jobs to check, maintain, and optimize your SQL database files. In general, if there are pre-existing standards for SQL backup, index maintenance, and other DBA-heavy activities, stick with those.

There's usually a belt-and-suspenders approach to backing up SharePoint. Although SharePoint's intrinsic tools, discussed above, are a good first step, larger content database backups from SharePoint can overrun the timeframes for overnight maintenance. SQL backups are more scaleable. Also, as noted above, you can use the SQL backups for **Unattached Recovery**, letting you extract selected lists or libraries to recover from accidental file deletions.

However, the following elements are a good framework. Set up three SQL maintenance jobs in SQL Enterprise Manager. The jobs are designed to perform extensive weekly updates and full backups on system databases (master, tempdb, msdb, model) and user databases (everything else – i.e. SharePoint), with a nightly differential backup and light maintenance on the SharePoint databases.

Weekly [Full] 2am Sundays – User DBs
- Check Integrity
- Rebuild Index [Keep Online]
- Update Statistics
- Full Backup
  - Root and subs
  - Save as bak
  - Keep 4 wks
- Cleanup History
- Maintenance Cleanup
  - Remove bak files after 4 wks

Nightly [Diff] 2am Mon-Sat – User DBs
- Differential Backup
  - Root and subs
  - Save as bak
  - Keep 2 wks.
- Transaction Log Backup
  - Root and subs

- o   Save as trn
- o   Keep 2 wks
- Cleanup History
- Maintenance Cleanup
  - o   Remove trn files after 2 wks

Weekly [Full] 3am Sundays – System DBs
- Check Integrity
- Update Statistics
- Full Backup
  - o   Target directory and subs
  - o   Save as bak
  - o   Keep 4 weeks
- Cleanup History
- Maintenance Cleanup
  - o   Remove bak files after 4 wks

Backing up the databases to local disks can use up a lot of disk space. In addition, you have a problem with keeping the backups on the same server, so most enterprises at least run a subsequent process to transfer the backup files to moveable media for offsite storage. If you keep the backups on the system as production, and you lose the server, you won't have the backups for recovery. Alternately, many data protection systems provide a way to directly transfer database backups to tape, freeing up disk space and saving a step in the process. Backup software is more powerful and robust, but isn't part of the base SQL Server installation.

RBS and related technologies also need to be considered for SQL maintenance. Although RBS moves the file contents outside SQL, the contents are still aligned to SharePoint content databases. If you are using RBS, you have the advantage of being able to run a separate backup and recovery process – but it IS a separate process, since the SQL database backups shouldn't touch the BLOB store. Also,

Microsoft strongly recommends that their free RBS Filestream provider not be used in production environments – in part because of the maintenance headaches; Over time, the BLOB store can be lose perfect synchronization with its parent content database. In particular, files deleted from SharePoint can be left behind in the BLOB store, especially if the BLOB store was offline during the deletion. Theses "orphan BLOBs" can be cleaned up through T-SQL scripts, or as part of a third party RBS provider's interface.

You also need to consider how to handle database transaction logs. Transaction logs provide a journal of all events that change the database. By default, SQL creates all databases as "fully logged", which allows you to roll a database back to any point in time, not just the most recent backup.   This can be a good tool, but you also need to make sure you are truncating the logs after they are backed up. If not, they can grow huge. Even a comparatively small database like SharePoint_Config, typically about 50MB, can rapidly generate a 40GB transaction log. Transaction log runaways are a common cause of filled up local disks. Alternatively, you might run the database in simple recovery mode (no logs) which avoids the runaway transaction logs entirely but also removes the ability to perform a point in time rollback.

User Profile

Configure the User Profile Service

The User Profile Service ("UPS") is responsible for synchronizing user identity information from other sources, such as Active Directory of HR systems, with SharePoint's own user database. User properties are intrinsic to My Sites and People Search. Many user properties are now stored in SharePoint as MMS field values. The synchronization can work two ways, allowing users to modify details like their home fax number, and, with the right security, update the remote systems automatically, such as AD. Powerful stuff!

However, UPS was completely overhauled in 2010. User profile "sync" was really a modification of a search crawl in older versions, and it's been replaced with a true identity management service. As a result, the User Profile Service is a more complex SSA than some of the others.

In general, we configure it from the inside out. Although it uses the baseline Windows Forefront Identity Manager service as well as the SharePoint "Service on Server", we need to start with the SSA to get our User Profile Service application running smoothly.

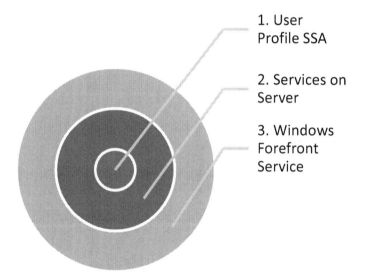

1. User Profile SSA

2. Services on Server

3. Windows Forefront Service

So, we need to configure the UPS service application in Central Administration. Assuming you're starting by pulling directory information from AD, two details are essential – the service account and the Active Directory container. At a minimum, the account requires the following permissions in AD. These steps assume you have access to make changes on an AD domain server.

Membership in Pre-Windows 2000 Compatibility Group

- Using Active Directory Users and Computers, expand the domain and the Builtin container
- Add "Everyone" to the membership of the Pre-Windows 2000 Compatible Access group, "Check Names" to assure the account is valid, and click OK.

Service Account Permission for Directory Changes

- Again using Active Directory Users and Computers, click Advanced Features on the View menu.
- Right-click the domain ("e.g. domain.com") and select Properties form the context menu.
- If the service account isn't listed on the Security tab, add it.
- Select the service account's properties, and make sure the Replicating Directory Changes check box is selected.
- Save changes

Service Account Replication Permissions

- On the AD server, run ADSIEdit.msc – the console can be started from that entry on the command line or the Run option in Windows Explorer. (ADSIEdit allows advanced configuration of AD properties.)
- Connect to the Configuration node, and right click it to display properties.
- On the Security tab, give the account Replicating Directory Changes permissions.

Make sure there's a schedule for when full and incremental synchronizations will run.

After that, if it's your first time in UPS, the service application will finish provisioning. This can sometimes take hours – although later cumulative updates and service pack versions are faster. Once that process completes, make sure the SharePoint service is stared inn

Services on Server. Finally, make sure the Forefront Identity Manager Service was properly configured and started.

Activity Feed Timer Job

Even if all this is running, users won't see anyone else's actions on their My Sites Newsfeed until you turn on the timer jobs that processes activity broadcasts.

In Central Administration, Monitoring | Timer Jobs[20], review Job Definitions. We're looking for "User Profile Service Application - Activity Feed Job" – it's listed alphabetically and is unlikely to be ion the first screen. Running it hourly is recommended.

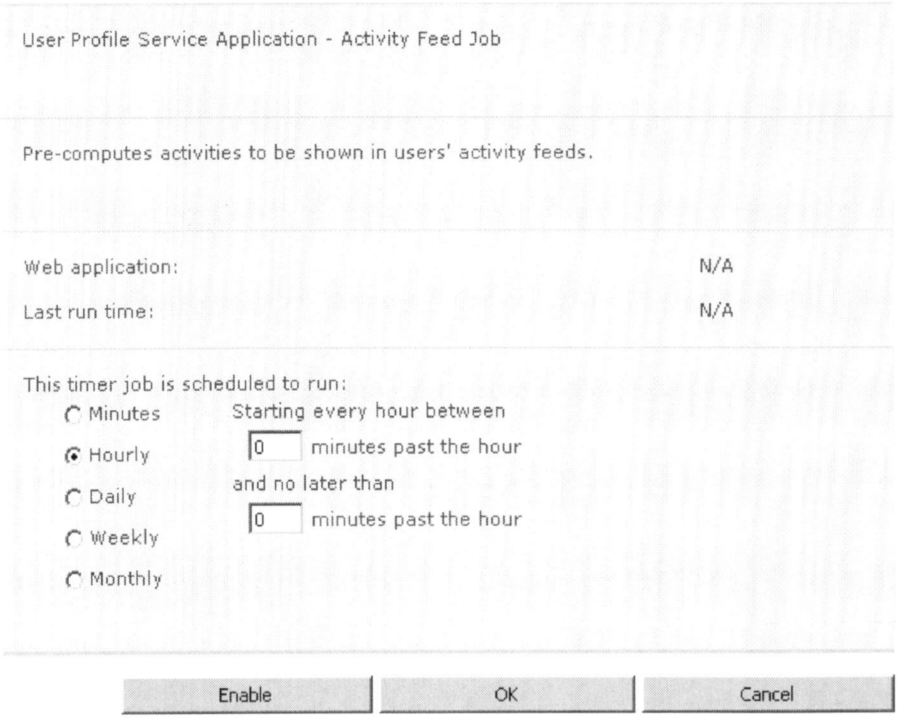

User Profile Service Application - Activity Feed Job

Pre-computes activities to be shown in users' activity feeds.

Web application:	N/A
Last run time:	N/A

This timer job is scheduled to run:

- ○ Minutes
- ● Hourly
- ○ Daily
- ○ Weekly
- ○ Monthly

Starting every hour between

[0] minutes past the hour

and no later than

[0] minutes past the hour

Enable	OK	Cancel

Figure 27 - UPS Activity Feed Timer Job

---

[20] The Timer Service runs all the background tasks, processes and workflows, hundreds a minute in some cases, on SharePoint.

Documentation

Finally, new SharePoint installations should always be documented. At my old consulting firm, we established a template to document new SharePoint installation and configuration work as a standard client deliverable. The actual format is less important than information. As-built documents also establish a valuable basis for turning the system over to a production "go live" team – either in-house or at a client.

In my experience, key elements include:

- Client Name and Date
- Table of Service Accounts and Roles
- Table of Servers, IP, Roles
- Installation Steps & Settings – Basic Installation and Wizard
  - Central admin port, farm account, passphrase
- Screen shot of topology
- Table of web applications
- Table of custom scheduled events (e.g. profile imports, crawls, backups) – days and times
- SQL Server key information – data, logs and backup
- SharePoint backup scripts and schedule
- SQL Maintenance Jobs summary
- Summary of database names and uses
- Table of Web applications and site collections
- Custom configuration elements
  - User profile import
  - SMTP configuration
  - Disable the loopback check
  - Acrobat configuration – PDF icons and iFilter
  - Large file upload support
  - Look/feel customization and themes
  - Regional settings / time zone
  - URL Mappings (Alternate Access Mappings)

     o   Miscellaneous configuration steps

Although system documentation should be updated with significant changes, it's also important to "freeze" the first configuration document as an archival, "as-built" document.

Upgrade and Migration

We've already set up an entirely new SharePoint farm. In some cases, you might start using it right away or you might be upgrading from a SharePoint 2007 system. There are two basic in the box techniques:

The first, appropriate for smaller, braver sites, is to perform an in place upgrade. It is highly recommended that the legacy site be running at least MOSS 2007 SP2 (October 2009 CU even better) so you can run the command line checker **stsadm -o preupgradecheck**. The preupgrade check will give you a read about the suitability of your system for upgrade, features needed on a new build, etc. One critical issue - all systems must be running Windows 2008 or 2008 R2 X64, so there is no in place upgrade available for 32 bit SharePoint 2007.

The alternate technique is to build an empty, new 2010 system, 64 bit, and then attach your 2007 databases. In this technique:

- Build a new, empty SP2010 farm
- Build a new web app with a deleteable content database and drop the content database in Central Admin
- Copy (detach/attach) the old content databases to a new server or name.
- Prescan the database using the PowerShell command **Test-SPContentDatabase -Name [database] -WebApplication [url]**
- Attach the new database to the web app using the command line: **stsadm -o addcontentdb -url [URL] –databasename [database] –assignnewdatabaseid**
- Review the migrated database content

Alternatively, if you have more exotic upgrade needs (e.g. 2003-2010), non-SharePoint migrations (Notes, file systems), needs to restructure content, etc. - third party tools from ISVs like Quest, Metalogix, Echo or AvePoint may help. So, let's walk through the most likely upgrade path – database attach.

PreUpgrade Maintenance

There's a lot you can do to align the information architecture and databases in 2007 prior to upgrade. At a minimum, content and sites that are obsolete should be archived and or deleted.

Site cleanup

One too-common behavior in 2007 was to allow legacy My Sites site collection to be scatter across multiple databases. In 2007, and in 2010, site collections can be transferred among different databases in the Central Admin UI. But you may have a lot of My Sites you'd like to consolidate into one database, or move out of a primary content database to one dedicated to My Sites. You can use a few command tricks to do this.

First, we dump a list of all the sites we want to move in a given database to an XML file. (You run this command on the 2007 server):

```
Stsadm -o enumsites -url http://MYSITESWEBAPP -databasename
EXTRADBNAME > mysites.xml
```

Review the XML file, and remove any references to any sites you DON'T want to move to the target – such as collaboration site collections, or sites for obsolete users (you might also delete those!) Then, the following command line sequence will transfer the site collections defined in the XML file from the source to a target database.

```
Stsadm -o mergecontentdbs -sourcedatabasename EXTRADBNAME -
destinationdatabasename TARGETDB -operation 2 -filename
mysites.xml
```

TIP: *The command above assumes that STSADM is on the PATH environment variable for your 2007 server. Otherwise, you may need to use the full path to STSADM.exe.*

Pre-upgrade checker

The pre-upgrade checker is a command-line tool to run in a MOSS 2007 farm to find any potential issues before you upgrade. As a prerequisite, you need SharePoint 2007 SP2 minimum, and the October 2009 CU is strongly recommended for more comprehensive compliance checks.

```
STSADM.exe -o preupgradecheck
```

By using the pre-upgrade checker, you can find information such as the following:

- Servers in the farm and whether the servers meet the minimum upgrade requirements of 64-bit hardware and Windows Server 2008.
- Alternate access mapping URLs
- Installed site definitions, site templates, features, and language packs
- Unsupported customizations, such as database schema modifications
- Database or site orphans.
- Missing or invalid configuration settings, such as missing files, bad host names or service accounts
- Database readiness tests, confirming the databases are set to read/write, and that any databases stored in Windows Internal Database are not larger than 4 GB.[21]

---

[21] This is less likely, but can happen if you were running the "free" local Windows Internal Database for SharePoint 2007. That database is now mapped onto a SQL Server Express installation, and although Windows Internal Database had no size restrictions, SQL Express has a maximum size of 4GB.

The command line gives you summary results on screen, as shown below:

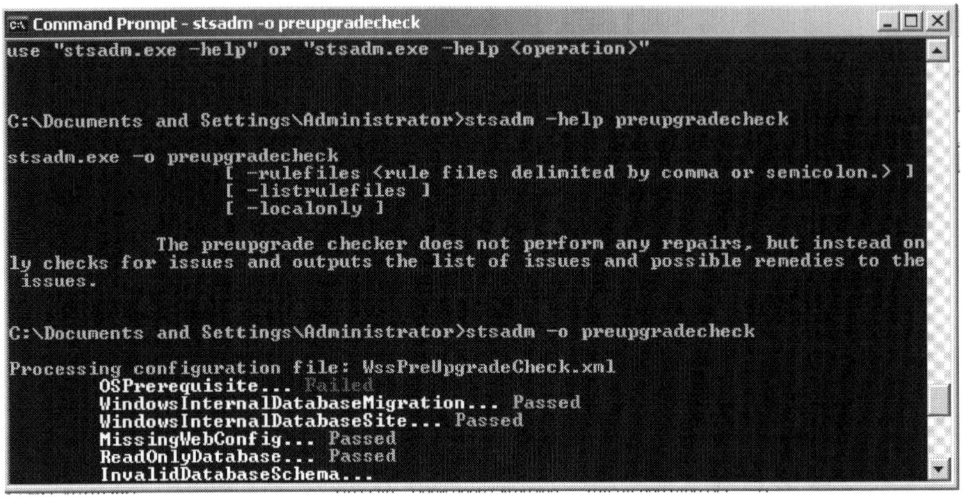

Figure 28 - PreUpgradeCheck Command Line Outout

But you don't need to worry about a screen shot – the Pre-Upgrade Check also creates a more nicely formatted HTML report, as shown below:

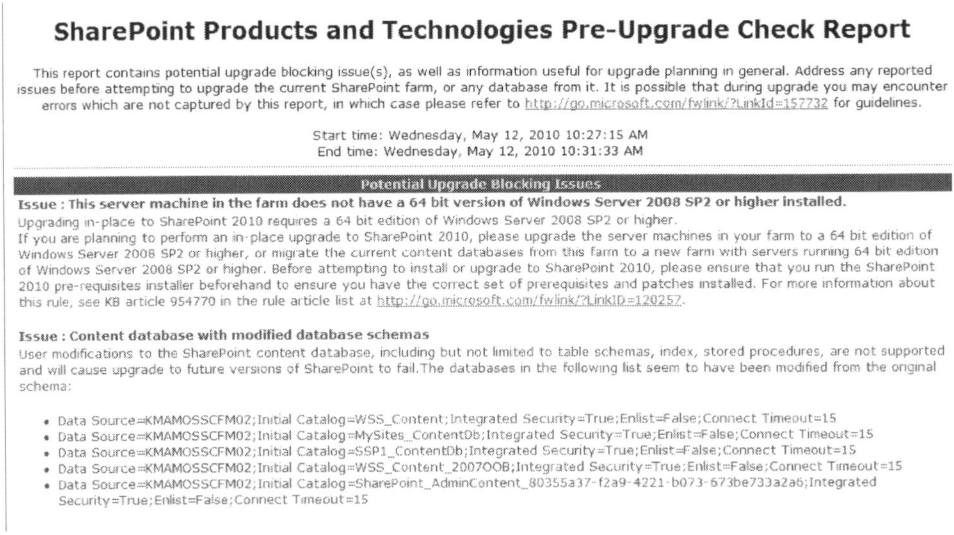

SharePoint Products and Technologies Pre-Upgrade Check Report

This report contains potential upgrade blocking issue(s), as well as information useful for upgrade planning in general. Address any reported issues before attempting to upgrade the current SharePoint farm, or any database from it. It is possible that during upgrade you may encounter errors which are not captured by this report, in which case please refer to http://go.microsoft.com/fwlink/?LinkId=157732 for guidelines.

Start time: Wednesday, May 12, 2010 10:27:15 AM
End time: Wednesday, May 12, 2010 10:31:33 AM

Potential Upgrade Blocking Issues

Issue : This server machine in the farm does not have a 64 bit version of Windows Server 2008 SP2 or higher installed.
Upgrading in-place to SharePoint 2010 requires a 64 bit edition of Windows Server 2008 SP2 or higher.
If you are planning to perform an in-place upgrade to SharePoint 2010, please upgrade the server machines in your farm to a 64 bit edition of Windows Server 2008 SP2 or higher, or migrate the current content databases from this farm to a new farm with servers running 64 bit edition of Windows Server 2008 SP2 or higher. Before attempting to install or upgrade to SharePoint 2010, please ensure that you run the SharePoint 2010 pre-requisites installer beforehand to ensure you have the correct set of prerequisites and patches installed. For more information about this rule, see KB article 954770 in the rule article list at http://go.microsoft.com/fwlink/?LinkID=120257.

Issue : Content database with modified database schemas
User modifications to the SharePoint content database, including but not limited to table schemas, index, stored procedures, are not supported and will cause upgrade to future versions of SharePoint to fail. The databases in the following list seem to have been modified from the original schema:

- Data Source=KMAMOSSCFM02;Initial Catalog=WSS_Content;Integrated Security=True;Enlist=False;Connect Timeout=15
- Data Source=KMAMOSSCFM02;Initial Catalog=MySites_ContentDb;Integrated Security=True;Enlist=False;Connect Timeout=15
- Data Source=KMAMOSSCFM02;Initial Catalog=SSP1_ContentDb;Integrated Security=True;Enlist=False;Connect Timeout=15
- Data Source=KMAMOSSCFM02;Initial Catalog=WSS_Content_2007OOB;Integrated Security=True;Enlist=False;Connect Timeout=15
- Data Source=KMAMOSSCFM02;Initial Catalog=SharePoint_AdminContent_80355a37-f2a9-4221-b073-673be733a2a6;Integrated Security=True;Enlist=False;Connect Timeout=15

Figure 29 - PreUpgradeCheck Report

Restore database from backup to new system

The next step is really important. Outside the context of SharePoint, we need to backup the content database in SQL, and restore or transfer it, using SQL techniques to the new database server. If your older SQL environment meets minimum standards, you could upgrade the original database – but the in-place upgrade changes the database schema so that it can't be used in 2007 anymore. That's why backup and restore is strongly, strongly, strongly recommended!

Check Database

Now we're getting to the new 2010 stuff. There is one final pre-flight check that compares the restored, unaltered copy of the 2007 database to the target farm to make sure any required features already exist on the new farm. This check requires PowerShell, so make sure that the account you're using for upgrade has at least dbo permission to the new SharePoint _Config database. (Remember, "spadmin", not "spfarm"!)

This command should be run from the SharePoint Management Shell, and not the general PowerShell window, to make sure the right SharePoint snapin cmdlets are loaded.

```
PS C:\Users\cmcnulty> Test-SPContentDatabase -Name
WSS_Content_200700B -WebApplication http://kmamssd01
```

And you will get output to the command line (redirectable if you know PowerShell.) The critical issues are identified as "UpgradeBlocking: True" in the output. Review and make sure that you have none of these. Also, you should try to resolve as many other non-critical errors if feasible. Here's some sample Pre-Scan output:

```
Category        : SiteOrphan
Error           : True
UpgradeBlocking : False
Message         : Database [WSS_Content_200700B] contains a site (Id =
[f78c83ee-20d9-4b87-93d1-e1d640da6633], Url = [/]) whose url is already used
by a different site, in database (Id = [2cc0fc28-c1ff-4311-ac68-
```

```
918229f5d834], name = [WSS_Content]), in the same web application. Consider
deleting one of the sites which have conflicting urls.
Remedy           : The orphaned sites could cause upgrade failures. Try detach
and reattach the database which contains the orphaned sites. Restart upgrade
if necessary.

[…]

Category         : MissingSetupFile
Error            : True
UpgradeBlocking  : False
Message          : File [Features\PortalLayouts\Images\searchresults.gif] is
referenced [1] times in the database, but is not installed on the current
farm. Please install any feature/solution which contains this file.
Remedy              : One or more setup files are referenced in the database, but
are not installed on the current farm. Please install any feature or solution
which contains these files.
```

Create Web Application

On the new farm, in SharePoint Central Admin, create a new web
application, with the right URL host header, for our migrated content.
The database is going to be discarded, so a name like
"WSS_Content_DeleteMe" is a good reminder in case you forget to
clean up SQL later.

Next, in Central Admin, click the name of the content database to
open up its properties, and click the checkbox to drop the content
database. Bye-bye, brand new empty database! Take note – this only
"unregisters" the database with SharePoint – it's still out there in SQL,
so don't forget to drop the database on SQL later.

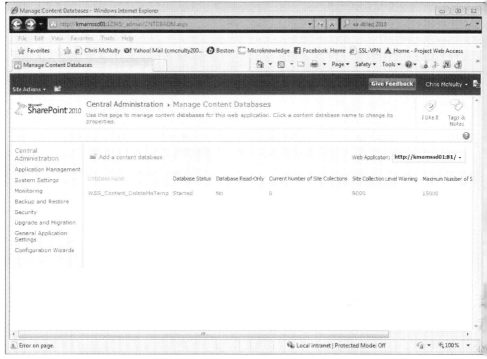

Figure 30 - Drop temporary database

Add new Content Database

And this is it. We add the old content database to our new web application, and SharePoint goes off and does its magic. This can take minutes, or hours – it all depends on the size of the database. A tiny database runs in a few minutes. Of course, the hardware specs matter, but 50-100GB of content has been observed to run from 2-6 hours. There are two ways to add the content database – STSADM or PowerShell. Both are listed below. No judgment if you decide to stay with STSADM! For now.

```
stsadm -o addcontentdb -url http://kmamssd01:81 –databasename
WSS_Content_200700B –assignnewdatabaseid
```

```
Mount-SPContentDatabase –name DATABSENAME –WebApplication
"http://WEB-APP-URL" -assignnewdatabaseid
```

TIP: *For lab or testing purposes you can't keep reading the same databases over and over – the assignnewdatabaseid parameter* *generates a new internal ID on each attach to prevent local conflicts in the new farm.*

The command line will show progress as the database upgrade continues. You can also monitor progress and Review Database Status from Central Admin | Upgrade and Migration: You select Review Database Status – and then clicking on the Status summary (e.g. "Upgrade In Progress" gives you more detailed information.

Check Upgrade Status

Figure 31 - Database Upgrade Status

In case you're curious, the browser GUI sometimes lags a few seconds behind the command line in its reports of percent complete.

When the database upgrade completes, your system is almost ready for use. Two final steps – checking the site collection administrators and confirming the user interface level.

Check Site Collection Administrators

In most cases, you've brought content over from sites that may not use the same list of site collection administrators, or even be part of the same domain. You can double check the site collection administrators in Central Admin to make sure you have valid users listed for primary and secondary admins.

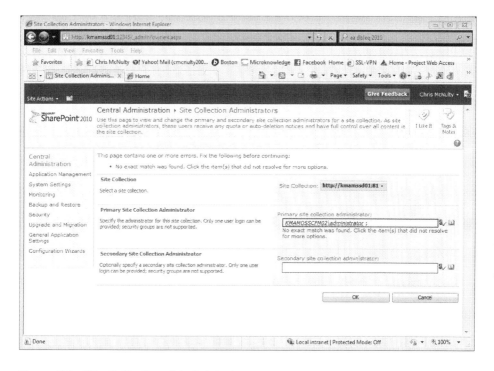

Figure 32 - Site Collection Administrators

Visual Upgrade

Finally, you may have noticed that your new environment, looks almost exactly like your old 2007 look and feel. That's because the database upgrade leaves the UI alone. You may want to train users on new feature before surprising them! In any event, Visual Upgrade is available inside the UI on a site-by site basis under Site Actions. Visual Upgrade allows you to temporarily update to the 2010 look and feel for testing (this is reversible.) When done, you can permanently commit the changes, which is not reversible. Here's a sample of what it does:

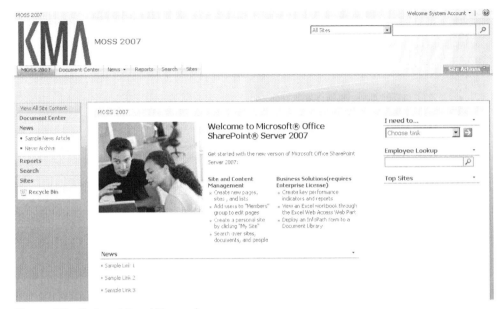

Figure 33 - Before Visual Upgrade

Figure 34 - After Visual Upgrade

Some users like the idea of separating the platform upgrade from the user interface – visual upgrade. This lets you preserve the look and feel from 2007 until you can train and "socialize" the changes. Other users would prefer to move to the 2010 UI from the start. Resetting the UI for a few sites is fine, but it can be tedious to manually reset every site in a large installation. The good news is that PowerShell can do this easily. Open up the SharePoint 2010 Management Shell, and type each of these lines separately (substitute your own URL for http://sitename!)

```
$webapp = Get-SPWebApplication http://sitename
foreach ($s in $webapp.sites)
{$s.VisualUpgradeWebs() }
```

That's it! FYI, this makes the change permanent, so don't do this if you're still toggling back and forth among the 2007 and 2010 look and feel.

Welcome to SharePoint 2010.

Business Intelligence

SharePoint 2010, along with SQL Server, makes major strides in delivering rich business intelligence ("BI") and self-service data discovery to users. Regardless of the time required or sophistication of the users, there is something in SharePoint BI to cover most anticipated uses.

Think all the way back to the oldest days of greenbar paper and line printers. Business intelligence, or, as it was known then, "reports", had the same two ambitious goals it retains today:

- Answering the known questions about our business
- Allowing users to self-discover patterns and answers to questions we haven't yet been asked

SharePoint 2010, along with SQL Server 2008 R2, takes us a lot closer to that second goal. Self service functions are available on the 2010 platform, especially with integrated SQL reports. SQL Server 2012 adds a whole new dimension of self-service with Power View.

The irony of most BI solutions is that they fall victim to the carousel paradox. Most data begins in Excel at some point in its lifecycle. It goes through exports, imports, queries, mashups, reports and the like. After all that, usually, a requirement for most end user reporting interfaces is that the data has to be exportable to Excel. You can't just give back the same spreadsheets they gave you originally. The carousel paradox reminds us of the importance of transforming the data – with cross references, correction visualization or insight – even if it seems we're only going in a circle. Remember to take users on a ride.

Figure 35 - Data needs to do more than move in circles

Before we go further, acronym watch! The database and BI world have their jargon. Here are some common terms used in SharePoint business intelligence:

- **SSRS** – SQL Server Reporting Services
- **Cube** – a prebuilt matrix of data aggregations, hosted in SQL Server Analysis Services
- **WCF** – Windows Communications Framework
- **Dallas** – a city in Texas. Also the code name for Windows Azure DataMarket, a Microsoft initiative to create publicly subscribed data services hosted on Azure and accessed via WCF, PowerPivot, etc. (http://www.sqlazureservices.com)

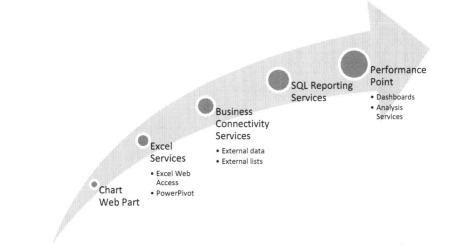

Figure 36 - SharePoint Business Intelligence Evolution

SharePoint provides a spectrum of solutions from simple end user charting tools – a wizard based web part – to sophisticated self-service exploration of SQL Server Analysis Services ("SSAS") cubes with Performance Point. Each of these tools has strengths and weakness. For example, an Excel Services based view may only take a few minutes to configure since it's based on existing Excel data. On the other hand, Performance Point dashboards can require true coding and development to use effectively. But Performance Point can also deliver interactive data exploration against high volume, external data. To sum up, there are broad ranges of BI tools of varying complexity and capacity. Pick the right tool for the right job.

Also, each of the major business intelligence systems has its own sub-system requirements. BCS, for example, relies on the Secure Store Service. Using many of the BI features presumes the proper use and configuration of other elements, like Excel Services or Kerberos. And some of the functions in SQL 2012, like Power View or SSRS Alerts, have even more prerequisites.

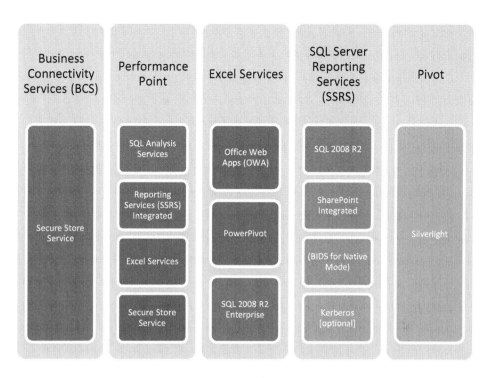

Business Connectivity Services (BCS)	Performance Point	Excel Services	SQL Server Reporting Services (SSRS)	Pivot
Secure Store Service	SQL Analysis Services	Office Web Apps (OWA)	SQL 2008 R2	Silverlight
	Reporting Services (SSRS) Integrated	PowerPivot	SharePoint Integrated	
	Excel Services		(BIDS for Native Mode)	
	Secure Store Service	SQL 2008 R2 Enterprise	Kerberos (optional)	

We'll talk a lot more about SQL 2012 at the end of the chapter. But now, let's start with the Chart Web Part.

Chart Web Part

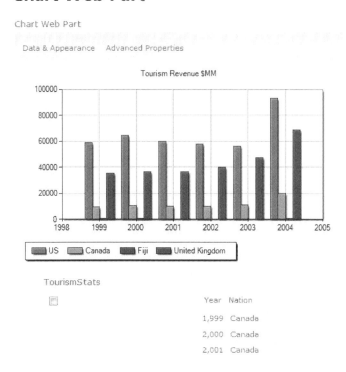

Chart Web Part

Data & Appearance   Advanced Properties

Figure 37 - Sample Chart Web Part

SharePoint Server 2010 Enterprise finally includes a native Chart Web Part. The Chart Part is a code free solution, and allows any user with design permissions to create live data visualizations. The Chart Web Part is pretty simple to configure once you add it to a web page. When in the page is in Edit mode, the Insert section allows you to pick a Web Part from the Site Collection Gallery. The Chart Web Part can be found under the Business Data category.

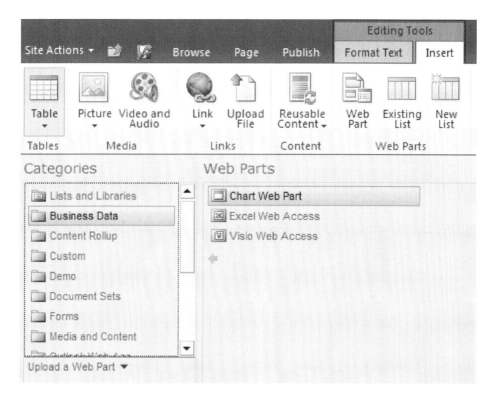

Figure 38 - Adding the Chart Web Part

On the new Web Part, select **Data and Appearance** to open up the configuration wizards. We'll start with **Connect Chart to Data**.

Customize Your Chart

This wizard will help you set your chart's look and feel.

Connect Chart To Data

This wizard will help you connect your chart Web Part to a data source.

Figure 39 - Chart Web Part Wizards

The wizard allows us to connect to another Web part, to a SharePoint list, to BDC data, or Excel Services. Although I sometimes use the

BDC, let's keep things simple and connect to another list. The next dialog allows you to pick any site in the current site collection, and then pick any list on that site.

Figure 40 - Choosing SharePoint Lists

The next screen allows you to preview the data and add optional filters. Filters are useful for large data sources, but the filters are "static" – you can't select a range of data or dynamic conditions.

Step 3: Retrieve and Filter Data

In this step, you can view the data retrieved from the selected list and filter the data by using an existing column as a parameter.

⊞ Filter Data

BITool	Votes
Chart Web Part	5
Excel Services	10
PowerPivot	4
Pivot	2
Business Connectivity Services	3
SQL Server Reporting Services	1
Performance Point	4
Custom Mapping	8

Preview: First **8** of **8** records.

Figure 41 - Data Preview

Finally, you can bind the chart to the data, picking X and Y fields, groups and series. The wizard even gives you visual cues about what it means to be an X-field, series, Y-field, or a series (see below). You can add custom fields, and apply a sophisticated set of statistics (e.g. moving average, detrended price oscillation, Bollinger bands, etc.)

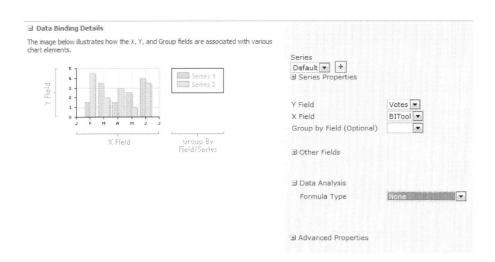

Figure 42 - Bind Data to Chart

Ta-da – you now have a chart! So far, it's not much.

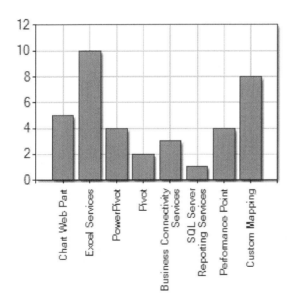

Figure 43 - Initial Chart Web Part

Now we can go back to **Data and Appearance** and choose a different chart type if we want further customizations. The **Customize your Chart** wizard allows you to select from any of the following chart types:

- Bar
- Area
- Line
- Bubble
- Financial
- Pie
- Radar

- Polar
- Gantt
- Range
- Error Bar
- Box Plot
- Funnel
- Pyramid

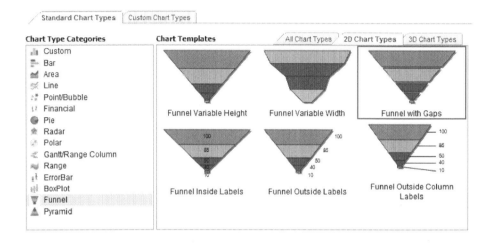

Figure 44 - Selecting Chart Types

Subsequent steps in the wizard allow you to change colors, size, add legends and labels, giving us the following chart:

BI Tools

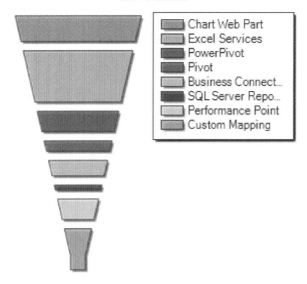

Chart Web Part
Excel Services
PowerPivot
Pivot
Business Connect..
SQL Server Repo..
Performance Point
Custom Mapping

Figure 45 - Chart Web Part, Configured

In practical terms, the Chart Part is sometimes used to give a quick visual display for data from another SharePoint list. For example, several different client organizations use a simple task list as the ticket tracker for small IT help desk operations. The chart web part gives a quick summary of how many tickets are new, pending, active and resolved.

The chart part also provides sophisticated statistical analyses. It's a great choice for quick and dirty graphing, and takes only minutes to set up. It's wizard based, so users who can use Excel chart wizards can probably be trained quickly. On the other hand, there's no print function, and the Chart Web Part isn't suited for truly massive recordsets – 5000 and up. As a result, it gets used less in the field than SSRS, Excel, PowerPivot or Performance Point.

SQL Server Reporting Services (SSRS)

SQL Reports are admittedly more complex than some of the Excel based techniques. But since SSRS reports are also a good base data source for PowerPivot models, I'll cover them first.

SQL Reports have been around since their debut as a feature add-on in SQL 2000. The good news is that the current version, included as part of SQL Server 2008 R2, is significantly enhanced when it's been integrated with SharePoint 2010. And there are even more end user features coming with SQL Server 2012 (see the end of this chapter!)

SSRS can report on data from a very broad range of sources:

- SQL Server
- SQL Server Analysis Services for MDX, DMX, & PowerPivot
- SQL Azure
- Oracle
- SAP NetWeaver BI
- Hyperion Essbase
- SharePoint List
- Teradata
- OLE DB
- ODBC
- XML

Traditionally, SSRS reports were built in a specialized version of Visual Studio, and saved as .rdl files in a customized web site directly on the SQL server. These sites used a completely different security model and interface from SharePoint, as shown below:

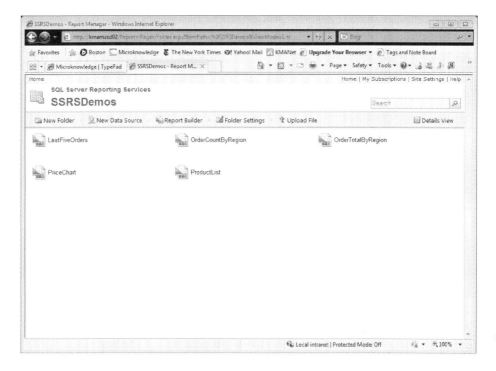

Figure 46 - SSRS Native Mode

In older instances, Reporting Services usually lived on a SQL Server. This configuration is called **Native Mode**. Native mode is simpler to configure since there isn't really much to do on the SharePoint side. For example, let's assume that our SharePoint server is named http://sharepoint, and SQL Reporting lives as http://sql/reports. Typically, native mode SSRS reports are accessed from SharePoint:

- As links to the reports on a SharePoint web page. The URL link might look like http://sql/reports/folder/MyReport.rdl
- Using the Reporting Services Web Parts – basically, an iFrame-type of control that frames the report. The SQL Reporting server still hosts and executes the report file, but from the user's perspective, the URL is something like http://sharepoint/sites/department/pages.reports.aspx. On that page, the user sees a control like the one shown below. (Usually, these web parts take up the full screen except for top navigation.)

Figure 47 - Native Mode SSRS Web Parts

There is a very small CAB file that ships with SQL Server that can be used to set up native mode SSRS web parts on a SharePoint server. The file is located at **C:\Program Files (x86)\Microsoft SQL Server\100\Tools\Reporting Services\SharePoint** in the SQL image (SQL 2008 example). This file can be installed on SharePoint using PowerShell or legacy STSADM:

```
STSADM.EXE -o addwppack -filename "RSWebParts.cab" -globalinstall
```

Older versions of SSRS required development tools – specifically, Business Intelligence Developer Studio ("BIDS"). BIDS comes "free" with SQL Server, and is a slimmed down version of the Visual Studio 2008 development environment.

However, in SQL Server 2008 R2, Report Builder is also supplied as an on-demand, browser downloaded component – but you need to configure Reporting Services to run in **SharePoint Integrated** mode.

Quick note for developers – BIDS remains a Visual Studio 2008-based approach, making it something of an oddball for development for

SharePoint 2010, since Visual Studio 2010 remains the preferred tool for developing SharePoint 2010 code. However, Microsoft has committed to making BIDS compliant with Visual Studio 2010 and/or the next version as part of the BI support delivered with SQL Server 2012, codename "Denali", expected in the first half of 2012.

In SharePoint 2007, integrated mode was a little difficult – but it's really simple in 2010. When Reporting Services is running in integrated mode, report definitions (.RDL files), models, and connections are all stored in SharePoint libraries. User security and the interface are also delivered on the SharePoint interface. But there's an important architecture design concept. Integrated mode servers need to participate as members of the farm. In smaller environments, the SQL Reporting Services instance is typically installed on the web front end server. In larger farms, especially with multiple WFEs, Reporting Services in usually installed on one (or two) dedicated servers.

To sum up:

- **Native Mode** – the SharePoint farm connects to a separate SQL instance of SQL Reporting Services. Report files live on the SQL server.
- **Integrated Mode** – SSRS is installed into the SharePoint farm, and report files live in SharePoint libraries.

Although there are two modes, you can't just toggle back and forth between them. Switching from native mode to integrated mode requires you to reinstall a new Reporting Services instance. So, let's walk through setting one up.

Reporting Services Installation and Configuration

For this example, let's assume that we are establishing a brand new instance of Reporting Services in our SharePoint farm. You can install this directly on the WFE server in a smaller build, or use a dedicated server for a larger installation, but remember - the server must already be part of the SharePoint farm.

TIP: *I often name this Reporting Services instance "RSInt" to distinguish it from the base SQL Database Engine or a traditional Native Mode Reporting Service build (shown above.)*

Setting up Reporting Services has three aspects:

- Installation of SQL Reporting Services
- Configuration of the RS Instance in SharePoint Integrated Mode
- Configuring SharePoint Central Admin to use the new instance of Reporting Services

(**Note**: this process will chance significantly with the new version of Reporting Services in SQL Server 2012 "Denali". I review that in the SQL 2012 section starting on page 214.)

Install SQL Reporting Services

The basic setup of SSRS happened during the SQL installation process. Since we are installing in Integrated Mode, remember we are installing Reporting Services into a SharePoint farm (rather than connecting SharePoint to a SQL-hosted web application, as is the case for Native Mode).

We do NOT need to install any other SQL services at all on the SharePoint server. Since we are setting up a new instance, we should choose "**New Installation...**" The wizard will run through a preflight check, install setup support files, and run a rules check to make sure installation will succeed.

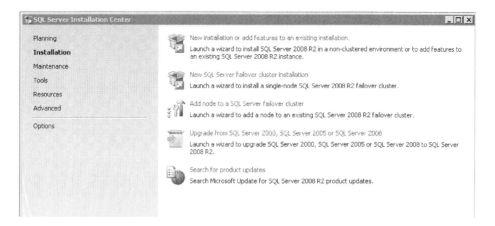

Figure 48 - SQL Server Installation Center

The next part of the process will show you any previously installed instances (e.g., the Database Engine, PowerPivot), and here we specify that we're creating a new instance.

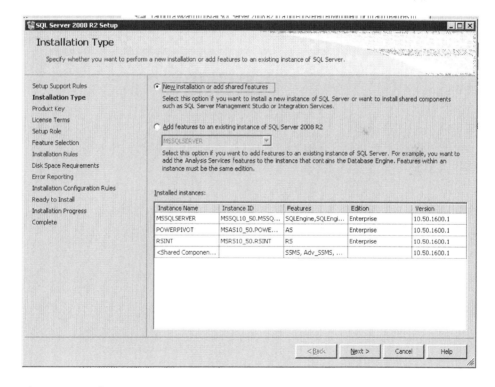

Figure 49 - Select SQL Instance

Next we enter the product key, accept the license, etc., and are brought to a screen where we can select "SQL Server Feature Installation". Accept this screen and proceed to feature selection, where we pick **Reporting Services**:

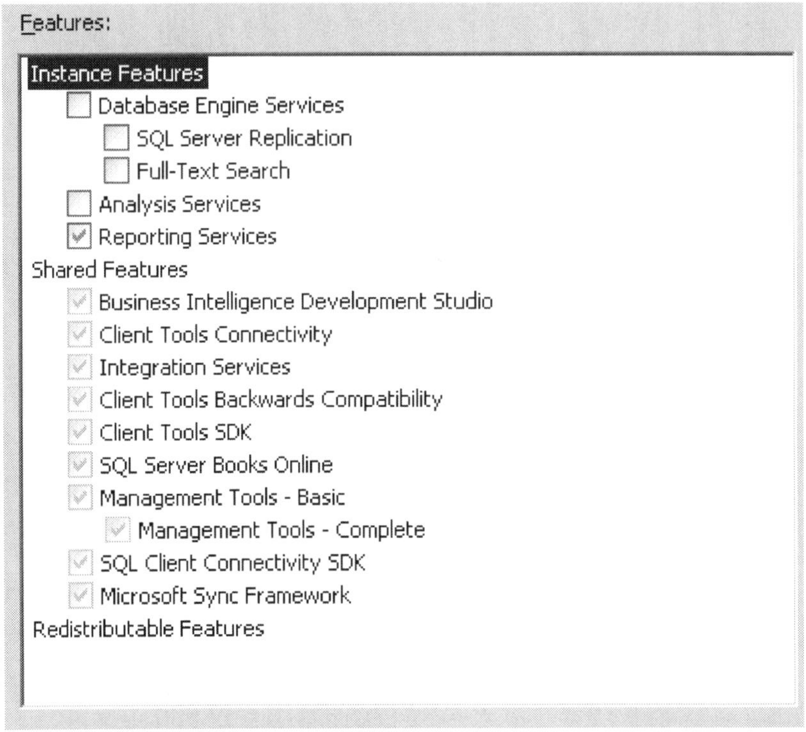

Figure 50 - Feature Selection

After that, we name the instance – and as mentioned above, I like to name it "RSInt" to distinguish it from other SSRS instances that may run in the same environment.

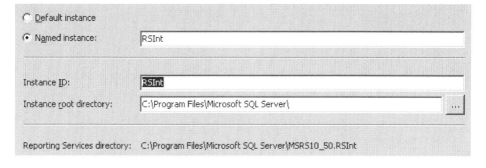

Figure 51 - Naming the RS Instance

The remaining steps for the wizard include:

- Confirming the disk space usage
- Specifying the account to use to run Reporting Services – which is sometimes the same as the SQL service account.
- A reminder that we are installing but not yet configuration Reporting Services
- Error reporting
- Final installation rules check
- Confirmation to kick of the installation process

Configure Reporting Services

Reporting Services, once installed, needs to be configured. The configuration wizard is installed into the Start Menu under Microsoft **SQL Server R2 | Configuration Tools | Reporting Services Configuration Manager**. Choose the instance we defined during installation above (remember, I suggested "RSInt"?).

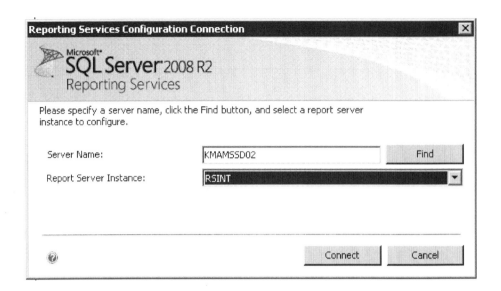

Figure 52 - Reporting Services Configuration Connection

Essential elements in this configuration include:

Service Account – choose an appropriate account to run the Reporting Service. This is mostly typically a SQL service account.

Configure **Report Service Web Service** [Hint – expand the dialog if you're unfamiliar with this screen -- the **Apply** button is off-screen by default in most screen resolutions.] Remember the URL that gets created here – you're going to need it when connecting SharePoint Central Admin to Reporting Services.

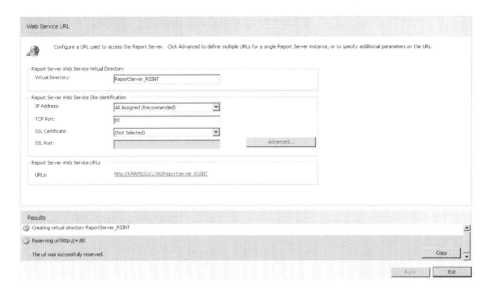

Figure 53 - RS Web Service Configuration

Database – Each Reporting Service instance needs its own configuration database. Changing/creating a database launches a mini wizard that allows you to specify the database server, name, and credentials. It's really important here to note whether the database should be created for Native or Integrated mode. Once you specify this, you need to create a new instances and a new database to change modes. It's recommended to reflect the "mode" in the database name itself, such as "ReportServerInt" (shows below.)

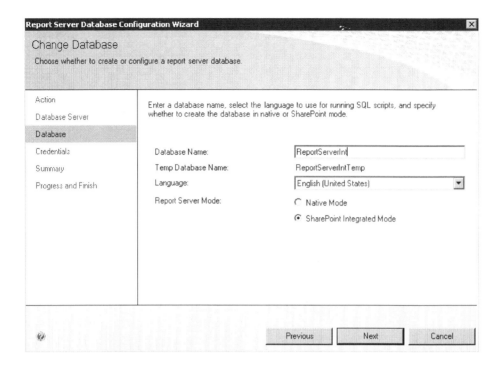

Figure 54 - RS Database Configuration

Report Manager URL – Again, allow the system to generate this value and apply it.

Email settings aren't needed unless you are allowing users to subscribe to reports. For this to work, you need to specify the "sending" address and, most importantly, the host name or IP for an SMTP server that will accept email from this server.

Execution account -- The execution account represents the default credentials used when report data connections don't otherwise specify credentials, or when they don't pass through end user credentials. Specifying a highly privileged account, such as the SQL service account or the SharePoint farm account, will "work" but may also expose database security unnecessarily.

Encryption keys should be generated and saved. If you need to rebuild or restore the server, all saved passwords etc. will be unusable without the original encryption key. Finally, scaled out deployments are used if you have multiple servers supplying Reporting Services for your farm.

Once you've finished these setting, you're ready to **Apply** the change and proceed to SharePoint Central Administration.

Configure SharePoint Integration

Finally, we need to go into SharePoint Central Administration and connect the farm to our Reporting Service instance configured in Integrated Mode.

In SharePoint Central Administration, go into General Settings for the Rerouting Service Integration module. This screen asks you to supply the URL for the Report Server Web Service (I **told** you we'd need it again!)

Figure 55 - RS Integration in Central Admin

Next we have to choose between Trusted Account mode (one account that acts on behalf of all users) or Windows Authentication (each user's credentials are passed through to the reporting service separately.) The first case is easier, and minimizes the use of Kerberos, but can also open up your report data more widely than might be anticipated.

Finally, you can specify the site collections where the Report Server Integration feature should be activated. (You can adjust this later.) In general, I tend to activate it on specific, shared, content site collections – not Central Admin or My Sites.

When you click OK, your choices are validated to make sure the Report Server service account has access to SharePoint configuration and content databases. In addition, the service account is added to the WSS-WPG Windows group, and the feature is activated on all selected site collections. At the end, you should see a screen that looks like this. Congratulations!

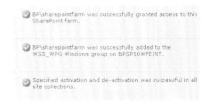

Database Access
Displays whether the Report Server service account was successfully granted access to the SharePoint configuration and content databases.

WSS_WPG Membership
Displays whether the Report Server service account was successfully added to the WSS_WPG Windows group.

Reporting Services Activation State
Displays site collections for which feature activation or de-activation failed, or displays whether it was successful in all specified site collections.

BP\sharepointfarm was successfully granted access to this SharePoint farm.

BP\sharepointfarm was successfully added to the WSS_WPG Windows group on BPSP10WFEINT.

Specified activation and de-activation was successful in all site collections.

Figure 56 - RS Integration Success

Reporting Content Types

Reporting Services Integration relies on three specific content types to be used in libraries where reports and connections are saved.

- Report Data Source
- Report Builder Model
- Report Builder Report

If this is working properly, when you create new documents in the library you should see the following dropdown choices:

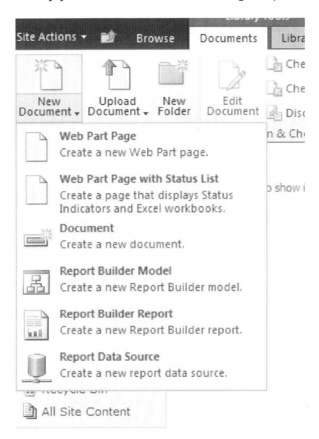

Figure 57 - Reporting Content Types in a Library

If you create a new library for reports or a new site AFTER you've connected to the Reporting Service, you might not have all of these. Here's how to add them.

First, confirm that Performance Point is enabled, especially if you plan to embed your reports inside dashboards. Performance Point needs to be enabled first at the Site Collection level, and then for each specific site where dashboards will be used. You can enable the SSRS content types for all document libraries in any Business Intelligence Center by disabling and re-enabling the Report Server Integration feature at the Site Collection level.

But let's just turn those content types on for a specific library.

1. Go to the library and choose **Library Settings** from the Ribbon.
2. Under General Settings, choose Advanced Settings. Under Content Types, select Yes to allow management of content types, and click OK
3. Now, in Library Settings, we can add the Content Types under that Content Types section. Click Add from existing site content types.
4. In the section to **Select Content Types**, click the arrow to select Reporting Services. We want to select Report Builder Report, Report Builder Model (less commonly used) and Report Data Source. Click Add, and when finished click OK.

Building an SSRS Report

Now, let's build a simple report. In our example, we're going to connect to an external database used by Project Server to deliver report data. You don't need Project Server – you could use any possible data source. First, we create a new Report Data Source in the library. RS Data Source files are saved with an .rsds extension. To do this, from the Library Ribbon, choose New Document | Report Data Source.

Next, we define the data source:

Data Source Type will be Microsoft SQL Server

Connection string will vary based on the Source Type. For many situations, the syntax:

```
Data Source=SERVERNAME; Initial Catalog=DATABASENAME
```

will work, substituting the SERVERNAME and DATABASENAME to match your actual environment.

Credentials allows you to choose among:

- Windows Authentication (pass through from the end user)
- Prompt for Credentials at run time. This can get to be a nuisance for users, and prevents you from using the report data source in automated activities like subscriptions or Alerts (in SQL Server 2012).
- Stored Credentials
- Credentials Not Required (in which case the Trusted Account will be used).

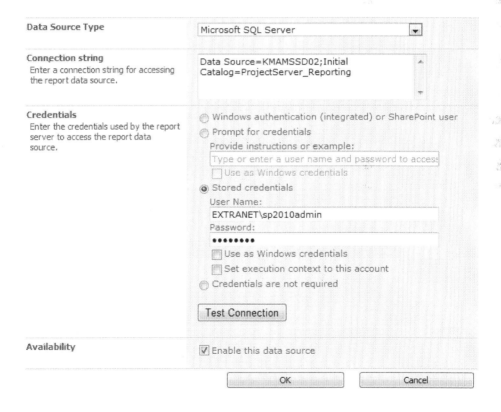

Figure 58 - New RS Data Source

Make sure the data source is enabled in **Availability** and test the connection. If all is ready, click OK and save the Data Source File.

Now we can create our actual report. We start just as we did for the Data Source file, except now we are creating a new document of type **Report Builder Report**:

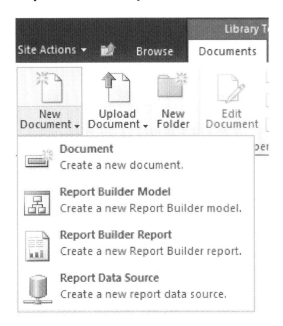

Figure 59 - New Report Builder Report

Once we choose this, your browser will download a component to let you design reports directly inside the site – no Visual Studio needed. Then, a Wizard opens up to help guide us through creating a report.

We're going to build a very simple report, so let's choose Table or Matrix Wizard.

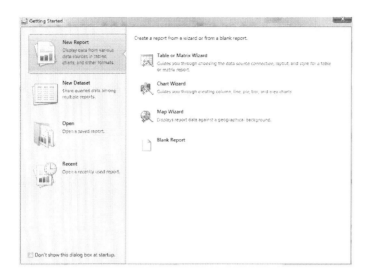

Figure 60 - New Report Wizard

Next we need to define the dataset to be used by the report. We're creating a new dataset, but we being by pointing to the shared data source we just created. (Based on your security environment, you may be prompted to reenter passwords during this part of the process.)

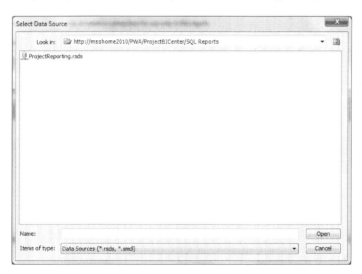

Figure 61 - Select Data Source

TIP: *You sometimes might have a report that connects to a unique data source. In such cases, you can define the data source directly inside the report. Obviously, this technique is tedious if you have a lot of reports -*

- each with individually defined connections – but the technique can sometimes be useful for unique reports or during prototyping.

Figure 62 - Embedded Data Connection

When asked, we're going to save the credentials with the report. Next we're asked to design the query. This screen opens up an outline view of the database table, views, and procedures. Here, we pick some fields out of a common SQL view. You can add grouping, totals, etc. using the field listing at the top right of the dialog. Once our fields are chosen, we can preview if we like, and then choose Next.

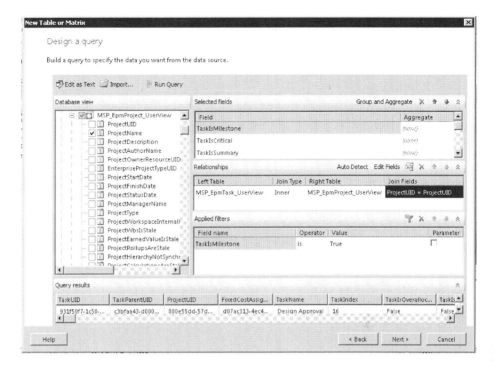

Figure 63 - SSRS Query Design

After that, we're presented with a list of all the fields we've selected. You can drag and drop individual fields to Values, and optionally add them to Row or Column Groups. In my example, I'm querying a list of project events ("Milestones") so I'm grouping by ProjectName and TaskName, and adding the TaskUID (and later, Date) to the Values section.

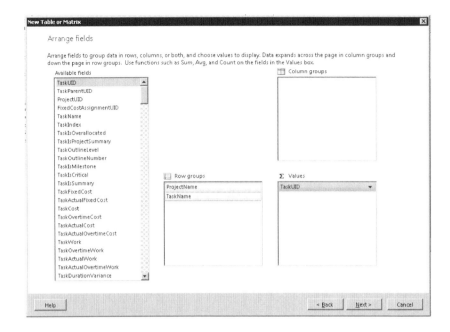

Figure 64 - SSRS Field Arrangement

We're headed for home! The penultimate step in the wizard asks you to choose a layout if you want to display hierarchies, subtotals or Grand Totals.:

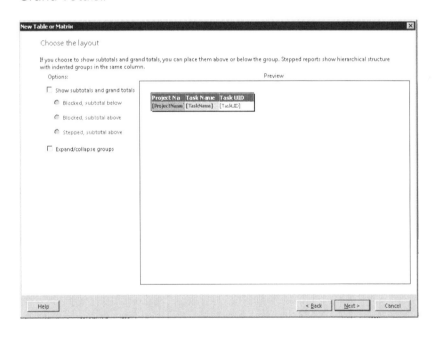

Figure 65 - SSRS Report Layout

This final screen allows to you apply a range of predefined styles (fonts and colors) to your report. After you select one and click Next, you are brought into your "finished" report in the designer. You may make changes to fields, fonts, colors, etc.

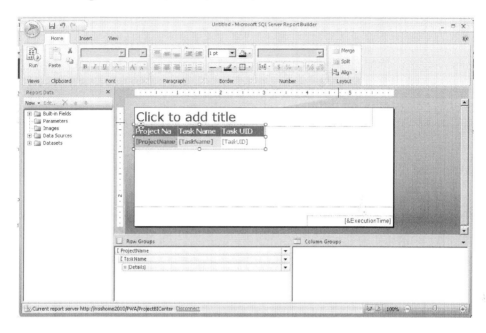

Figure 66 - SSRS Report Designer

We're done! You should now save the report back to the library FIRST, and then click the RUN button on the Ribbon to preview the results. (Why save first? I'm superstitious...)

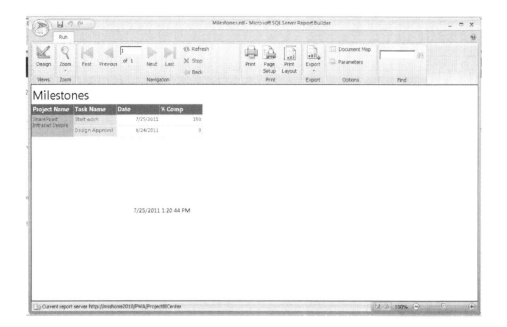

Figure 67 - SSRS Report Preview

Once that's done, users can run the report directly by clicking on it from the library:

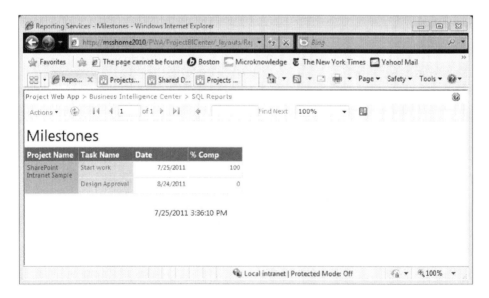

Figure 68 - SharePoint Integrated Access to SSRS Report

I'll have another example of building a report later when we discuss PowerPivot, since SSRS reports can be a good source for PowerPivot models. That walkthrough starts below on page 170, and uses a simple SQL table as its source.

Excel Services

Microsoft offers **two** ways to use Excel to develop business intelligence interfaces in SharePoint – Excel Services and PowerPivot. Why? Well, as Microsoft loves telling folks, Excel is the world's leading business intelligence tool. It's ubiquitous on almost all PCs. And with Excel 2010, the native tools offer powerful interface elements for BI. For example, Sparklines provide a simple one-cell trend line chart to display alongside data.

What's the difference? In Excel Services, the data lives **inside** a spreadsheet, while in PowerPivot, you can model extremely large datasets, greater than 1 million rows, which live **outside** Excel in external databases.

Excel Services is closely related to the browser-based version of Excel included as part of Office Web Applications. Excel Services are usually integrated as Excel Web Services web parts that display part or all of a spreadsheet. On top of that, Excel Services can also use native SharePoint Status Indicators (KPIs) (which can also display KPIs based on list data). Excel Services is a great choice when some users are skilled in data modeling and display in Excel 2010 (e.gl. Slicers), and data is already in spreadsheets, but not all users have Office 2010

PowerPivot

PowerPivot began as Microsoft's "Project Gemini". User access to business intelligence has always been a challenge. In many ways, Excel is the world's leading tool for data manipulation. Excel is ubiquitous on almost all business desktops. But it's not designed to handle extremely large recordsets. How might Excel be used on recordsets of 1-10 million rows that live outside of traditional spreadsheets?

PowerPivot is Microsoft's tool, released as part of SQL Server 2008 R2, which allows fast, in-memory access to multimillion row data sets in Excel 2010 and SharePoint 2010. The Excel client add in can be downloaded at http://go.microsoft.com/fwlink/?LinkId=155905 [requires Excel 2010]. Once installed, you can work with SharePoint hosted PowerPivot just by uploading the spreadsheet to a PowerPivot Gallery on SharePoint. And it works on 100 row datasets too – any data that live outside the spreadsheet.

PowerPivot solves that challenge by adding in a slimmed down version of the Analysis Services engine for data manipulation. PowerPivot is composed of two elements:

- An "free" Excel add-in that connects spreadsheets to those large SSAS recordsets
- A SharePoint add-in that allows a SharePoint server to handle PowerPivot data in an Excel spreadsheet through Excel Services. This was released as part of SQL Server 2008 R2.

"Traditional" Excel Services displays data stored in an Excel spreadsheet. PowerPivot connects to one of the broadest range of data sources including;

- SQL Server
- Analysis Services Cube
- SSRS Report
- Access
- Other PowerPivot and Excel files
- Data Feeds (XML, Atom, Azure, WCF OData, Dallas)
- Oracle, Teradata, Sybase, DB2
- ODBC
- Text files (CSV, etc.)

Why use PowerPivot? One of the strongest reasons is your technical culture. If you have a cadre of users who are really good at Excel and are able to work site remote data sources, it's a good fit. Often, enterprise data **has** to stay inside its source system (Oracle, SQL etc.) Moving and copying it around to local files is impractical or even impermissible under certain compliance rules.

SSRS Reports as a PowerPivot Data Source

When developing SharePoint business intelligence solutions, most of the time the data connections are fairly routine. However, I was once building a PowerPivot solution where some of the data modelers, working in PowerPivot, lived in a different Active Directory domain from the source database and SharePoint farm. Also, this environment didn't use Kerberos. Kerberos, as you may recall, is a security protocol that allows users to request and receive authorization "tickets" across multiple server hops – from machine to machine, and across domains. Because of its occasional complexity, the protocol was named after Cerberus, the three-headed beast of ancient Greek mythology.

Figure 69 - Hercules captures Cerberus. (Hans) Sebald Beham, 1545

OK, let's not slay any monsters! Let's just suppose we want to enable Excel users to develop PowerPivot models against a remote, cross-domain SQL data source for publication to a remote domain's SharePoint farm. How best to proceed?

Multiple data hops (client – server – server – database) usually require Kerberos security configurations. However, not all organizations are sufficiently mature to have implemented Kerberos. In these cases, using SSRS as a data source can reduce or eliminate extra hops. In particular, SSRS under SQL Server 2012 makes it simple to expose sections of an SSRS report as XML data feeds to be reconsumed by other subscribing applications. Since PowerPivot can connect directly to a SQL Server Reporting Services report as its data source, in addition to remotely addressing the SQL Server.

Add the data to a SQL Server Reporting Services report.
This is pretty simple. In this case, we're already running SSRS in SharePoint integrated mode. And let's assume we already have a library that supports Report Server Reports and Report Data Source files, and that our data source was built and published to SharePoint as an .rsds file. When we set up the report, we're going to grab all the data we think we want in the report. We can filter later in Excel.

1. Create a new report in SharePoint library by selecting **New Documents | Report Builder Reports** from the library Ribbon
2. Select the **Table or Matrix Wizard.**

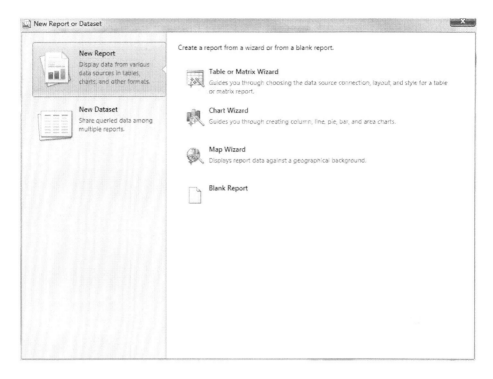

Figure 70 - Report Wizard

3. On the next screen, choose 'Create a dataset'.

4. Select the data connection, and, if re-prompted, login.

5. On the **Design a query** screen, select the source table or view and choose **Next**.

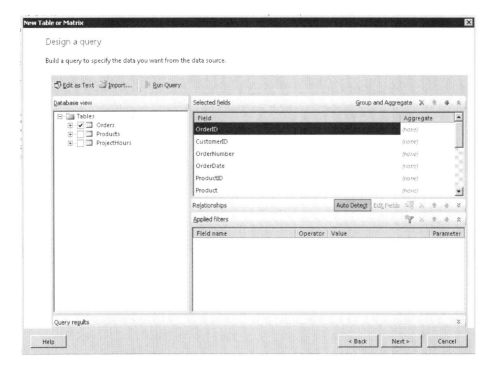

Figure 71 - Query Designer

6. On the **Arrange fields** screen, select all the fields and drag them into the **Values** section at lower right. Choose next.
7. Choose **Next** on the Layout screen (if you're getting all the data and adding it to the Values section, there should be no options for grouping or subtotaling.)
8. Pick any color scheme – it doesn't matter to PowerPivot.

Your report is built! Now save it back to the SharePoint report-document library, and remember what you named it and where it was saved for the next steps. Again, we don't really intend to run or print this report, so the formatting etc., doesn't matter. It's just a data source.

Create a PowerPivot model in Excel 2010

Click the PowerPivot menu item, and select the PowerPivot button in the Ribbon. From there, select the **From Report** option in the **Get External Data** section of the PowerPivot window.

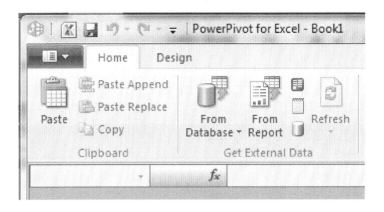

Figure 72 - PowerPivot External Data

In the **Table Import Wizard**, click the browse button and find the SSRS report we saved in the first half of this exercise. The report will render in preview mode – click **Next**. The next step will show the table – the "Tablix" – we built in the report. You may choose to eliminate columns from the **Preview and Filter** button, or click Next to open up the source data in PowerPivot.

And that's it! You can slice and dice your PowerPivot model as you like now. Just don't wake up the sleeping three headed dog on your way back to the SharePoint document library...

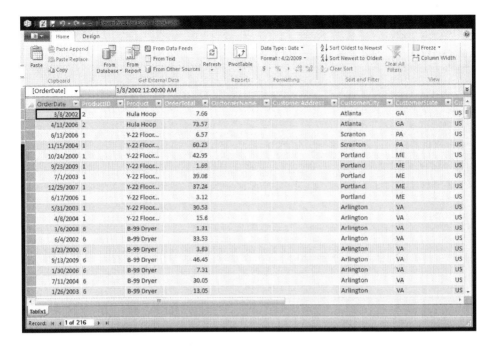

Figure 73 - PowerPivot Window

PowerPivot Tips

For troubleshooting, make sure the add-in is not just installed but enabled in Excel. Also, you can disable spurious error messages by adding the following environment variable:

```
VSTO_suppressdisplayalerts = 0
```

Pivot

Pivot is a unique graphical query interface released by Microsoft Live Labs in 2010. Microsoft certainly seems to love the word – this follows in the wake of PowerPivot and PivotTables, two very different business intelligence subsystems.

Pivot is entirely different. When originally introduced at Microsoft's Worldwide Partner Conference 2010, speakers described it as "powerful, informative and fun". Fun? Yes, I think it is!

Pivot lets you build an interface to items that can be represented with a graphical tag. As you drill into the items, the pictures dynamically fly around the screen to rearrange themselves according to your query. Pivot provides a local client, an Excel design interface, and Silverlight controls to allow you to integrate Pivot into your SharePoint site. I've pasted a screenshot below – you can also "play along" with the interactive demos online at http://www.microsoft.com/silverlight/pivotviewer/

Figure 74 - Pivot Viewer

Let's walk through building your first Pivot collection and viewing it through a Silverlight control from your SharePoint site. Since one of my hobbies is digital photography,[22] I used Pivot to build a simple viewer for some of my favorite pictures.

Step 1: Install the Excel Add-In
The simplest way to start building a Pivot Collection is to install the Excel Add-In from

---

[22] See www.flickr.com/photos/cmcnulty for more.

http://www.silverlight.net/learn/pivotviewer/download-excel-tool/ The Excel Add-In add the Ribbon control to allow you to create a New Collection. What's a collection? A collection is maintained in an Excel spreadsheet, but is exported to Pivot as a .cxml file and related directory that contains all the related support fields and graphic element required by the Pivot interface.   You use Excel to maintain the data, and then users can query the data using the Pivot Collection.

Once you've installed the add-in, select New Collection from the Pivot Collections tab. The Pivot template gives you two spreadsheets in your workbook:

- **Collection Items.** This is the main screen where you will add image files and define the principal columns for data exploration.
- **Collection Properties** The tab allows you to define collection-wide information, such as Collection Title, Icon, Brand Image, Additional Search Text, and Copyright.

Use Import Images to browse for pictures you want to add to the Collection. (You may note that some columns are hidden by default.) Once the photos are imported, you need to start adding data for the existing columns:

- **Name** – A title for the image
- **HRef** – A link to follow if the image is clicked
- **Description**

Pop-up help reminds you about each of those columns on the header line. Most important, you can add additional columns to the right of the Description Column. Here's what our sample collection looks like after I imported photos and added several additional columns for State, Time (of day) and Year:

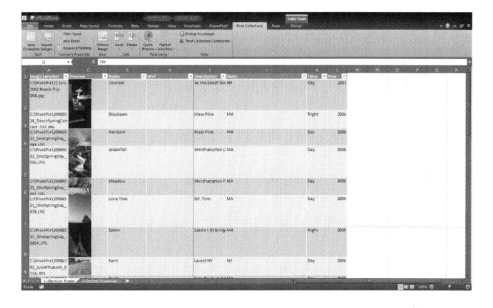

Figure 75 - Pivot Collection

Once the collection is defined, you can play with it by using the Quick Preview option (which actually doesn't show the images, just the query.

Sept 2: Publish Collection

First, save your Excel file – and it doesn't need to be in the location where the finished collection will live. Then, choose the Publish Collection item. Pick a new local folder, and give the Collection .CXML file a name. This process can take a few minutes while the engine parses and resizes all the graphical elements. Once it finishes, your collection should open up in a new Pivot Viewer local window. You can explore your data and test to make sure your collection is ready to share.

One of the things you may note is that you're not limited to "check box" queries – if you define number values the Pivot query interface lets you use a slider control to filter a range of values.

Step 3: Publish to Web

The first thing to do is to copy the entire Collection directory to your SharePoint server – somewhere on the file system, outside of SharePoint. There are a LOT of files, so this process can take a while. In our example, I created a new C:\Pivot directory. The entire collection goes into C:\Pivot\PivotPix.

You're also going to need to download the sample Silverlight Pivot viewer and viewer page from Microsoft (see http://www.silverlight.net/learn/pivotviewer/release-notes/) In our example, we put the XAP file (a compiled Silverlight app) and HTML page in C:\Pivot\Viewers. We're really taking a shortcut here – however, recompiling a new viewer is pretty simple in the Silverlight 4 Toolkit.

Step 4: IIS Configuration

Now the web server needs to know about the files we just added. In IIS7 manager, I add two virtual directories:

- Pivot – mapped to the location of the viewer files
- PivotPix – mapped to the location of the CXML file and the rest of the collection

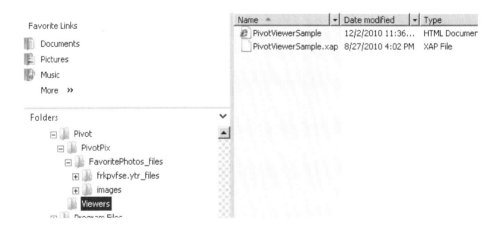

Figure 76 - IIS Virtual Directories

To do this:

- Right click on the web site where you want to add the alias
- Select Add Virtual Directory
- Enter the Alias and Directory as needed

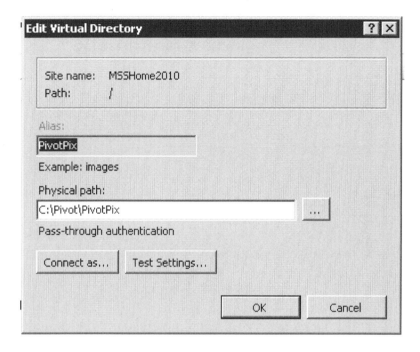

Figure 77 - IIS Virtual Directory

Step 5: Edit the HTML File

There's a lot in the sample HTML file, but the key line is:

```
<param name="initparams"
value="initialCollectionUri=http://msshome2010/PivotPix/FavoritePhotos.cxml"
/>
```

Change the value of the initialCollectionUri to match the "http://website/alias/nameofcollection.cxml" path for your local server. (Substitute your own local server name and alias.)

Step 6: Add links on SharePoint

Test the path to your edited HTML file – it should be http://yoursite/your-alias/PivotViewerSample.HTML [match to your own actual server names .] If you've set up the aliasing correctly, add a link in SharePoint and you should get your browser to render the Silverlight view to your collection:

Figure 78 - Pivot model in the browser

What next? There's a lot more you can do. You may start by adding custom columns to your collection. Also, you'll want to redesign and recompile the Silverlight viewer to patch your interface requirements but we'll leave that for another day.

Pivot SharePoint Web Part

You can get even better integration with the Silverlight Pivot Viewer for SharePoint on Codeplex http://pivotviewersp.codeplex.com/ This control is designed to let you skip the Excel collection generation and IIS process entirely. Instead, this solution consumes its images and data directly from:

- A picture library
- The User Profile List
- Site navigation

The web part is not hard to figure out once you've downloaded and deployed the WSP. (Hint – although the documentation tells you how to install it using STSADM, why not look forward and use PowerShell: Add-SPSolution and Install-SPSolution).

Anyway, once you've installed the part and added to a page, you can connect to a library, and get almost the same experience as you had using the HTML-hosted XAP file:

Figure 79 - Pivot Web Part

Have powerful, informative fun!

Business Connectivity Services

Business Connectivity Services, or BCS, began in SharePoint 2007 as the "BDC" (Business Data Catalog). The BDC was usually restricted to a single column of read information to be used in searches or lockups. BCS empowers s a new Content Type called "External List". External Lists refer to a data set -- such as orders, customers, products – that live in an external database but look like a read/write SharePoint list in the browser. BCS is also newly able to write data – an extension to the read only functions in the 2007 BDC. BCS adds three great new capabilities:

- Read write access to remote data sources
- Exposing remote SQL tables (and other sources) as editable, native SharePoint lists to use datasheets, RSS feeds, etc.
- Republishing BDC data to other applications, such as Office 2010. This means you could have a remote contact list in your CRM system, link it as an editable list in SharePoint 2010 and republish the list as a Contacts list in Outlook.

Although the data connection can be read-write, for many line-of-business systems, you will want to disable write functions. For example, if you're pulling a list of general ledger codes from a SQL-based accounting system, you may not want to give users the ability to inject new billing codes directly into the accounting system without going through that application's interface.

On the SharePoint side, the External List looks indistinguishable from a native SharePoint list:

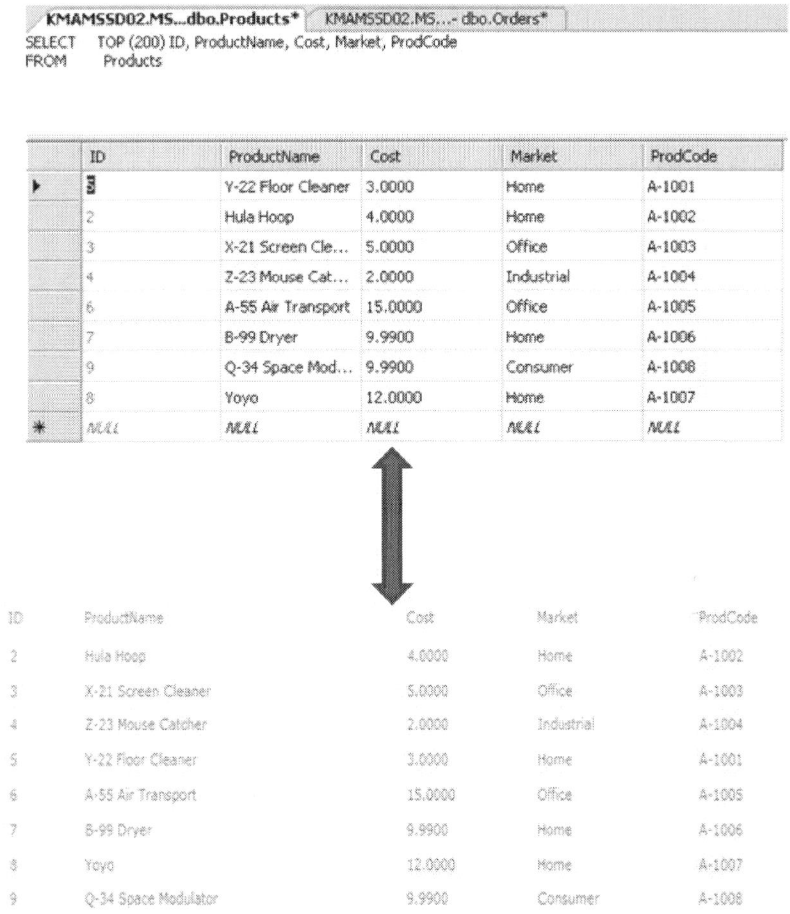

```
SELECT   TOP (200) ID, ProductName, Cost, Market, ProdCode
FROM     Products
```

	ID	ProductName	Cost	Market	ProdCode
▶	5	Y-22 Floor Cleaner	3.0000	Home	A-1001
	2	Hula Hoop	4.0000	Home	A-1002
	3	X-21 Screen Cle...	5.0000	Office	A-1003
	4	Z-23 Mouse Cat...	2.0000	Industrial	A-1004
	6	A-55 Air Transport	15.0000	Office	A-1005
	7	B-99 Dryer	9.9900	Home	A-1006
	9	Q-34 Space Mod...	9.9900	Consumer	A-1008
	8	Yoyo	12.0000	Home	A-1007
*	NULL	NULL	NULL	NULL	NULL

ID	ProductName	Cost	Market	ProdCode
2	Hula Hoop	4.0000	Home	A-1002
3	X-21 Screen Cleaner	5.0000	Office	A-1003
4	Z-23 Mouse Catcher	2.0000	Industrial	A-1004
5	Y-22 Floor Cleaner	3.0000	Home	A-1001
6	A-55 Air Transport	15.0000	Office	A-1005
7	B-99 Dryer	9.9900	Home	A-1006
8	Yoyo	12.0000	Home	A-1007
9	Q-34 Space Modulator	9.9900	Consumer	A-1008

Figure 80 - BCS Illustrated

BCS natively supports remote data formats including SQL Server, .NET Framework, and WCF-based web services such as the "Dallas" Windows Azure DataMarket. (This means that if you want to tie into remote data in Oracle, DB2, etc. you will need to write a custom web service to expose the data first.)

Let's walk through how to set up a simple External List Connection in SharePoint Designer 2010. There will be three major aspects:

- Define the BCS External Content in SharePoint Designer 2010

- Establish Permissions in Central Administration
- Test the BCS connection in Internet Explorer

BCS Definition

Let's get started!

1. Open up SharePoint Designer and connect to the site that will store the definition for the BCS connection. (This is usually the root site of a site collection, and will appear through the Designer screens as the "Namespace".)

2. Highlight External Content Types in the left navigation bar, and from the Ribbon, click the left most button to create a new External Content Type.

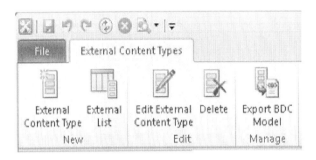

Figure 81 - New Content Type

3. Create a name and a display name for your BCS connection under **External Content Type Information**. Next, click the link next to **External System** to build a connection to the data source.

External Content Type Information	^

Key information about this external content type.

Name	Products2012
Display Name	Products2012
Namespace	http://sp2010
Version	1.0.0.0
Identifiers	There are no identifiers defined.
Office Item Type	Generic List ▾
Offline Sync for external list	Enabled ▾
External System	Click here to discover external data sources and define operations.

Figure 82 - External Content Type

4. Click the **Add Connection** button. On the screen that prompts us to choose a connection type, pick SQL Server (not .NET or WCF) and click OK

5. Fill out the SQL Server connection dialog and at a minimum, use the **Database Server** and **Database Name**. For now, leave the settings on *Connect with User's Identity*. (It's not that hard to use the Secure Store to define an Application ID for this connection and a saved set of credentials for the Impersonated Identity, but we'll leave those aside for now since this is our quick-and-dirty build.)

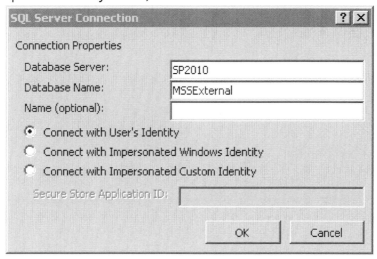

Figure 83 - SQL Connection

6. Next we need to define the Operations that BCS will use to retrieve and update single rows, or all rows in our source. There's a quick template wizard we can use here to create them. Right mouse click on the table name and select **Create All Operations**.

7. The most important thing to make sure we select on this wizard is the Identifier, to define the unique key for accurate record retrieval. In the screen shots below, we designate the ID field as the Identifier. The second most important thing is to identify which fields show as record identifiers in the Picker dialog. Here I'm using **ProductName** under **Show In Picker**. Make any needed change to other field definitions and click through the rest of the wizard. You may notice filter parameters as a possible adjustment – and although these may be needed for large recordsets, we'll exclude them from scope for now.

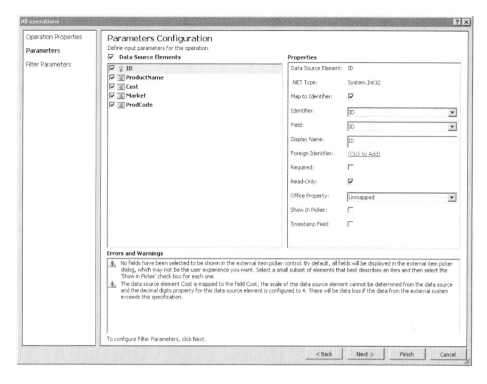

Figure 84 - BCS Parameters

8. Click On ribbon, choose Lists & Forms | Create Lists and Forms
   Pick a new name for the list.

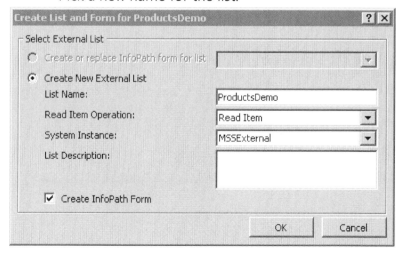

Figure 85 - Create External List and InfoPath Form

Permissions

9. In SharePoint Central Admin, go to Application Management. Select Manage Service Applications, and then click on the name of your BCS service application (by default, "**Business Data Connectivity Service**").

10. In the next screen, click on the name of the BDC entity (we used "**Products2012**" above.)

11. On the next screen, you can see the entity definition in the service application. On the Ribbon, click on **Set Object Permissions**.

12. On the Set Object Permissions dialog, pick the appropriate user accounts or groups in the top portion of the screen. After these are "resolved", use Add to move those users into the second section, and add permissions with the check boxes in the bottom of the dialog.

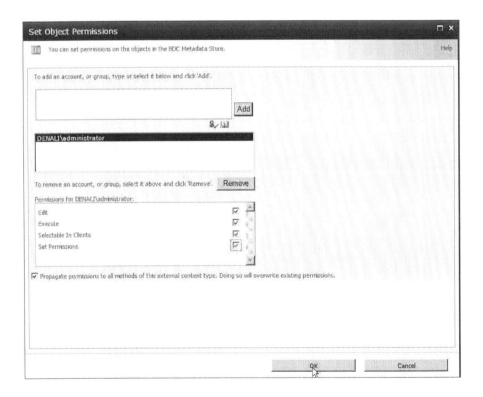

Figure 86- BCS Permissions

Once this is done, you should be able to use the new list to add data using the new form.

PerformancePoint 2010

Performance Point is the pinnacle of SharePoint's intrinsic business intelligence subsystems. Performance Point allows you to combine Excel Services, SSRS and native Performance Point elements into multi-tabbed dashboards, scorecards, and interactive charts. For example, this screen shot shows the second page of a four page dashboard, combining a Performance Point KPI scorecard with three SSRS Reports.

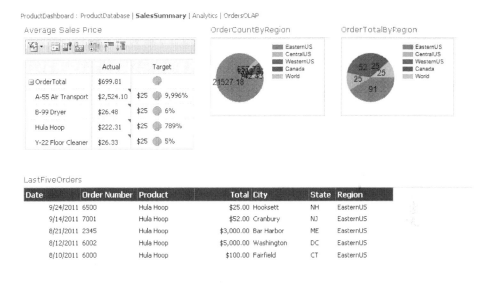

Figure 87 - Performance Point Dashboard

One of the highlights of Performance Point is its Decomposition Tree, which lets users interactively drill down through the hierarchies of data underlying of its Analysis Services based charts. Performance Point works best with SQL Analysis Services based data, but can also work wonders with Excel Services, SharePoint Lists, and SQL.

Performance Point alone is a huge topic. There are whole volumes already published on its detailed use. We're going to be a little more focused. Here, I'll walk you through the elements of creating a dashboard, adding SSRS elements and KPI scorecards, and how to add an Analytic Chart to enable the Decomposition Tree.

Performance Point can combine elements from SSRS reports and Excel Services in addition to its own native components. Performance Point native elements provide the most interactivity when they use SQL Analysis Services cubes as their data source. Decomposition Tree, for example, is unavailable if the data source is a simple SQL table for example. Designing an Analysis Services cube can be a significant development effort. It requires the use of a custom version of Visual Studio 2008 – Business Intelligence Developers Studio ("BIDS"). SSAS cubes usually require true SQL development. However, some systems, such as Microsoft Project Server 2010, come with prebuilt SSAS cubes. And there's a lot you can do in Performance Point without writing code. Let's start building dashboards from SSRS reports.

Before we start doing anything in Performance Point, though, let's make sure the service applications are established.

PerformancePoint Service Application

The PerformancePoint SSA has very few settings. There's an interface that allows you to import Performance Point 2007 elements, and an interface to specify trusted locations for data sources and PerformancePoint libraries. But the most important part of this screen is the Service Application Settings.

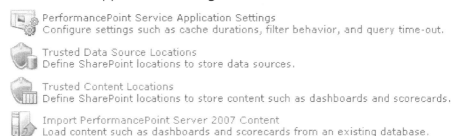

PerformancePoint Service Application Settings
Configure settings such as cache durations, filter behavior, and query time-out.

Trusted Data Source Locations
Define SharePoint locations to store data sources.

Trusted Content Locations
Define SharePoint locations to store content such as dashboards and scorecards.

Import PerformancePoint Server 2007 Content
Load content such as dashboards and scorecards from an existing database.

Figure 88 - PerformancePoint SSA

This screen allows the administrator to set various throttles and timeout values for data retrieval, Decomposition Trees, filters, and comments. But the most important settings to configure are those for the Secure Store Service. Secure Store Service maintains an encrypted vault of user accounts and password to be presented when applications need to use single sign-on. Here, we need to enter the name of the Secure Store Service SSA, and the account that should be used for Unattended Service Account access. The Unattended Service Account credentials are used whenever a data source in PerformancePoint doesn't have its own security credentials or use the user's individual login.

Figure 89 - Secure Store Settings

As you might expect, for this to work, you need to have already configured the Secure Store Service SSA. Secure Store will automatically map and configure a Performance Point target application when you run the post-installation configuration of

SharePoint using the Farm Wizard (the so-called "white" wizard. See page 97 for more.)

	Target Application ID ↑	Type	Target Application Name
☐	5fd8a7cd-d768-45fd-952c-c4009cb434ab-PPSUnattendedAccount	Group	PerformancePoint Service Application
☐	MSSExtSQL2010	Group	MSSExtSQL2010

Dashboard Designer

Performance Point dashboards are built with Dashboard Designer. Dashboard Designer is a free component that downloads and runs from your browser to any Business Intelligence Center-based site on SharePoint.

Adding SSRS Reports to Performance Point

First, launch the Dashboard Designer from the home page of the Business Intelligence Center.   Dashboard Designer downloads file locally and then launches an app that runs locally.

TIP: *Although Dashboard Designer may prompt you to save the elements of a Dashboard "Workspace" locally", all elements are actually saved and registered on the Performance Point Content list of the BI Center site. The "local save" just represents personalization and pointers to the SharePoint-hosted elements.*

When the Designer opens, highlight the PerformancePoint Content node on the left hand side under Workspace Browser. Then, on the

Ribbon, you can choose the Create Tab, and in the Reports section choose Reporting Services.

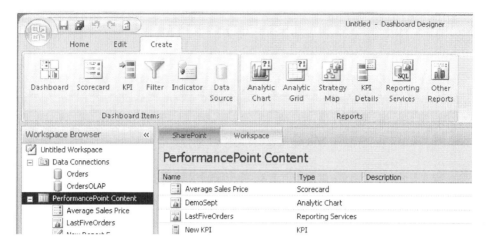

Figure 90 - PerformancePoint in Dashboard Designer

This brings up a screen where we can specify the SSRS report we want to link into Performance Point. Critical elements are described below.

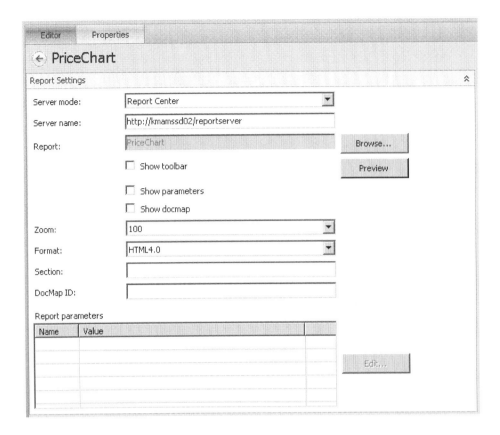

Figure 91 - Native Mode SSRS Integration

Server Mode – choose between Report Center (Native Mode) or SharePoint Integrated

Server Name – a misleading title, this is the URL to the Report Manager Web service. If you remember back to the process of configuring integrated mode, there are two web services that are created during the configuration (see page 151 for more). The format for a Native Mode service is often http://[SERVERNAME]/reportserver. For Integrated mode, it usually takes the form http://[SharePointServer]:80/reportserver_[InstanceName]

In SQL Server 2012, since Reporting Services is now a Shared Services Application (SSA) there's a change to the URL format. What was once

http://[server]/ReportServer

Is now, in SQL 2012 Denali:

http://[server]/_vti_bin/ReportServer

Report – the URL to the actual report we're adding

The remaining elements may or may not be relevant. Commonly, we turn the report toolbar off, and based on the report itself, you may or may not want to specify runtime parameters. Finally you will probably want to rename the report from its default name – "New Report 5" etc. You do this under the Properties tab.

TIP: *If you see the error "An unexpected error occurred. Error 11861", it means you're trying to develop a report in Dashboard Designer using a data source that hasn't been saved to the server yet. Save it!*

Creating a Dashboard and Embedding SSRS Reports

OK, now we want to build the web page that will contain our new report and other elements. Again, we start in Dashboard Designer with the Create Tab, and choose Dashboard

The next dialog opens a list of page templates:

- 1 Zone
- 2 Columns
- 2 Rows
- Three Columns
- 3 Rows
- Column, Split Column
- Header, 2 Columns

You don't need to worry too much about getting the perfect format. Once you pick a page, its relatively easy to right click in the

Dashboard Content Region of the desginer to add, delete, split or reconfigure a zone. And if you've worked with SharePoint Designer, you may think the page looks like a web part page. That's not a coincidence – they work the same way.

You can also add pages using the New Pages button in the Pages section of the middle screen. Each page appears as a navigation sub-tab on the Dashboard page. But for now, lets just stay with a single page dashboard.

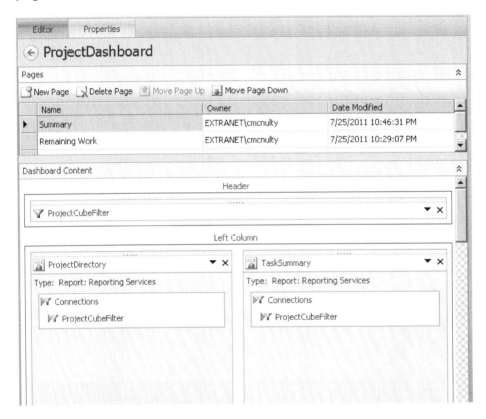

Figure 92 - PerformancePoint Dashboard

Next we're going to look at the Details section at the right. Open up the **Reports | PerformancePoint Content** node. Drag the Report you want to the right zone on your dashboard page. (If you have nothing in the other zones, they won't really take up space in the published dashboard.)

OK, before we move on there are two other aspects to consider. First, the Properties tab in the middle opens up a screen where you can rename the dashboard, and redirect the dashboard to publish to a different document library.

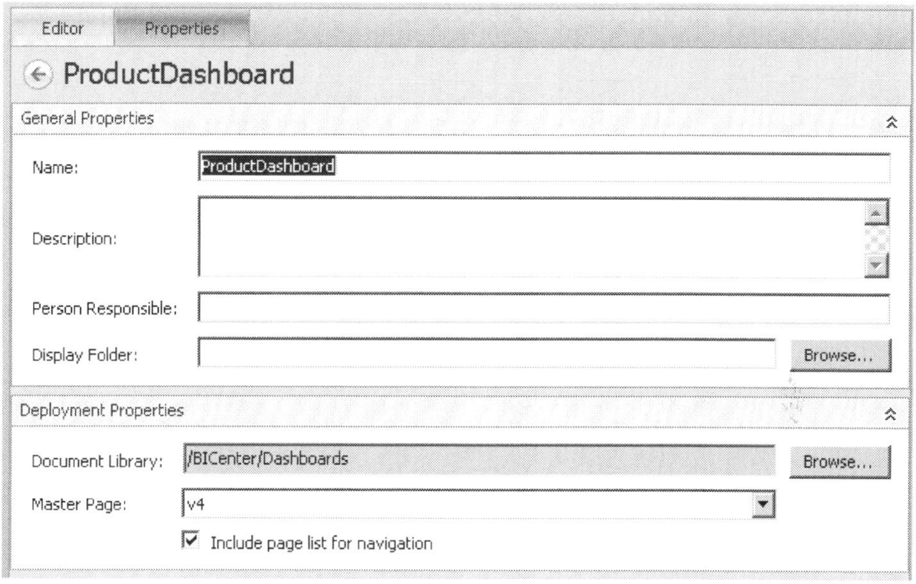

Figure 93 - Dashboard Properties

Second, when you click on the Properties tab, the Details pane switches to show you a list of all the elements – reports – data sources, filters, charts, etc. – used in the dashboard. If you have a large Performance Point site with a lot of similarly named elements, this can be invaluable to make sure you're editing the "right" pieces of your dashboard. Each of the elements of a dashboard is 'live' – that is, if you change the report or change the chart, the dashboard will automatically reflect that – it doesn't keep a snapshot of the elements.

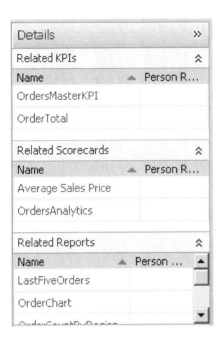

Figure 94 - Dashboard Details

Ok finally, we should save the dashboard by clicking on the disk icon at the top left, and then right click on the name of the dashboard. From that content menu, you can select **Deploy to SharePoint...** After the page publishes, the Dashboard will open up in a new browser window. Ta-da!

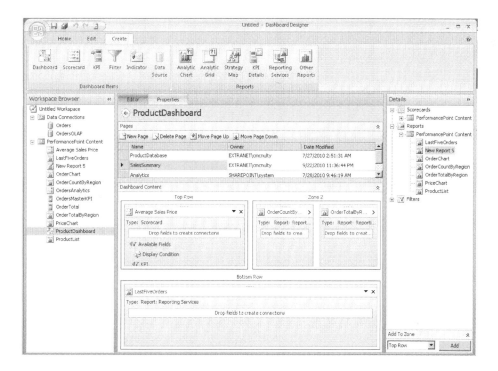

Figure 95 - Dashboard Deployment

TIP: *If your SSRS report uses real-time data, there's an obscure but useful URL argument that tells the report not to cache its data:*

```
"rs:ClearSession=true"
```

Performance Point KPIs and Scorecards

OK, here's where the magic happens! Performance Point is "happiest" with an Analysis Services data source, since cubes support dimensions, KPIs, and other complex data elements. But that doesn't mean you're out of luck if you have a SQL database, and no SQL Analysis Services developers can be found. There's a lot of power in Performance Point to create dimensions and scorecards, even with non-cubed data. Let's plunge in!

Scorecards are a native part of Performance Point. For all the "native" elements, you need to start by adding a data source. There's a lot you can do even with a simple SQL table to approximate the dimensional slicing that's built into data cubes. This process has three phases:

- Define and model a data source
- Build a KPI to compare actual values and targets in the data source
- Add the KPI to Scorecard and add that to a dashboard

We begin as before by defining a new data source from the now-familiar **Create** tab on the Dashboard Designer ribbon. This time, let's select SQL Server Table.

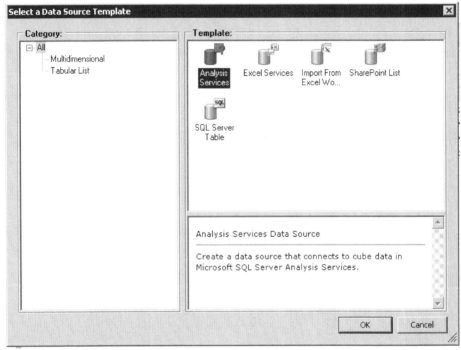

Figure 96 - Dashboard Data Source

The subsequent screen controls the key data properties. Although you could define an advanced connection string, let's begin by specifying a server, database and table. Under **Data Source Settings**, we have a choice of using Per-user identity (assuming each user has direct permission to the table.) Or we can set up the Shared Service

Application to use the Unattended Service Account, which we discussed earlier as part of the SSA configuration.

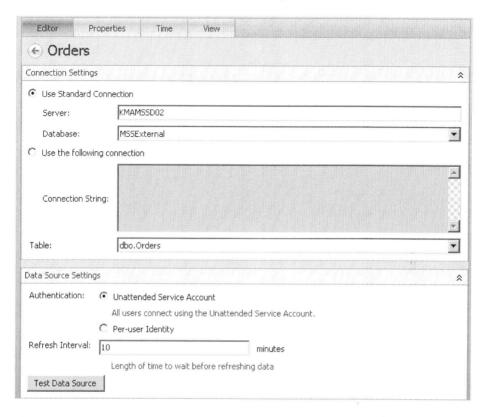

Figure 97 - SQL Table Data Source

Once you establish and test the connection, switch to the View tab and click **Preview Data**. This will open up a view of the columns and values. You can click on columns to select them for the right hand Details tab, and this is where you need to characterize each of the columns by what kind of data it contains. This is a simplified version of the process that developers use in Visual Studio to build data cubes:

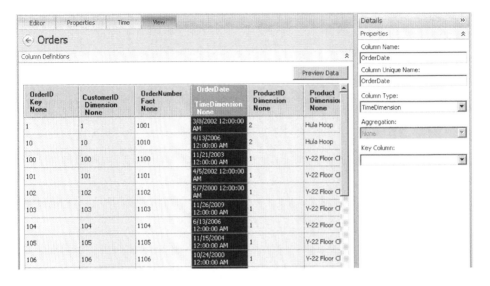

Key – the unique ID to be used to retrieve records. It really speeds things up if the column is already indexed in SQL Server, and this may be a native SQL "Key" data type column.

Dimension – data to be used for grouping and aggregation, such as locations, products, projects, staff names

Time Dimension – Similar to regular dimensions, Time Dimensions allow you to group rows by ranges of dates (week, months, quarters, years, etc.)

Fact – The default characteristic for most columns, Fact columns flag data to be displayed or calculated in groups. Dollar values, for example, are facts that can be totaled, averaged, or have other calculations on them.

When you are modeling the kinds of data for a SQL data source, it's also important to identify the **KeyColumn** to be used to pull back the data for that dimension.

Finally, the **Time** tab is used after you've identified a TimeDimension column or columns. Here, you can specify the ranges to be available for date groupings (year, month, week, etc.)

Save the data source. Now we can build a KPI to add to a scorecard. The process of building a KPI will vary greatly based on source data and calculations. KPIs usually evaluate actual data against a derived or prebuilt target goal.

Begin by using the Create tab to add a new KPI. This opens another, duh, wizard, and we can walk through the following selections:

Create a new Blank KPI

On the next screen, click on the Data mappings link on the Actual row. You'll see a "fixed" mapping for a value of 1.

- Click the Change Source button to open up a dialog to point to our known data sources.
- Select the SQL-based data source we just created and click OK.
- On the Dimensional Data Source Mapping dialog, select a **Measure** from the drop down at the top of the screen. These will be based on numerical Fact columns we noted during the data modeling above. Click OK.
- Repeat the same process to define a data mapping for the Target values. For targets, you can also establish a Scoping Pattern and Indicators – to show what ranges are good and bad, and how to display the results (stoplights, thermometers, trend lines.) [Yes, there's a wizard for that, too!]

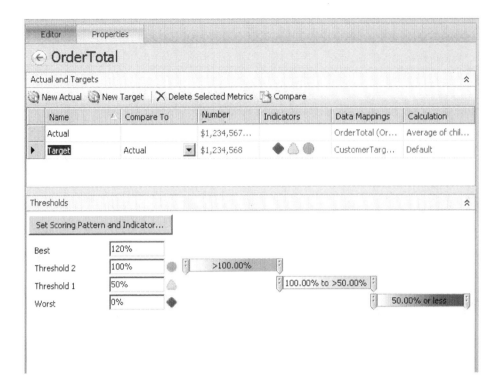

Figure 98 - KPI Configuration

Finally, we're going to create a new Scorecard. We start with a Tabular scorecard based on SQL Server Tables.

- Pick our SQL table data source.
- Select the KPI we just built.
- Filters are not strictly necessary.
- You don't need to pick a measure dimension yet. Finish the wizard and the scorecard will open up in a Designer screen.

From here, you can open up the right hand details tab to drag a dimension onto the scorecard, dragging it just to the right of the name of the KPI in the left column. In this example, we've dragged a Time Dimension for Year onto the scorecards. Save and refresh, ,and you should see a view that looks like the scorecard below.

OrdersAnalytics

	Actual	Target	
⊟ OrdersMasterKPI	$154.64	⬤	
2000	$16.91	$25 △	-32%
2001	$19.77	$25 △	-21%
2002	$32.49	$25 ⬤	30%
2003	$23.89	$25 △	-4%
2004	$27.63	$25 ⬤	11%
2005	$23.99	$25 △	-4%
2006	$31.30	$25 ⬤	25%
2007	$23.28	$25 △	-7%
2008	$25.98	$25 ⬤	4%
2009	$27.29	$25 ⬤	9%
2010	$1,448.55	$25 ⬤	5,694%

Figure 99 - PerformancePoint Scorecard

Now we have another dynamic Perfomance Point element that can be added to a dashboard as we did for SSRS reports earlier. See – all without cubes!

Analytic Chart Design

OK, I've postponed it long enough! Let's describe how to build Performance Point elements using Analysis Services. Finally!

Creating an Analysis Services Cube

SSAS is usually a prerequisite for the most powerful functions in Performance Point. Here's a summary of the process for creating a cube from an Excel file:

- Import the data into a SQL database table using the Import Wizard
- Create a SQL View to wrap around the data table
- In Business Intelligence Developer Studio, create a new Analysis Services project
- Add the table as a data source
- Add a Data Source View
- In the Data Source View, create named queries for each proposed dimension
- Add the named queries as cube dimensions
- Build and deploy the cube

TIP: *If you are importing an Excel file into SQL 2008 R2, you may see the error:*

```
The 'Microsoft.ACE.OLEDB.12.0' provider is not registered on
the local machine.
```

It turns out that not all the Office file based data drivers were originally made available on 64 bit platforms, so you need to download an extra component. The critical component is the 2007 Office System Driver: Data Connectivity Components, which adds support for Excel Imports to the SQL Import Wizard and to SSIS.

http://www.microsoft.com/download/en/details.aspx?displaylang=en&id=23734

OLAP Data Source

Most of the data modeling complexity has already happened inside the Analysis Service cube. So our first step is to create a new data source – this time, choosing Analysis Services instead of SQL. You'll note that we pick a "database" which is the actual Analysis Service database. However, instead of a table, we select a cube. Save this data source.

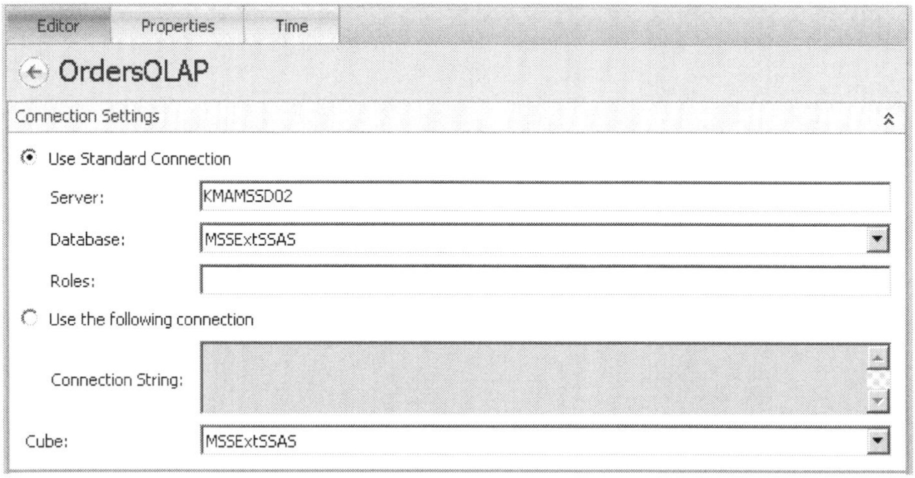

Figure 100 - Analysis Services Data Source

Analytic Chart

The next step is to create a new Analytic Chart in Dashboard Designer. The first step in the wizard asks us to select a data source. Make sure you choose the cube data source we just set up. That's it – it's not the biggest "wizard".

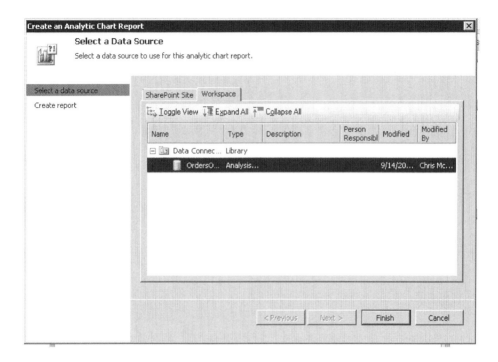

Figure 101 - Data Source Wizard

You're prompted to change the default name, and then you have an empty Designer screen. To keep things simple, drag a Measure to the Series pane, and a Dimension to the Bottom Axis pane. Save the report and add it to a dashboard.

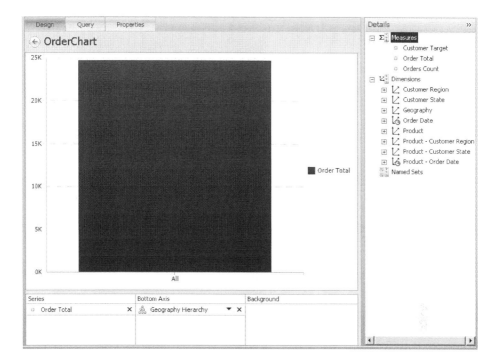

Figure 102 - Analytic Chart

You're done. Seriously. Add this report to a dashboard, save, and publish the dashboard as discussed earlier.

There's a lot more you can do with Performance Point customization, but for now, we've given you enough of a roadmap to explore on your own. Let's take a look at what we've built in action:

Open up the dashboard page containing the Analytic Chart report. Click on the name of the report in the header bar to let the report take over the full available screen space. On the toolbar, switch to the pie chart view. From here, if you right click you can Drill Down to one of the dimensions or grouping in the cube. Here, I've chosen a product dimension.

All

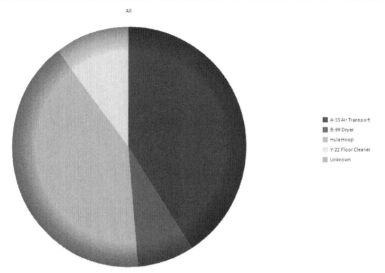

A-55 Air Transport
B-99 Dryer
Hula Hoop
Y-22 Floor Cleaner
Unknown

Figure 103 - Analytic Chart as Pie Chart

Again, the chart is a live data explorer. If I right click on any product, one of the available actions is **Show Details**. It gives you a tabular grid that can be directly exported to Excel. (Here comes that carousel!)

Details: Hula Hoop, All, Order Total - Windows Internet Explorer

Export to Excel   Page 1 of 1   All

Order ID	Product.Order ID	Customer Region.Order ID	Customer State.Order ID	Product - Customer Region.Order ID	Product - Customer State.Order ID
1	1	1	1	1	1
10	10	10	10	10	10
11	11	11	11	11	11
12	12	12	12	12	12
13	13	13	13	13	13
14	14	14	14	14	14
15	15	15	15	15	15
1500	1500	1500	1500	1500	1500
16	16	16	16	16	16
17	17	17	17	17	17
18	18	18	18	18	18
19	19	19	19	19	19
2	2	2	2	2	2
20	20	20	20	20	20
203	203	203	203	203	203

Figure 104 - Data Details for Export

Finally, again with a right click, we can open up a Decomposition Tree. The Tree lets users explore all the subgroupings and details in a given slice:

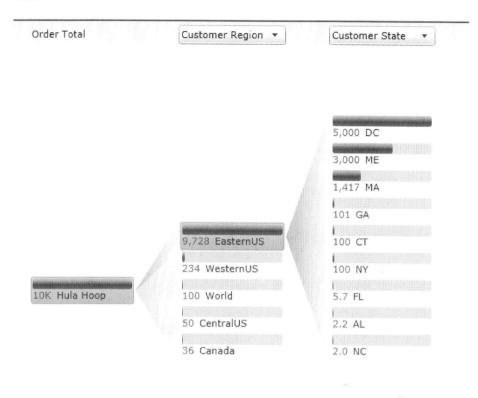

Figure 105 - Decomposition Tree

PerformancePoint and the iPad

The December 2011 CU added Apple iPad support for most of the SharePoint BI stack. BI is highly visual, and the large glass on a tablet gives a far better user experience than a smartphone. But until now there hasn't been a good story for the iPad. Microsoft has added details on TechNet http://technet.microsoft.com/en-us/library/hh697482.aspx. The support isn't universal – you can't run Dashboard Designer, Decomposition Trees, Strategy Maps or ProClarity reports. But you finally get support for:

- Business Intelligence Center

- Dashboards with filters and links
- Excel Services Reports
- Scorecards
- KPIs
- Analytic Charts (my favorite, if you've seen my presentations!)
- Web Page Reports

SQL Server 2012

The newest additions to SharePoint's business intelligence stack come from SQL Server 2012, scheduled for release in March 2012. We're going to walk through its latest incarnation at press time, Community Technology Preview 3 ("CTP3")[23].

Earlier, I discussed Always On (near continuous availability for SQL servers and databases) and upgrades as part of infrastructure planning. (See page 46 for more). Here we're going to look at the two most exciting parts of SQL 2012 Business Intelligence – SSRS Alerts and Power View.

Integrated SSRS reports are great – but how can a user be expected to keep checking all their reports to see what's changed? With SSRS Alerts, users can pick data on any reports and set up their own rules to email them if anything of interest changes.

---

[23] For the most up to date information, check Microsoft's site at http://www.microsoft.com/sqlserver/en/us/future-editions.aspx

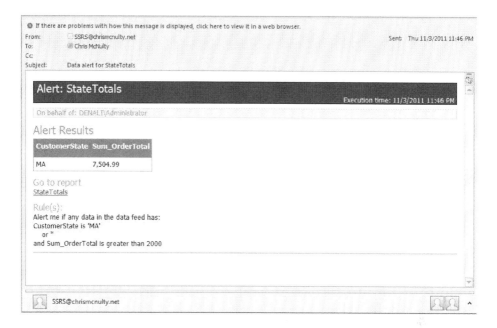

Figure 106 - SSRS Alerts

Similarly, Power View puts the ability to design reports in the hands of users. Power View provides a browser based "Canvas" for drag and drop reporting against almost any conceivable range of data sources.

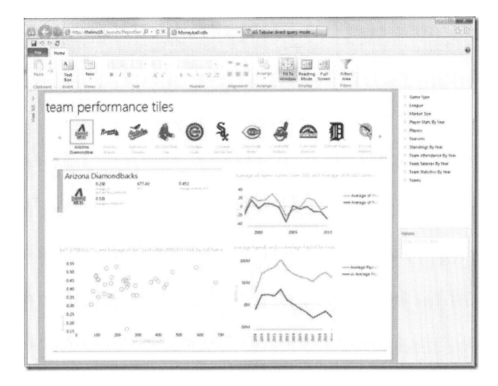

Figure 107 - Power View

SQL Server 2010 CTP3 can be downloaded from https://www.microsoft.com/betaexperience/pd/SQLDCTP3CTA/enus/d efault.aspx

Let's look at how to set up and use these great new features!

SQL 2012 Reporting Services

SSRS in SQL 2012 uses a very different architecture than previous versions. SSRS has two new components. One is a simple web add-in for the WFE servers. The more extensive change is the core Reporting Service – it's now a full SharePoint Shared Services Application ("SSA").

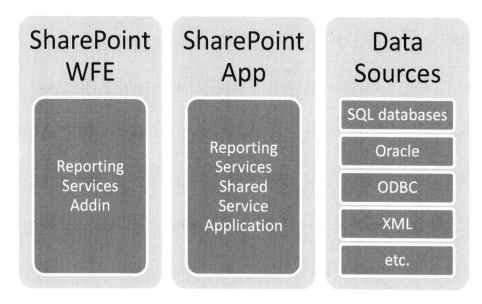

SharePoint WFE	SharePoint App	Data Sources
Reporting Services Addin	Reporting Services Shared Service Application	SQL databases Oracle ODBC XML etc.

Figure 108 - SQL 2012 Reporting Services Architecture

Here's a quick summary of the installation process.

1. Install SQL Server 2012 onto the SharePoint application servers. Install only the Reporting Services engine, and specify that the reports server should run in SharePoint integrated mode.

2. If you have separate WFE servers, download and install the Reporting Services Add-in for the web servers from http://www.microsoft.com/download/en/details.aspx?id=2677 9

3. Open the SharePoint Configuration Shell (PowerShell) on the app server and run the following commands to install the Reporting Services SSA:

```
Install-SPRSService
Install-SPRSServiceProxy
get-spserviceinstance -all |where {$_.TypeName -like "SQL Server
Reporting*"} | Start-SPServiceInstance
```

4. Configure the Reporting Services Shared Service Application. In **Central Admin | Application Management**, select **Manage Service Applications**

5. On the Ribbon, select **New | SQL Server Reporting Services Service Application** (that's a mouthful!)

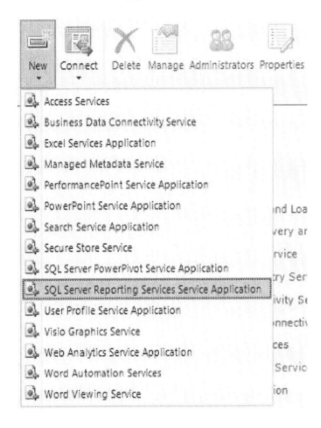

Figure 109 - Creating a new SharePoint 2010 Shared Service Application

6. On the dialog box, enter the properties for your new Reports Services service application.

    a. **Name** – choose a new name for the Service Application. "SQL Reporting Service" as a good suggestion here.

    b. **Database** – Database Server & Name – choose a unique name for the database. But please don't use

GUIDs or spaces! "SQLReportingService" is a fine suggestion.

   c. Pick the **IIS App** pool to run the service – SharePoint Web Service Default or another choice.

7. Pick the SharePoint web applications to associate with the SSA.

8. Set permissions and add Reporting Services content types (as above)

9. Make sure SQL Agent is running on the SQL Server that is storing the databases created for the RS SSA instance we just configured to process the alerts.

10. Configure the SSA. Confirm that outbound SMTP services are configured. Inside the list of Service Applications, click on the name of the SSA we created above.

Figure 110 - Reporting Services SSA Settings

   a. Select **Provision Subscriptions and Alerts.** Make sure SQL Server Agent is running, and either provide credentials to the agent, or download a T-SQL script to give account access.

b. Select **E-mail settings.** Give SMTP server and sending address

At this point, you should be able to create reports and then start working with alerts. Creating SSRS reports is pretty much the same as our prior examples in this chapter – but Alerts are new.

OK, so let's open up a typical report. When users view the report, under Actions, they can set an Alert by choosing New Data Alert.

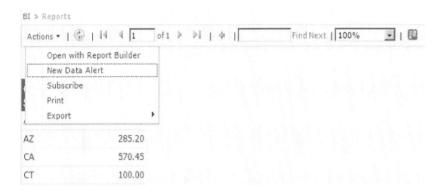

Figure 111 - New Data Alert

The New Data Alert dialog lets the user view the data in the report and add a rule to be evaluated on a regular, recurring basis. In the example below, we're going to check every hour to see if we ever get any sales in Alaska (CustomerState is AK).

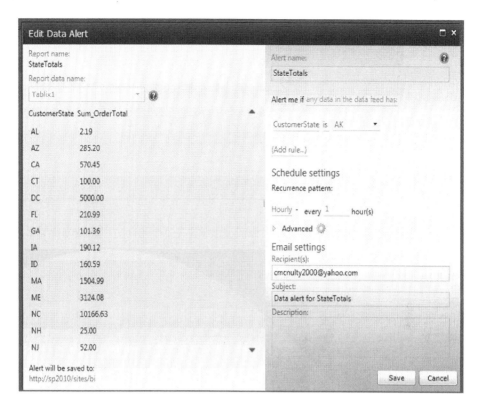

Figure 112 - Edit Data Alert

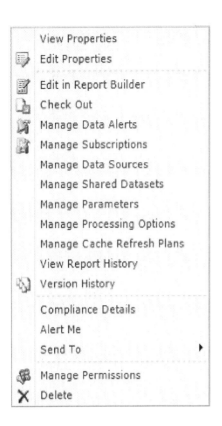

View Properties

Edit Properties

Edit in Report Builder

Check Out

Manage Data Alerts

Manage Subscriptions

Manage Data Sources

Manage Shared Datasets

Manage Parameters

Manage Processing Options

Manage Cache Refresh Plans

View Report History

Version History

Compliance Details

Alert Me

Send To ▶

Manage Permissions

Delete

Figure 113 - Report Context Menu

Each report's context menu also allows you to Manage Data Alerts. This option opens a screen where you can list ALL the alerts defined in the library. In addition to editing the alerts, and reviewing the history, you can force the alert to rerun for testing.

Figure 114 - Manage Data Alerts

Alerts are email based. Recipients get a formatted message showing an excerpt of the report that matches the rule, along with a summary of the rule and a link to open the full report.

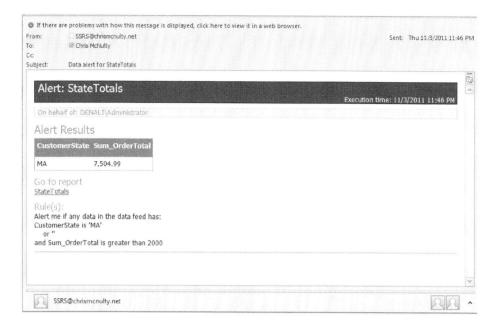

Alert: StateTotals

Execution time: 11/3/2011 11:46 PM

On behalf of: DENALI\Administrator

Alert Results

CustomerState	Sum_OrderTotal
MA	7,504.99

Go to report
StateTotals

Rule(s):
Alert me if any data in the data feed has:
CustomerState is 'MA'
or "
and Sum_OrderTotal is greater than 2000

SSRS@chrismcnulty.net

Figure 115 - SSRS Alerts in SQL Server 2012

Finally, when you run SSRS reports, you can now open the report as an XML data feed – that's this button:

This lets you open the data as a live XML stream. And if you have in it configured locally in Excel 2010, the data will open in PowerPivot.

PowerPivot v2 and Power View

Microsoft launched its "Project Crescent" to greatly enhance end user self-service for Business Intelligence. Now titled "Power View", it uses the PowerPivot data model as its core foundation. So getting ready for Power View means updating PowerPivot.

Just as before, PowerPivot has Excel and SharePoint components. You'll save a lot of trouble by updating both the client and the server to the latest version.   PowerPivot originally shipped with SQL Server 2008 R2, and was described internally as version "10.5"...for example "10.5.2500.0" Make sure you get the latest version ("11.x") of

PowerPivot – both the client and server versions – for CTP3[24] (v2) from http://www.microsoft.com/download/en/details.aspx?id=26721. For example, if you are still running the 10.5 version that shipped w SQL 2008 R2, you will see error messages that "PowerPivot can't load the Vertipaq engine" and that "data may be corrupt."

To open up Power View, create a PowerPivot model as we did before:

- Create a PowerPivot model in Excel
- Upload to a PowerPivot Gallery document library
- View the PowerPivot v2 Model in the browser

On the view for each model (shown below) click the middle button on the grey Title bar to open up a Power View Canvas (f/k/a "Crescent Report").

Figure 116 - Report Button

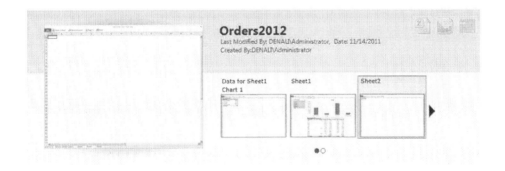

Figure 117 - PowerPivot Gallery v2

---

[24] CTP3 means Community Technology Preview 3 – which comes before Release Candidate 0 ("RC0") and the official release version – dubbed "RTM" for Released To Manufacturing.

The Canvas is a drag and drop end user report designer. It shows all the available fields in the data source for user to drag ad insert into a report.

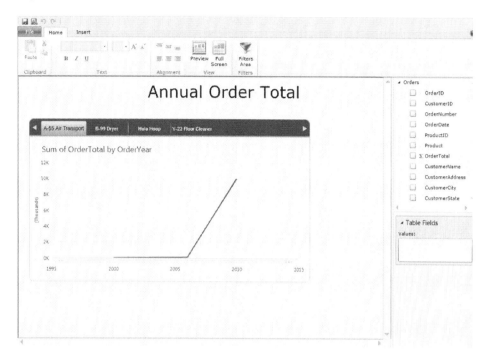

Figure 118 – Power View Report Creation 'Canvas'

Power View reports have a lot of new functions, including Presentation View (a live full screen view intended for projection during meetings). Another promised feature (not yet ready in CTP3 but confirmed in later builds) is the ability to export a live report (not just a picture) into PowerPoint for full presentation readiness.

It's way, way too early to know all the recommended best practices here, but we can extrapolate one now. In PerformancePoint, most of the hard work actually happens inside the data cube and Analysis Services. If that's done properly, it makes matters much simpler for the report builder. Expect the same rule to hold true for Power View! I recommend that PowerPivot designers avoid the temptation to go quick and dirty and drop all the columns into their model without renaming them. Stick to the fields you need, and keep the names and measures business user friendly.   The Power View experience is much friendlier if users can grab a field named "WorldRegion" than "txtGeoCode10".

SQL Azure DataMarket - Project Dallas

We've covered a lot of ground on SharePoint business intelligence. Although most of our data sources have been inside SharePoint or SQL, there's no need to be limited to that horizon. As part of the ever-expanding Azure initiatives, Microsoft has created a common web-based data platform for published reference datasets. This was originally dubbed Project Dallas, and now goes by the slightly less mellifluous name "SQL Azure DataMarket"

The DataMarket is Microsoft's ambitious project to host public reference datasets on Azure – on a public domain and or subscription basis. In their architecture, all the datasets are directly referenceable for download, browser view, and access from PowerPivot in Excel and/or SharePoint. Also, you can easily code .NET solutions to them using OData since they're also URI addressable as WCF endpoints.

Enough geek speak – just visit at http://www.sqlazureservices.com. For example, here's recent information on global ice cream production from the UN on "Dallas", umm, "SQL Azure DataMarket".

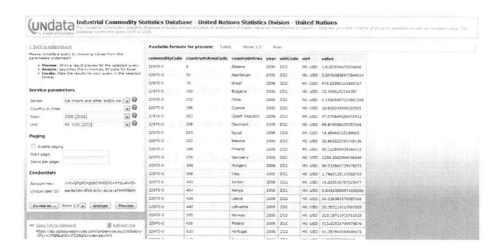

Figure 119 - Azure DataMarket

Introduction to Metadata

The Managed Metadata Service, or MMS, is one of the most eagerly awaited new features in SharePoint 2010.

What is metadata? Literally, "meta" is derived from the Greek μετά, meaning "beyond" or "after"[25]. So metadata is "beyond" data, or data about other data. In the SharePoint world, it means properties and tags that help define and classify documents and list items.

Tagging documents with standard metadata is not new. Almost as soon as SharePoint was introduced in 2001, users began developing ways to standardize the metadata across multiple document libraries. With the arrival of SharePoint 2007, the capacity and number of libraries used in a typical enterprise configuration exploded, and standardization became essential.   In SharePoint 2007, we often used custom site columns and Business Data Catalog connections to standardize values across many libraries and sites.

Now, with SharePoint 2010, MMS lets you establish term stores -- central hierarchical databases of document tags and groups. Terms stores can then be shared across multiple farms in the enterprise. There's also support for watching end user-defined tag trends ("folksonomy") and promoting commonly used terms to the enterprise standard store.

Since the Managed Metadata Service is new, let's introduce some new terminology:

- **Hub** – A site collection which operates as a central source to share content types across the enterprise
- **Content Type Syndication** – Publishing content types across multiple sites, site collections, web application and/or farms

---

[25] http://en.wikipedia.org/wiki/Meta

- **Taxonomy** – A formal hierarchy of terms and tags, usually centrally administered and defined
- **Folksonomy** - Informal list of ad-hoc tags or terms, usually built up over time through user defined keywords
- **Ontology** – A depiction of knowledge as a set of concepts inside a domain, and the relationships among those concepts
- **Term Store** – A database that houses taxonomies
- **Term Set** – The "second level" of a taxonomy
- **Term** – (a/k/a "tag") An element of the defined taxonomy

I've been asked the best way to sum up metadata. Managed Metadata tags and terms can be simply thought of as a central set of lookup fields. The fields are defined in one enterprise master hierarchy. Most users don't see the hierarchy – they see a field where they can type in a value or pick from an ordered list. Here's what it looks like in a document properties dialog box.

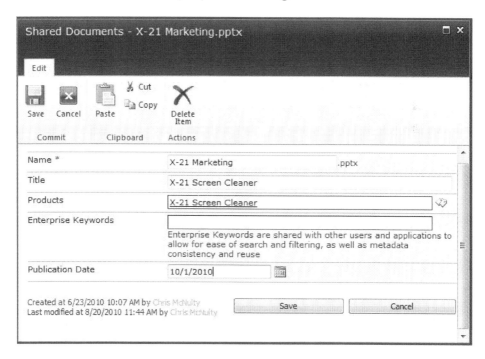

Figure 120 - Document Edit Properties Dialog

In the example above, **Products** is a Managed Metadata field, added to a Document Library; **Enterprise Keywords** is another Metadata field designed for users to type in their own keyword tags. These fields live right alongside other standard fields, and other custom fields. For example, **Publication Date** is a custom non-MMS field coexisting with the other standard fields and MMS fields in this library.

MMS tags and ratings are also exposed throughout the user interface as navigational controls, both in document libraries and in search results. You can reach across content anywhere in your farm to find all documents tagged with "SharePoint" – or just "MOSS" – for example.

Figure 121 - MMS Taxonomy Navigation

Metadata fields can also be used like any other field in library views for sorting, filtering, or grouping.

	Type	Name	Modified	Modified By	Products	Publication Date
		HumanResourcesBanner4	7/7/2010 8:49 AM	Michael Gilronan		
		New Text Document	7/12/2010 9:36 AM	System Account		
		SharePoint 2010 Consultant	8/20/2010 12:15 PM	Michael Gilronan	X-21 Screen Cleaner	
		X-21 Marketing	8/20/2010 11:44 AM	Chris McNulty	X-21 Screen Cleaner	

Add document

Figure 122 - Document Library View with MMS Fields

Also, metadata fields are equally at home in data lists – they're not just for document libraries. For knowledge management, this means you can define your knowledge taxonomy independent of a physical or organization hierarchy, to be able to find relevant information wherever it lives.

OK, you're thinking, but what does that all mean? Why might you use this? Let's consider a typical scenario.

Growth of Information Architecture

Suppose we've just started a new company, and our first mission is to develop new products to bring to market. Our first product is the "X21 Screen Cleaner". So we set up a new SharePoint site – it's a collaboration site with a document library linked off our home page for the products group. On that site, we set up a folder for product information. Logically, it looks like this:

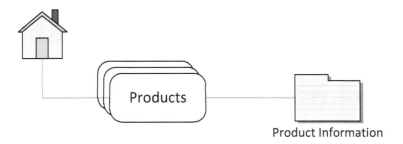

Figure 123 - Initial SharePoint 2010 Logical Collaboration

After a few months, we hire a marketing specialist, who begins writing product information sheets and other documentation to help sell newly developed products. Since it's a new role, the products team adds a new folder to their library, giving us a structure that looks like this:

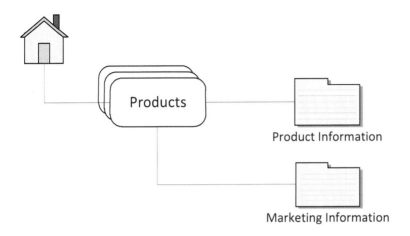

Figure 124 - SharePoint 2010 Collaboration by Folders

So far, so good, everything's kept in one place, and it's easy to find things.

However, over the next six months, the Marketing department continues to grow. Eventually they get their own site, looking like this:

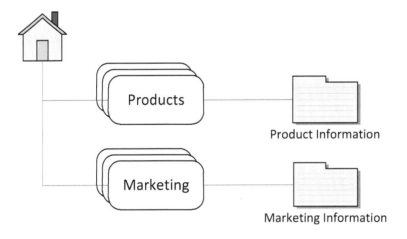

Figure 125 - SharePoint 2010 Collaboration - Multiple Sites

At first glance, this is pretty common – we have multiple departments, each with their own sites and libraries. But this structure opens up a whole range of new questions.

- "I'm in the marketing group, and I just finished a new product sheet for the X-21 project – do I keep it on my department site, or on the products site, or save it to both places?"
- "I'm in the marketing group, and there's a product information sheet for the X21 Screen Cleaner here – is that the most recent version, or do I have to double check on another site?"
- "I'm searching for information on the X-21 product – do we call it 'X21', or 'X-21'? Why can't we use both?"

Sound familiar? With the Managed Metadata Service, these questions become a lot less common. We can use the taxonomy to define a standard list of products that is defined in one term set in the MMS. And once it's defined uniformly, we can make sure that those tags are uniformly maintained so we can find all the X21 Screen Cleaner documents wherever they are.

That's a lot to consider at the moment. You may come back to this later on, but for now, let's walk through setup and configuration for MMS.

New Managed Metadata Service Application

The Managed Metadata Service is installed by default as one of the standard Service Applications for a new SharePoint 2010 installation. In case you didn't install the service originally, or if you want to establish a new Shared Service Application, let's show you how to set up a new Managed Metadata Service.

1. Open Central Administration.
2. In Application Management, select Manage Service Applications

Figure 126 - SharePoint 2010 Central Administration

3. On the Ribbon, select New | Managed Metadata Service

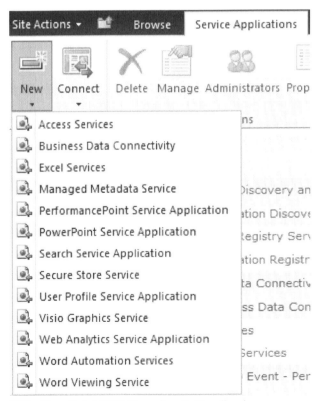

Figure 127 - Creating a new SharePoint 2010 Shared Service Application

11. On the dialog box, enter the properties for your new Managed Metadata service application.
    a. **Name** – choose a new name for the Service Application
    b. **Database**
        i. Database Server & Name – choose a unique name for the database.

TIP: SharePoint 2010 generates many databases – usually one for each separate service application. If you are using a common database instance for multiple SharePoint applications, choose names that help you identify which database corresponds to the service.

        ii. Database Authentication – Windows Authentication is usually the appropriate choice

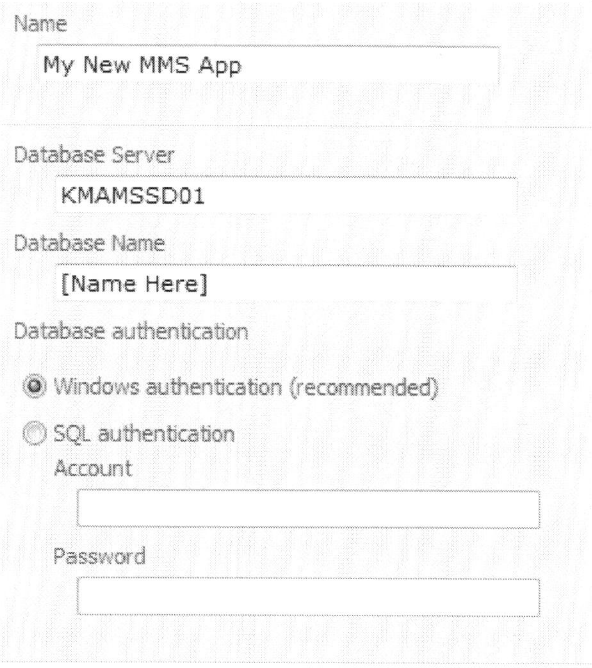

Name

    My New MMS App

Database Server

    KMAMSSD01

Database Name

    [Name Here]

Database authentication

⦿ Windows authentication (recommended)

◯ SQL authentication
    Account

    Password

Figure 128 - MMS Database Connection

iii. **Application Pool** – decide whether or not to reuse an existing pool or create a new pool. If you expect to open up the administration of terms and taxonomies to a number of nontraditional administrators, such as professional knowledge managers or librarians, it may make sense to use a separate pool and or credentials to support the MMS service application.

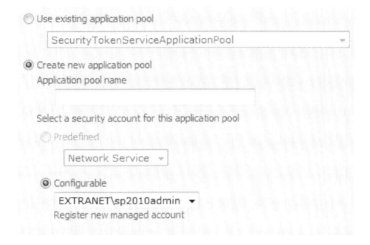

Figure 129 - MMS Application Pool Settings

c. Under **Content Type Hub**, choose the master site collection that will be publishing common content types across the enterprise

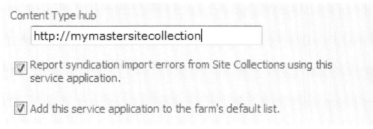

Figure 130 - MMS Content Type Syndication Settings

d. Click OK.

That's it! You now have a new Managed Metadata Service application. Let's talk about how to configure it before we start adding term sets and terms.

Configuring the Managed Metadata Service

To configure the Managed Metadata Service, we first need to make sure we have administrative permissions. From Central Administration, select the Manage Service Applications section. Highlight the Managed Metadata Service application in the list of service applications, and then choose the Administrators button.

Figure 131 - SharePoint 2010 Manage Service Application Ribbon

Ok, now that we have permissions to work with the application, let's get started! Again, from the Ribbon, choose **Manage**.

Available Service Applications

Since a site can use multiple metadata service applications, we need to pick which one to configure. (If you have only one Managed Metadata Service, it's selected by default.) Having multiple MMS applications is rare. It's usually only seen in extremely large global enterprise implementations, with a central service farm handling global metadata, search, user profiles etc., and regionalized service application that define metadata fields particular to a divisional or regional SharePoint farm. However, in almost all cases, one MMS application will suffice.

Sample Import

The Managed Metadata service can import a predefined hierarchy of terms in a term set from a CSV text file. You can view a sample import file directly from the admin screen. Here's an excerpt:

```
Term Set Name,Term Set Description,LCID,Available for
Tagging,Term Description,Level 1 Term,Level 2 Term,Level 3
Term,Level 4 Term,Level 5 Term,Level 6 Term,Level 7 Term
Political Geography,"A sample term set, describing a simple
political geography.",,TRUE,"One of the seven main land masses
(Europe, Asia, Africa, North America, South America, Australia,
and Antarctica)",Continent,,,,,,
,,,TRUE,"Entity defined by people, not visible to the naked
eye",Continent,Political Entity,,,,,
```

The standard import file allows you to nest terms up to seven levels deep. SharePoint is capable of defining term hierarchies more deeply, but in practice most implementations only need five or six levels of depth.

Term Store Administrators

You can enter users, groups, or emails. These users can create new groups of term sets and assign users to manage them.

Default Language

This is the default language for all metadata in the system.

Working Languages

If you support other languages in your SharePoint installation, you can also specify other languages to use in the term. For example, a "USA" term can be displayed as "E-U" (or "Etats-Unis") for French users in a multilingual environment. Using other languages requires installation of the appropriate multilingual language support pack.

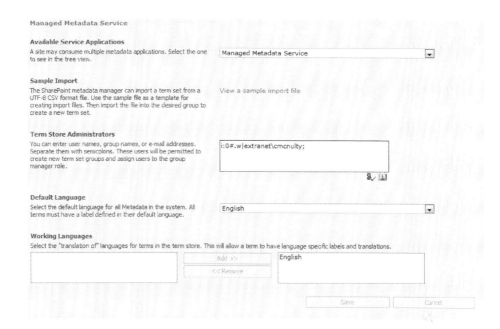

Figure 132 - MMS Configuration

System and Keywords

In the MMS configuration screen, before you begin creating any custom groups for term sets, you'll see the **System** group. The System group is the default home for Managed Keywords – the user generated set of terms.

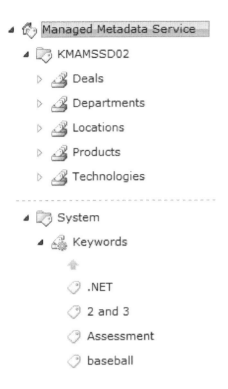

Figure 133 - MMS Keywords

Keywords, as you may recall, are an aggregation of terms and tags created by end users as they add their own keywords to content through SharePoint. Keywords can be moved or deleted from the item context menu. In addition, a term can remain defined, but unavailable by selecting the term in the tree view, and disabling the check box. Why does this matter? Suppose that you find a common typo – "porduct" instead of product. If you delete the term, someone else could repeat the mistake in the future. Leaving it defined but unavailable prevents the next user from using the incorrect keyword.

1968

Available for Tagging

Select whether this term is available to be used by end users for tagging. When unselected this term will be visible but not enabled in tagging tools.

Figure 134 - Sample Settings for a Single Managed Keyword

Site Collections

Most taxonomy management is done at the site collection level. It may help to remember the basic hierarchy of elements in the service:

- Site Collection
  - Group
    - Term Set
      - Terms (multiple levels deep)

And remember, a group of term sets in one site collection can be accessed from multiple site collections across the enterprise.

At the site collection level, you can edit the following properties for the service:

- **Group Name** – Descriptive name for the groups of term sets in this site collection.
- **Description** – Optional additional information about the site collection groups.
- **Group Manager** – These users can define new groups, and term sets. They can also control who's allowed to add new terms to the store. If you have non-technical librarians or knowledge managers who will be responsible for maintaining the tags and terms, they would usually be entered here.
- **Contributors** – Contributors cannot set up new groups, but can set up new terms and edit the terms in those sets.

For Group Managers and Contributors, you can enter users, groups or email addresses, but remember to use the checkbox icon to validate the entries before proceeding. In addition, the "book" icon allows you to browse the user base for SharePoint to pick users.

Term Sets

In addition, from the tree view, you can create a new term set. The first thing you're prompted to add is the name of the set. For our example, here, let's call it **Products**.   You can modify the properties of the term set as noted here:

- **Term Set Name** – Limited to 255 characters of standard text
- **Description** - Self-explanatory
- **Owner** - Defaults to the creator, and identifies the user most responsible for this set of terms
- **Contact** - This is an email address for users to propose new terms or provide comments about the terms they see here. For example, you may not want users to be able to add new product terms on the fly. However, the feedback process allows a user to propose a new product term and have that information passed to the librarians or managers who can determine how to handle the request.   Users can still propose changes to "closed" term sets; however, only managers can make those changes.
- **Stakeholders** – This is a tracking field to identify users and groups that may have an interest in changes to the term set.
- **Submission Policy** – Controls whether or not end users can add tags directly on-the-fly as they tag documents and content. If the term set is closed, only managers can add new terms.

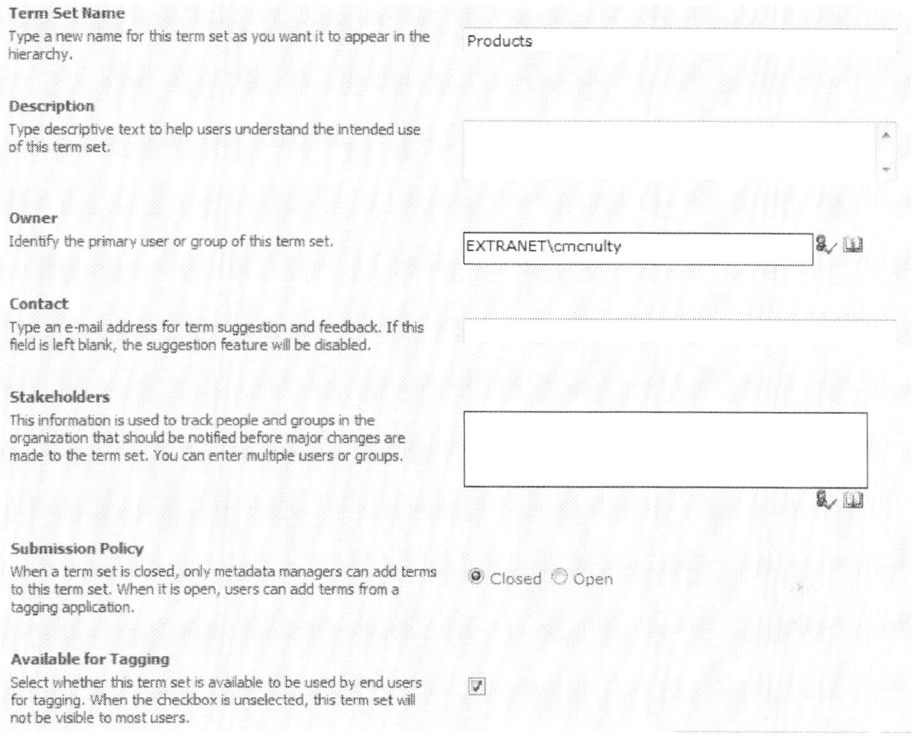

Term Set Name
Type a new name for this term set as you want it to appear in the hierarchy.

Products

Description
Type descriptive text to help users understand the intended use of this term set.

Owner
Identify the primary user or group of this term set.

EXTRANET\cmcnulty

Contact
Type an e-mail address for term suggestion and feedback. If this field is left blank, the suggestion feature will be disabled.

Stakeholders
This information is used to track people and groups in the organization that should be notified before major changes are made to the term set. You can enter multiple users or groups.

Submission Policy
When a term set is closed, only metadata managers can add terms to this term set. When it is open, users can add terms from a tagging application.

◉ Closed ○ Open

Available for Tagging
Select whether this term set is available to be used by end users for tagging. When the checkbox is unselected, this term set will not be visible to most users.

☑

Figure 135 - Term Set Configuration

TIP: *Interface Customization -- it's not crystal clear in the UI, but you can also specify a custom sort for the elements of the term set. This can be especially useful if you have a larger set and some elements should rise to the top of the list for user convenience. For example, you may want to move "United States" to the top of a country term set if you have a largely U.S.-based user population.*

Terms

From any term set or term, you can click on the term name to bring up a menu of custom actions. Using the **Products** term set you've already created in the previous example, let's add the *X-21 Screen Cleaner product*. Select **new term** on the Products term set.

Once we do that, the right hand side of our screen changes to show what we can edit about the term. Most of these settings should be familiar, but probably the most important is **Other Labels**. Other Labels defines the synonyms that are available when users are selecting this term.

Once we attach this term set to a document library, SharePoint will use the entire list of synonyms to suggest the correct terms as users type, and gently redirect usage to the "preferred" name for the term.

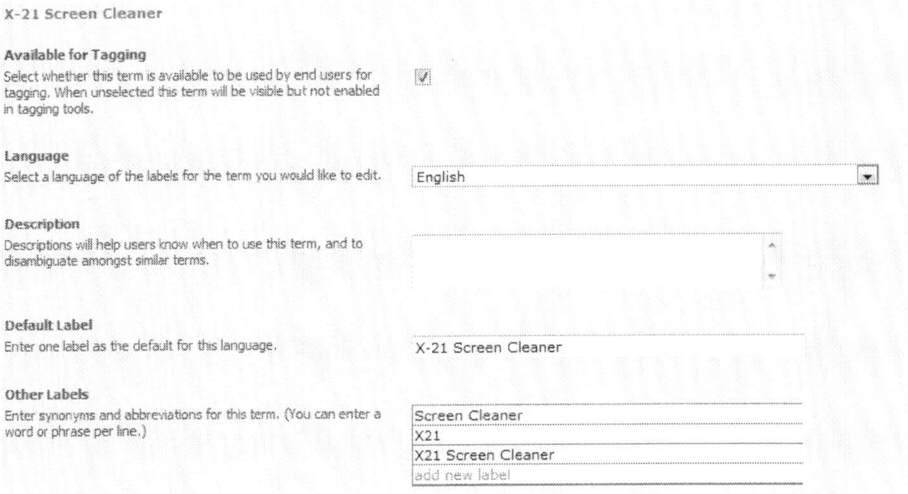

X-21 Screen Cleaner

Available for Tagging
Select whether this term is available to be used by end users for tagging. When unselected this term will be visible but not enabled in tagging tools.
☑

Language
Select a language of the labels for the term you would like to edit.
English

Description
Descriptions will help users know when to use this term, and to disambiguate amongst similar terms.

Default Label
Enter one label as the default for this language.
X-21 Screen Cleaner

Other Labels
Enter synonyms and abbreviations for this term. (You can enter a word or phrase per line.)
Screen Cleaner
X21
X21 Screen Cleaner
add new label

Figure 136 - MMS Term Configuration

Also, we can add multiple terms as children of a parent term, and continue nesting terms as deeply as needed. During testing against SharePoint 2010, we've been able to nest terms at least 21 levels deep.

Keep in mind that terms can be grouped hierarchically. In the example below, there is a higher level tag for "SharePoint" and then a series of child tags that correspond to specific version. When using a hierarchy, you can specify if parent tags can be used or only children. You can also determine whether or not to display the entire path to the tag on the document ("SharePoint:MOSS") or only the child tag label itself ("MOSS")

▷ 🗁 System

▲ 🗁 Site Collection - kmamssd01

  ▷ 👥 KMAClients

  ▷ 👥 Projects

  ▲ 👥 Technologies

    ▷ 🏷 Project Server

    ▲ 🏷 Sharepoint

      🏷 2001

      🏷 2003

      🏷 FAST

      🏷 MOSS

      🏷 Sharepoint 2010

      🏷 WSS 3.0

    ▷ 🏷 SQL Server

What if we stop making our "X-21 Screen Cleaner"? We might delete terms outright, but we can also **deprecate** them. Deprecation keeps the terms in place for existing usage, but prevents them from being attached to new documents going forward.

Design Considerations

We should describe a few design considerations for the Managed Metadata Service – in particular, data sources, security, openness, and usage.

External Metadata Sources

Early adopters have noted some of the limitations of the one-way data import format – it's a one-way, one-time import process. Many have asked if there's a way to define tags based on an external data source. The good news is that the technique used sometimes in SharePoint 2007 – the Business Data Connector – is still available. (Remember, it's called the BCS (Business Connectivity Services) in 2010.)

Once you've established a data source through the BDC service application, you can add a field to any given library to allow this metadata to be applied to each individual element. You don't need to link additional columns from the BDC source.

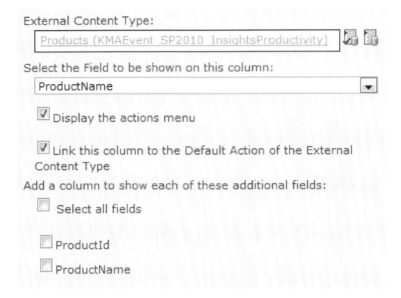

External Content Type:

Products (KMAEvent_SP2010_InsightsProductivity)

Select the Field to be shown on this column:

ProductName

☑ Display the actions menu

☑ Link this column to the Default Action of the External Content Type

Add a column to show each of these additional fields:

☐ Select all fields

☐ ProductId

☐ ProductName

Figure 137 - Adding a Business Data column to a library

Once this is defined, you can edit the properties of the document and pick a value from the BDC source.

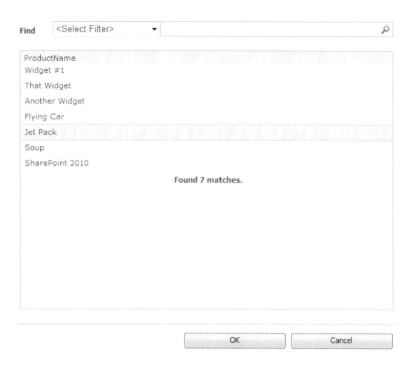

Figure 138 - Picking SQL-Based Metadata for a Business Data field

And remember, using a BDC data source means you can maintain those lookup values in the source database – either externally, or by publishing the source as an External List. External Lists act almost identically to native SharePoint lists in the UI.

ProductId	ProductName
1	Widget #1
2	That Widget
3	Another Widget
6	Flying Car
7	Jet Pack
8	Soup
9	SharePoint 2010

✚ Add new item

Figure 139 - SharePoint 2010 External List

There's a tradeoff, though. As a 2007 technique, although we're using "metadata", it's not really "Managed Metadata". So although you can add BCS data to document libraries, you can't use hierarchies, metadata navigation, tag profiles, or any of the other new features in MMS for SharePoint 2010.

Security

Security for metadata elements is a relatively simple model. We can control whether or not a group, term set or term is visible to users or not – but we don't get more granular than that. Let's think about what this means for certain potential term sets. Suppose your company has a Mergers & Acquisitions group. The M&A group keep a list of companies that are current acquisition targets. In many real world scenarios, there might be different teams of people working on each potential deal – and the names of the companies themselves might be highly privileged. What you get to do for security is limited at the term set level, and all child terms inherit this visibility setting.

What you **can't** do is this:

- **Tag (Viewers)**
- Northwind (Only Andy & Bob can see the term)
- Contoso (All Employees can see the term)
- Oracle (Executive Team Only – a custom security group – no one else sees the term at all)

User-generated tags and folksonomy

Openness is another design consideration. By default, Managed Keywords are usually "open", and allow users to add new terms interactively through tagging. Conversely, managed term stores are usually closed, and require administrators to add new terms. In general, keeping this split between open folksonomies and closed taxonomies is a good practice. It allows us to see trends in our casual social tags and determine if they need to be "promoted" to the formal taxonomy.

Conceptually, user tags are folksonomy – they "belong" to the people. And with a populist creation, we need to be careful about reworking terms that have meaning particular to their creators. We might not like "bobspostvacationpresentation" as a tag, but if that's how Bob finds his PowerPoint files, why delete it? Enterprise taxonomists have recommended that new terms should be added to a folksonomy, but almost never deleted, except in the case of "prohibited" words. Similarly, in taxonomy, we should be careful to add synonyms without deleting pre-established usage patterns.

Federated Administration

Finally, who should administer your term stores? Keep in mind that SharePoint 2010 has moved away from the 2007 Shared Service Provider. In 2007, the SSP was a single application that governed user profiles, search, business data, etc. Having privileges to administer the SSP gave you rights to administer all the shared services, so the SSP was usually kept in the control of IT administrators.

As we discussed earlier, SharePoint 2010 introduces the Shared Service Application ("SSA") architecture. Part of the reason for this was to allow a mix and match approach to only installing needed services for the enterprise. However, since each service application can run under separate security configurations, we can give control over the content for the taxonomy, or any subset of groups and sets, to a business user.

You may choose to still have SharePoint administrators control the Managed Metadata tags. However, SharePoint 2010 gives you flexibility to open up the term store to a corporate librarian or knowledge manager, if those roles are appropriate in your organization.

Using Managed Metadata

Now that you've built out architecture to support the MMS, how do we start using it? We've spoken a lot about the distinction between taxonomy and folksonomy. Folksonomy is the more loosely defined of these, and as a result, the easiest place to start.

Folksonomy – Enterprise Keywords

Here's how to start with a folksonomy on a document library. To turn on Enterprise Keywords, open Library Settings from the Ribbon. Under Permissions and Management, choose "Enterprise Metadata and Keywords Settings"

Permissions and Management

☐ Delete this document library
☐ Save document library as template
☐ Permissions for this document library
☐ Manage files which have no checked in version
☐ Workflow Settings
☐ Generate file plan report
☐ Enterprise Metadata and Keywords Settings

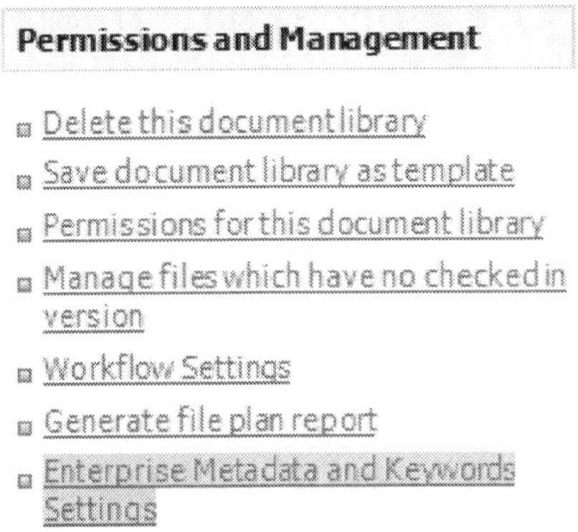

Figure 140 - Turning on Enterprise Keywords

Once there, you have two choices.

- **Add Enterprise Keywords.** This automatically adds a column for user supplied tags and terms, and ensures that "legacy" keywords already entered on Office documents will be automatically stored as Managed Metadata.
- **Metadata Publishing.** Selecting this option makes sure that any user supplied keywords also carry through on each user's profile page, My Sites, and other social networking features in

SharePoint 2010. Turning it off hides those tags from those community interfaces.

You're done! You can rename the column, delete it, or require unique values. Now, when users load a new document, they will also get "Enterprise Keywords" as a choice on their new document upload screen.

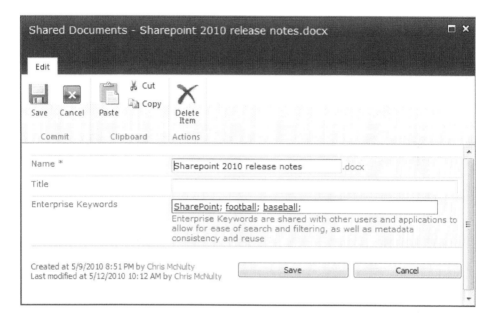

Figure 141 - MMS Enterprise Keywords

The Enterprise Keywords field is also a "type-ahead" or "auto-complete" field. SharePoint dynamically suggests other completed terms based on the first few letters. As you type, partial matches of other terms will be suggested. For example, typing "sha" in our sample environment will prompt you with a number of already-entered tags for keywords or formal metadata from a managed taxonomy.

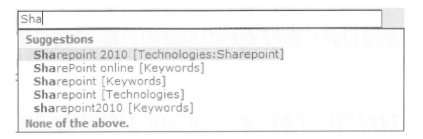

Figure 142 - MMS Auto Complete Dialog Box

Folksonomy & Social Networking

Social networking and online communities are a big part of SharePoint 2010. If you've spent any time in the SharePoint 2010 system, you've probably noticed the little "Tags and Notes" button hanging out in the top right hand corner of your screen. How is this different from what we just did? It's not – it's just a different way to get to the same tags.

Tags &
Notes

TIP: *You can annotate or tag web pages as well as individual documents – so make sure you've selected a particular document to "tag" with the check box before selecting the Tags and Notes button – otherwise your tag is for the page and not the document.*

The big distinction for the **Tags and Notes** button is social networking. Tags and Notes shows you not just the Managed Keywords described earlier, but also shows the history of each tag. It also let you control sharing your tags or keeping them private.

If a user has already used the Tags and Notes button on a page in SharePoint, you'll see it appears in color to provide a visual cue that there's information out there.

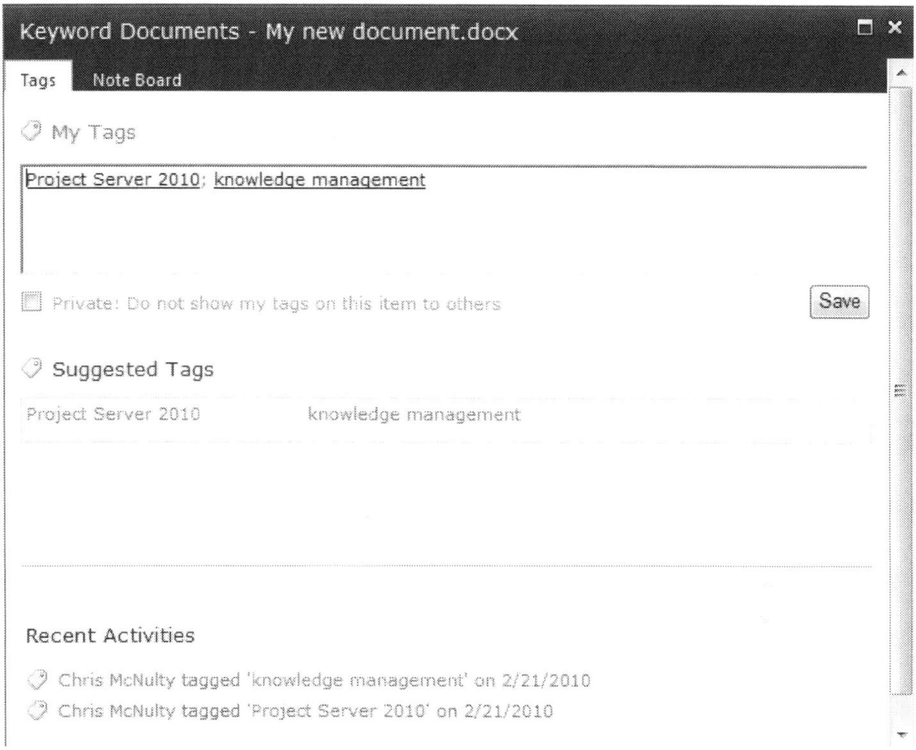

Figure 143 - Tags and Notes

TIP: *You can also add tags and notes to external site pages on the public Internet, whether or not they are hosted on SharePoint. See below for details.*

To tag external pages, you need to use the Tags and Notes button to open up the Tags/Note Board dialog. See where it says "Right click or drag and drop this link to your browser's favorites or bookmarks toolbar to tag external sites"? That's the link you need – add that link to your Favorites toolbar in Internet Explorer.

Figure 144 - Tag/Note Board Dialog Box

In Internet Explorer 8.0:

- Right mouse click the link
- Select Add to Favorites. You may get a security warning since you're adding a JavaScript link – but it's OK to continue.
- Rename the tag if you like and add it to the Favorites Bar folder.

Now, once you've done this, when you're on an external site, you click the button on your Favorites Bar to tag the page. The example below shows you how this looks on My Sites –the bottom tag links to a SharePoint page, but the top link is a tag on Microsoft's public SharePoint site, http://sharepoint.microsoft.com .

Activities for: ◀ August, 2010 ▶

🏷 Tagged SharePoint 2010 - the Bus... with SharePointInternet. 8/23/2010

    View Related Activities   ☐ Make Private   Delete

- -

🏷 Tagged Operations - Home with InfoPath. 8/23/2010

    View Related Activities   ☐ Make Private   Delete

Figure 145 - Tags as displayed on My Sites

As noted, tagging documents becomes part of your personal activity stream on your profile/My Sites page. If you're observant, you may have noticed that each of these tags or terms looks like a hyperlink. Where does this lead?

Just as people have expanded profiles in SharePoint 2010, tags and terms also get their own profile page (see below). You can use the tag profile to browse for other documents with the same keywords. You can also follow the tag on your profile page – think of the "Become a Fan" option on Facebook – and search for other people who follow the same tag. This helps you find expertise and knowledge in a non-linear, non-hierarchical pattern – driven not by a top down hierarchy but by the real world behaviors of real people. Leveraging this kind of information discovery is the essence of folksonomy.

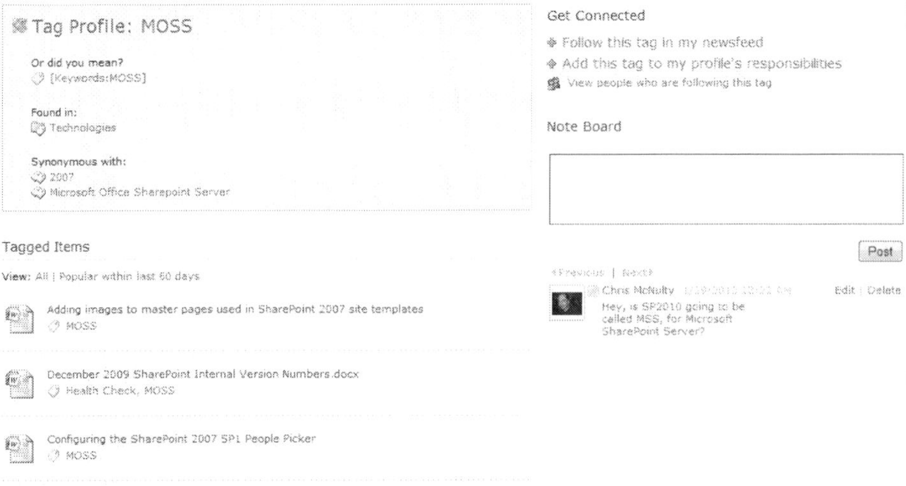

Figure 146 - MMS Tag Profiles

Using Formal Taxonomy

Folksonomy is fantastic for user-driven knowledge management. However, for larger pools of data, sometime you need more formal taxonomy, and here's where custom metadata fields come into play. (Remember, it's called **managed** metadata for a reason.)

Let's return to our earlier example, and suppose that we want to add our "Products" term set and a new column to a document library for our Products area. If you add a column to the document library, you'll see that you can now specify that the column contains **Managed Metadata**.

Column name:

Products

The type of information in this column is:

- ○ Single line of text
- ○ Multiple lines of text
- ○ Choice (menu to choose from)
- ○ Number (1, 1.0, 100)
- ○ Currency ($, ¥, €)
- ○ Date and Time
- ○ Lookup (information already on this site)
- ○ Yes/No (check box)
- ○ Person or Group
- ○ Hyperlink or Picture
- ○ Calculated (calculation based on other columns)
- ○ External Data
- ◉ Managed Metadata

Once you define the column type, you can specify some standard SharePoint properties – such as whether or not to add the column to existing content types, whether or not it's required, etc. We'll assume these are familiar to the reader.

TIP: If you expect anyone to load documents from outside a Web browser – such as older versions of Microsoft Office 2010 – DON'T make a managed metadata property a required field. Not all older applications can update this type of field, so making it required can prevent users from uploading new documents.

After this, you have a couple of MMS specific options:

- **Path/Hierarchy** – SharePoint taxonomy lets you define terms in a hierarchy – with parent child relations among terms and groups of related terms. You have a choice of displaying the whole term path (e.g. "Portals:SharePoint:SharePoint 2010") or just the term itself ("SharePoint 2010").

- **Managed Term Set / Custom Term Set** – Here you have the ability to pick a specific set of terms from the Managed Metadata Term Store. Usually, you'll be consuming a preexisting term set from the MMS. However, you also have the option for creating a new term set "on the fly". New term sets, if created here, will be stored in the default site collection for new term sets (configured in SharePoint Central Administration.)
- **Allow Fill-In Choices** – If the term set is marked as "open", you can let users use this column to add new terms when needed.
- **Default Value** – This is what you would expect – you can define a default tag value for new documents in the library.

Navigation

We've always been able to use folders to navigate a hierarchy in a SharePoint document library.   Now we have a second option, as SharePoint 2010 adds support for using metadata tags as additional navigation.

One quick note – before using navigation, you have to activate the Metadata Navigation and Filtering site feature in Site Settings. Once you've done this, you can configure library metadata navigation in the document library's Settings screen.

General Settings

Title, description and navigation

Versioning settings

Advanced settings

Validation settings

Column default value settings

Rating settings

Audience targeting settings

Metadata navigation settings

Per-location view settings

Form settings

Figure 147 - Library Configuration

Metadata can be used as two different kinds of navigation:

- Hierarchies
- Key Filters

By default, these are shown in the left hand navigation area below the Quick Launch bar.

Hierarchies can be displayed for any selected Managed Metadata field. In the interface users can drill down through the hierarchy of terms to filter the library contents progressively, narrowing or broadening their scope to find the right documents to display. You can display navigation for multiple managed metadata columns. In addition, single value choice fields and content types can be used as additional navigational fields.

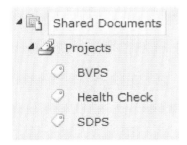

Figure 148 - Hierarchical Tag Navigation

Finally, "key filters" allow users to type in filter values for a predefined metadata column. These key filters can also be used for other field types, such as choice fields, date-time, or person fields.

Figure 149 - Tag Key Filters

Content Type Hubs

Content Types may be familiar to SharePoint 2007 users. Content Types can be thought of as a common classification for related documents – for example, a "Marketing Presentation". Content types can be used across multiple document libraries and sites. They can be given rules for document drop off libraries, Content Organizer, records management and retention policies. In addition, a content type can define a standard set of columns, including metadata columns.

SharePoint 2010 is more flexible in how it works with Content Types. In 2007, functions like Information Management Policy allowed admins to specify a separate retention policy for each content type. 2007 also allowed us to ship documents to be managed in a centralized Records Center site. However, this required separate document types for each unique set of terms and conditions. If "Legal Presentations" have a seven year retention policy, and "Marketing Presentations" only require three years' retention, each had to be a separate content type. However, in 2010, the rules engines are also "property aware" – meaning we could use one master content type of "Presentation" and retain them on different schedules based on a department field, record declaration and a publishing date. We expect that this flexibility will permit the creation of smaller numbers of Content Types in 2010, making better candidates for centralization and thus more easily syndicated.

If you think about it, this is consistent –since we can now centralize the definition of a custom column across multiple site collections, it makes sense to be able to centralize the definition of **sets** of custom columns as well.

Setting up content type hubs involves the following steps:

- Create a site collection, or use an existing one.
- Activate the Content Type Syndication Hub feature for that site collection. This feature can be activated in Site Collection Features, reached via Site Actions | Site Settings.
- Configure the MMS Shared Service Application to use that site collection as their source for published content types.
  - In Central Administration, select Manage Service Applications
  - Create a new Managed Metadata Service Application, or edit an existing one. If you edit a preexisting application, you get to this screen by highlighting the Service Application and selecting **Properties** on the Ribbon.
  - On the Properties dialog, enter the URL to the site collection where you activated the Content Type Hub Syndication feature. Once you define a hub for a service application, it cannot be changed easily – you have to create a new service application,

Content Type hub

☑ Report syndication import errors from Site Collections using this service application.

☑ Add this service application to the farm's default list.

Figure 150 - Content Type Hub Configuration

- Define content type in the primary site collection as "published". How do you do this?
  - ○ Open the content type gallery from **Site Actions | Site Settings | Content Type Gallery**. Or, navigate to http://[sitecollectionhostURL]/_layouts/mngctype.aspx
  - ○ Open up a content type, and from the settings screen, choose **Manage publishing for this content type**. On the next screen, make sure the content type is set to Publish or Republish, and click OK.

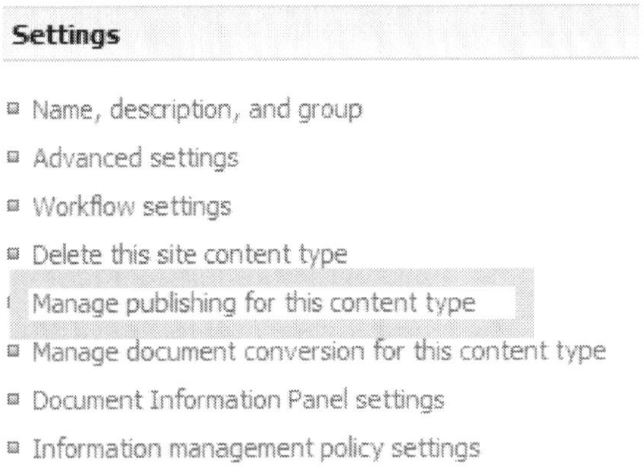

Settings

- Name, description, and group
- Advanced settings
- Workflow settings
- Delete this site content type
- Manage publishing for this content type
- Manage document conversion for this content type
- Document Information Panel settings
- Information management policy settings

Figure 151 - Content Type Configuration

- Create additional web applications, and configure them to use a connection to the MMS service application defined above. This is usually done during provisioning. Why? Usually the "source" is a site collection dedicated to hosting master content types, so you need somewhere to host subscribing site collections.
- On the "subscribing" site collections, you can check the source application, and the content types being published. This is done via the Content Type Publishing screen in Site Settings.

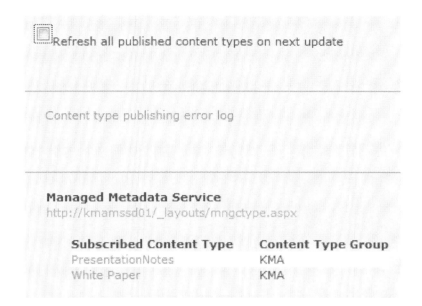

☐ Refresh all published content types on next update

Content type publishing error log

Managed Metadata Service
http://kmamssd01/_layouts/mngctype.aspx

Subscribed Content Type	Content Type Group
PresentationNotes	KMA
White Paper	KMA

Figure 152 - Site Settings - Content Type Publishing

Content type publication is triggered from a timer job that defaults to hourly refreshes. Keep in mind that on the target site collection(s), you should expect a mix of uncustomized, out of the box content types, locally defined custom content types, and well as published content types.

There are two design concepts to bear in mind. First, it's ideal to have the content type hub live independently of any end-user facing content web applications. It's OK to have the primary content application double as the content type hub. But I've seen implementations that start out using the root http://intranet as the Hub. Over time, other applications and URLs arise, and the organization would like to move or decommission that original site – but the syndication from it is hard to disrupt. My best guidance is to dedicate an independent web application as the hub – as part of a central services farm, for example. That way, http://cthub can be moved around without disrupting the syndicated URL. When you create it, make sure the site uses the Team Site template. It avoids a configuration nuisance, but more on that later.

Remember, I said it was difficult to move, but not impossible. You can't redirect a hub in the Central Admin UI, but you can with PowerShell. The command is

```
Set-SPMetadataServiceApplication "Managed Metadata Service" –
HubUri http://domain.com/
```

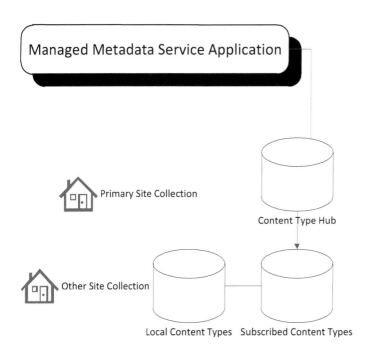

Figure 153 - Central and Local Content Types

A few quick tips on content type publishing:

- If you are using the document ID feature, it must be uniformly enabled on both the hub and the subscribed site collection(s) – otherwise the content types are never pushed out. (This is a site collection feature not just a site feature.)
- If content types aren't updating, check the logs. By default, the logs are available from the Site Settings screen through the content type publishing link under Site Collection Administration (http://[SITECOLLECTION]/ /_Layouts/contenttypesyndicationhubs.aspx)

- o If you've made a change to a content type, reset the content type's publishing setting to **Republish** (under **Manage publishing for this content type** in the Content Type settings screen.)
- o Restart the Content Type Hub timer job, followed by the Content Type Subscriber job for the target site.
- Site columns, especially choice lists, can behave unexpectedly. Column definitions and lookup values will be pushed out from the content hub.

Lookup values will be copied to each separate site collection – however, those lookup values can be locally edited and changed. They will reset to master values the next time the content type is published. In general, you may be better off using either a metadata column or avoiding edits to the local site column definitions.

I have a final example about moving the Content Type Hub. It's a nuisance to move or keep embedded inside obsolete content web applications. I've seen a web application named "http://mytestsite" live on because it was the hub for content types that were reused throughout other SharePoint sites.

So a client followed that guidance, and in setting up the new content type hub they used the "blank" site template. That makes sense, right, since no one's planning to put any other content there – it's just the syndication hub. Then they activated the Site Collection Feature for Content Type Syndication Hub.

Content Type Syndication Hub
Provisions a site to be Enterprise Metadata hub site.   Deactivate   Active

Figure 154 - Content Type Syndication Feature

Their term store was already built, so the next step was to start creating Site Columns to use in custom Content Types.   But as soon as they specified a Managed Metadata column type, they saw the lovely error in Term Set Settings shown below – "The required feature is not enabled for this column type."

Term Set Settings

Enter one or more terms, separated by semicolons, and select Find to filter the options to only include those which contain the desired values.

After finding the term set that contains the list of values to display options for this column, click on a term to select the first level of the hierarchy to show in the column. All levels below the term you select will be seen when users choose a value.

⊙ Use a managed term set:
Find term sets that include the following terms.

The required feature is not enabled for this column type.

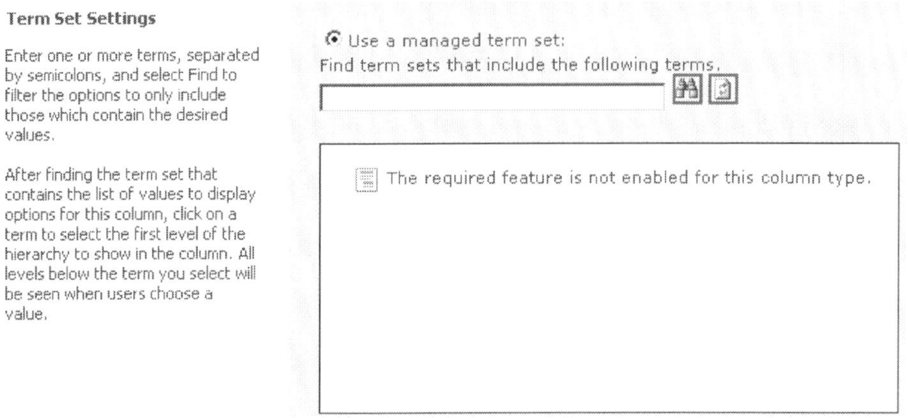

Figure 155 - Term Set Settings

Easy enough – must have missed a feature under Site Features – maybe Site Collection Features? Standard Features? Enterprise Features? Wait – which feature do they need to activate? Is it an SSA Proxy issue?

Stop looking – it's not a UI-based feature. It's a feature that is disabled by default on the Blank Site template. So, as always, PowerShell rides to the rescue! First, although there are utilities you can use to get this information, one single command line in PowerShell will list all the features installed on your farm:

```
Get-SPFeature | Sort -Property DisplayName
```

Review this output – you're looking to find the GUID of a feature named **TaxonomyFieldAdded.**

Then, also at the PowerShell command line, you can activate that feature by GUID:

```
Enable-SPFeature -id "[GUID-From-Prior-Step]" -url [http://your-
content-type-hub]
```

Growth of Information Architecture - "Scenario 2"

Let's return to the company information architecture scenario from earlier in the book. Remember, we started making a product called the "X-21 Screen Cleaner", and added products and a marketing department. Let's suppose it's a year later, and our company is using the Document Center feature in SharePoint 2010 to aggregate a large number of published documents. Our Marketing department publishes all its completed documents there, but may still keep early drafts or work products in its original team collaboration site.

How do we uniformly identify all the "Marketing" documents for our project, spread across a heterogeneous Document Center **and** a unified Marketing collaboration site? Now that we've walked through MMS configuration and setup, that's easy!

- Define a term set for all our departments

Figure 156 - Departments Term Set

- Add a Managed Metadata field in the document library of our Document Center for Department
- Add a new "Departments" managed Metadata field to the appropriate Content Types used in our collaboration sites and our Document Center, and set its default value to "Departments:Marketing" in the Marketing site libraries

Search

Search evolved rapidly during the evolution of SharePoint 2007. The Infrastructure Update in July 2008 added support for **federated search** – adding additional windows that retrieve search results from remote search engines – such as Google or Bing. In addition, many sites deployed CodePlex solutions for faceted search – allowing drilldown search refinements against an initial pool of search results.

To be clear, SharePoint 2010 crawls not just the document contents but also its properties, including tags and metadata. Users can search for the full text of any document as well as the full text of any tags. And search facets are now included automatically as refinements on the results screen, without any external tools.

Once initial results have been added, you can use tagged metadata to further drill into search results. By default, initial search results show a range of up to 6 possible refinements down the left hand of the results screen. (This can be configured to add additional refinements by editing the web part properties on the results page.)

Tags

Any Tags

collaboration

compliance

Health Check

show more ˅

Figure 157 - Search Refinements/Facets

Advanced Customization

There are even more ways to work with the Managed Metadata Service through custom code – XML, PowerShell and C# are all viable tools for coding.   We'll discuss those topics, and MMS customization, throughout the chapter on Development on page 287.

Search Refinements

Let's assume we want to add the Products field as a standard refinement for your search results page.   This is easy and you don't even need SharePoint Designer, although you need to edit a little XML.

1. From your Search Center, run any search to open up a search results page.
2. Edit the page, and select the "Refinement Panel" and edit the Web Part

Figure 158 - Search Results Customization

3. Expand "Refinement" and edit the Filter Category definition field. This is a lot of text – so hit the [...] button next to the field to open up a dialog box to get all the text. Copy and

paste the field contents into your preferred text editor –
Notepad, SharePoint Designer 2010, Visual Studio, etc.

4. In your text editor, find the existing Category Custom Filter
    definitions. Add the following text after the Category
    Custom Filters, but before the existing entries for Managed
    Metadata Columns and Tags.   This is usually entered as one
    line but is broken up here for readability.

```
<Category
Title="Products"
Description="Products managed metadata field"
Type="Microsoft.Office.Server.Search.WebControls.TaxonomyFilterGe
nerator"
          MetadataThreshold="3"
          NumberOfFiltersToDisplay="2"
          MaxNumberOfFilters="20"
          ShowMoreLink="True"
          MappedProperty="ows_TaxID_Products"
          MoreLinkText="More Products"
          LessLinkText="Fewer Products"
     />
```

Most of the XML is intuitive – except for that **MappedProperty** value.

MappedProperty is a unique name, used in search, for each crawled
metadata field. It can be looked up in Central Admin -> Managed
Service applications -> [Your Search Service Application].

Choose Metadata Properties from the left hand quick launch, and
browse to find your chosen field. This opens up all search managed
properties, and taxonomy fields all begin with "owstaxId" followed by
the column's internal name (which is the same as, or close, to its
display name!)

5. Paste the full XML text back into the field, save the part and
    the page.

MMS Design Recommendations

In summary, managed metadata shows up throughout SharePoint 2010 – in taxonomy and folksonomy, in information architectures, social networking and search.

I'd like to summarize of the design considerations discussed earlier – they'll make more sense now:

- Use BCS if tag definitions are best hosted outside SharePoint, such as general ledger codes from an enterprise accounting application
- Understand the limited security model for terms and term sets
- Determine when a term set should be "open" to end user additions, and when it should be closed
- Extend admin access to the terms stores for nontraditional administrators (e.g. corporate records staff) as appropriate
- Plan for and deploy centralized content types as a tool to define required metadata and document retention policies
- If security requirements are simple - and document sharing is important, use the Document Center to centralize document storage, and use content types and tags to classify docs in the Document Center. It's harder if you have a lot of variance in document security – that's a good case for using different libraries or folders.
- If you're syndicating content types, base the root in an independent URL location that can be moved without disrupting other user content.

MMS has a few technical constraints. These include:

- 1000 termsets per group
- 30,000 terms per term set
- 1 million total terms

And MMS can't go everywhere, not yet.   For starters, MMS is an object hierarchy, with few attributes on each element other than synonyms. This means you can define products and group them hierarchically, but you can't add a list price and then navigate or refine to find content by price. In addition:

- No granular security on tag definitions or tags as applied
- No meta-metadata
- Can't tag a tag, can't rate a tag, can't "like" a tag
- Can't organize "personal" tags

And although MMS is supported in many Office applications, that support isn't yet universal. SharePoint Workspace 2010 can read but not write MMS tags. And the InfoPath browser client can't read or write MMS tags – although other browser screens can, as can the full InfoPath client.

Where to get started? Start small. Avoid the temptation to define every potential term as a piece of formal taxonomy. Start with obvious categories:

- Office locations
- Departments
- Products
- Major Projects

Do NOT succumb to the temptation to put every part, every zip code, and every general ledger code in a term set – it's too much complexity for many initial rollouts. At the same time, introduce keywords/folksonomy to a subset of users who understand the benefits in using tags to navigate and retrieve content.

How do I get users to enter tags in the first place? Great question. One of the simplest new features in 2010 allows us to specify default values for tags. For example, in smaller organizations, you may not have a full-blown enterprise project management solution, but you might set up a series of team sites for each project – each with its own library. If you define a term set for your list of projects, you can make each project's tag a default value on all documents for that project's document library – and make the tag available throughout the organization. That way, the tag profile and searches for that project tag will always show you the project team site documents plus all the other documents tagged that way around the site – even if they are part of "Finance", "Marketing", or "IT."

Finally, take a look at usage patterns for keywords. This will tell you where to grow and where to prune your taxonomy trees. For example, unused typos in a keyword field (e.g. "holidya list") can be deleted since they aren't being used. Similarly, if you see a new project name showing up in a folksonomy open keyword column, that's a great candidate for being promoted to a formal taxonomy.

Taxonomy and Metadata Planning

MMS in SharePoint 2010 makes it easy to centralize taxonomy management while also empowering users to self-determine their own classifications. This can be fantastic – but it can also breakdown when users create too little, or too much, metadata.

A bit of upfront planning will help smooth the way to well-adopted and useful enterprise metadata patterns. Here are a few tips.

Start in 2D. Moviemakers spent decades filming in two dimensions before they tried 3D. Make sure you reach consensus on defining the major dimensions of your business - departments, location, products, projects – before attacking other details (e.g., zip codes, part numbers). And resist the temptation to turn every possible subcategory of meeting notes, presentation formats, etc. into an independent content type.

Plan to be unplanned. It's impossible to predetermine all possible end-user preferences for keywords and categories. Users can generate a lot of potentially redundant keywords, which is OK as long as clear boundaries are established. One of the less well understood features in SharePoint MMS is the synonym functions. Synonyms are available in term sets and taxonomies – but not for keywords. Create a few very general term sets – e.g., "Topics" – and promote frequently used keywords into the Topics term set so they can be merged and grouped with synonyms. That way, users can be gently steered toward a common syntax for a tag like "Office 365" if they type "O365" as a keyword.

Plan to be re-planned. As part of your overall strategy, you should anticipate reviewing search logs and usage patterns at least quarterly. Let your users vote with their feet, or at least their mouse clicks, about where to grow your information architecture.

The cost of the red asterisk. (*) SharePoint designates mandatory fields with a red asterisk on the interface. That's not to be used lightly. Getting users to enter metadata manually is an extra step for them. The best way to keep your content databases empty and manageable is to load them up with document libraries defining tons of mandatory fields. The red asterisk costs time. If it takes longer to save a document than it does to write it, why bother?

There are increasingly more third party tools to automatically tag or classify information based on content and context. FAST Search is able to automatically tag documents as it crawls them, and other autoclassification engines are able to identify even more subtle distinctions, such as resumes, credit card transactions or personally identifiable information ("PII").

Promotions. Taxonomy has richer management syntax than folksonomy – in particular, the use of synonyms and deprecation. It's usually a good practice to establish a few open ended term sets for topics or company names. That way, if someone creates a keyword for "BI" it can be promoted to a Topics term set, and merged as a synonym for Business Intelligence. The next time someone wants to add the "BI" tag, they'll be steered to a more managed keyword.

Enterprise Content Management

There's a rich range of Enterprise Content Management ("ECM")
features in SharePoint 2010. Here's a quick road map in order of
increasing complexity and organizational maturity.

ECM Configuration Roadmap

Function	Feature Scope	Where to configure it
Content Organizer	Site	Site Settings | Content Organizer Rules
Hold and eDiscovery	Site	Site Settings | Hold and eDiscovery Section
In place Records Management	Site Collection	Context Menu | Compliance Details
Send to Records Center	Define in Central Admin	Central Admin: General Settings | Send To Connections
ILM	Variable	Content Type definition; or override at library/folder level in library settings – Information Management Policy Settings

Document IDs

Document IDs are a very important attribute that's common (but optional) to all the SharePoint ECM tools. Document ID's are unique, unchangeable serial numbers that are permanently affixed to each document. When a document is first uploaded to SharePoint, the server assigns a unique identifier that follows the document throughout its lifecycle – even as it moves from site to site as part of workflows, organizer roles, or lifecycle management policies.

Document ID formats are specified in Site Settings | Site Collection Administration for each site collection. Document ID's are a site collection level function and need to be activated for each site that will use them. (Remember, if you use Content Type syndication, the hub and subscribing site collections need to agree on whether or not the feature is on or off.)

In Site Settings, you can configure the format of a prefix to be added to each document ID. This helps ensure uniqueness across multiple site collection – since you might start the intranet with *XYZ-Root-*, while the HR site collection could be prefixed with *XYZ-HR-*.

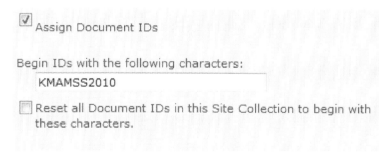

Figure 159 - Document ID Configuration

Once Document IDs are configured, they can always be viewed in each document's properties.

Name	Microsoft TechEd 2010 Day 1 Recap
Title	
Document ID	KMAMSS2010-28-2
Enterprise Keywords	
Rating (0-5)	☆ ☆ ☆ ☆ ☆
Number of Ratings	0

Content Type: Document
Version: 1.0
Created at 11/24/2010 6:03 AM by Chris McNulty
Last modified at 11/24/2010 6:05 AM by Chris McNulty

Figure 160 - Document Properties

The advantage of the document ID is that every document can always be retrieved by its ID value. Even as the document may be moved around a site by Content Organizer rules, workflow, or Information Management Policy, the ID remains consistent.

By default, some of the in-the-site templates, such as the Document Center, are preloaded to use the 'Find by Document ID" web part. This can also be easily added to any SharePoint page. You can find the part in the Search folder of the default Web Part catalog.

You can also always find a document by ID using the URL format:

```
http://[SITECOLLECTION]/_layouts/DocIdRedir.aspx?ID=[DOCID]
```

Substitute your own values for [SITECOLLECTION] and [DOCID].

That's helpful – but what if you don't know the document ID in the first place? You can always add the Document ID to any Office 2010 document. Make sure the document has been saved to a document library in a collection where the Document ID feature is active. Then, inside Word (for example), from the Ribbon, choose Insert | Quick Parts | Document Properties, and select the "Document ID Value".

Versioning and Metadata

Document versioning remains one of the oldest and strongest functions in SharePoint.   As users collaborate on a document, you can:

- Require the document be checked out to a user before edits
- Save a running copy of all draft and final published versions
- Require administrative approval before other users can see approved, published content
- Retain or delete prior drafts or published versions

In addition, you can – and should - use "Content Types" to establish sets of properties about a document – e.g. Draft/final, presentation date, subject keywords, etc. These types and properties will greatly help in using all the other features that let you manage content after it's created and/or published.

Let's revisit our site diagram used earlier. Here, we can now see that we're attaching different content types to different libraries in the information architecture. This means that the rules for what constitutes a "policy" – that it has a date, topic and owner; and its lifecycle/retention policy – are uniformly applier throughout the site. And our definition constrains "Policy" documents to be used only for HR, Legal, and IT – not Sales, since that content type isn't attached to that site's library.

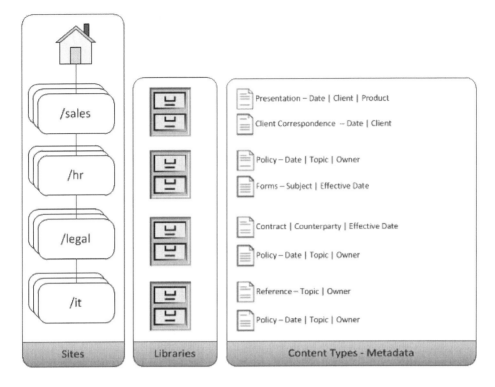

Figure 161 - Site Hierarchy

Document Sets

Document sets allow you to define and work with a collection of documents with common properties and workflow. For example, you might define a product portfolio to always include at least a product overview, sales presentation, and pricing spreadsheet. Here's one I built – notice that ProductAudience is a property of the set, and each element has individual properties.

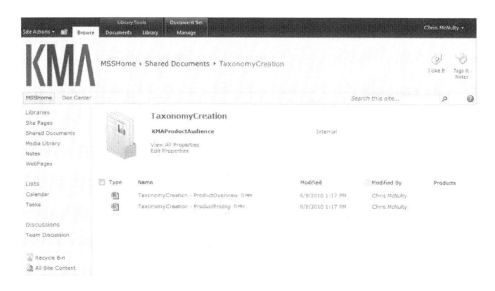

Figure 162 - Document Set

Drop off library and Content organizer rules

In large, complex sites, users who occasionally write new content are faced with a dilemma – where should I post this? They often pick one of two options:

- Post it nowhere for fear of "breaking" something
- Post it to multiple places – one of them is bound to be right.

The good news in SharePoint 2010 – users don't need to remember all the "right" places to post a document. Instead, by activating the Content Organizer, you can direct users to a single "drop-off library", and then use rules to route the document to the correct location. Rules are flexible, and can be driven by content types, document properties, titles, etc. I've listed an example below for a rule to route audio files to a media library if they are copyrighted in 1997:

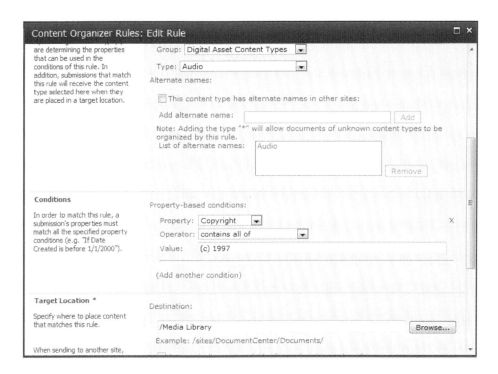

Figure 163 - Content Organizer Rule

It's powerful to write rules based on properties, and not just Content Type. In 2007, enterprises often had a proliferation of content types, or avoided them all together since that was the only way to route documents via Record Center document retention policies. The result was a separate content type for each department, subcategory etc. that needed a different policy. The new rule sets for Content Organizer and related ECM functions are more flexible. Before, you would have needed a new content type just for audio files from 1997.

Finally, Content Organizer functions have to be activated as site features.

eDiscovery and Hold

Hold and eDiscovery allow an administrator or compliance staff to "freeze" a document it place, or route it to a holding area. Holds can be implemented directly on a document. You can also preview a set of search rules, and let the system add documents to a "hold" automatically (it saves an Excel report when done!)

Although this sounds like a good way to prepare for a subpoena, and it is, this function can help outside of litigation support. For example, financial firms conducting due diligence use this when they need to find and purge documents from cancelled deals. The documents are moved to a pending area for review and then deleted.

Records Management

Records management was included in SharePoint 2007, but the functions were so limited that they seldom saw enterprise use. Essentially, you could copy content types to a new site collection and manage them as records there. However, the original documents were left intact, and could be edited further. SharePoint 2010 presumes you will do one of two things (most likely):

- Ship the document to a Record Center site collection and leave behind a link.
- Declare the documents to be a record "in place" and manage it there.

Here's another question – why? Simple. Once you've declared a document to be a record, you can more easily prevent the document form being deleted interactively, or exempt the record from other document retention policies.

Send to Records Center

Record Center is a custom, in the box site collection template that you can add to an existing SharePoint 2010 farm. Once you've established it, you can define a custom "Send To" action for the document context menu (the hove). These settings can be found in Central Administration | General Settings. You can pick a target location, and

decide whether documents can be copied, moved, or moved with a
link left behind.

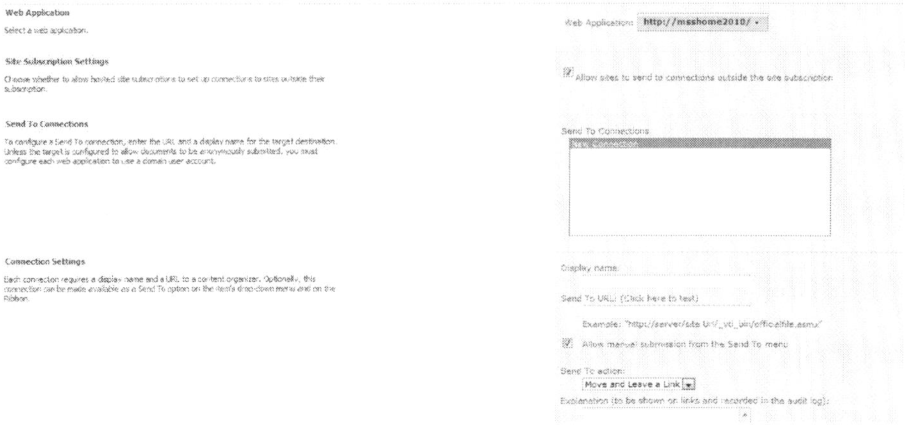

Figure 164 - Send To Settings

Records Center is best thought of as a high volume routing site. It
uses the same sort of rules we saw with Content Organizer. Here's a
snapshot of the default home screen:

Figure 165 - Records Center

Records Center is an appropriate choice for larger organizations that
already have some structure and definition about what constitutes a
record. Simple test – if you have a centralized document repository
for paper, if you have record managers on staff, if your information

architect has a degree in library science – if any of this is true, Records Center is a strong contender.

It really helps to understand what "being a record" means in your context. SharePoint provides tools for flagging records – but it's up to you to provide guidance as to what constitutes a record. Are all completed documents records? Is the approach transactional – you save the summary of each transaction but not the steps along the way? Is the approach reconstructive – the essential information required to recreate decisions, data and the context around them? Or is almost everything a "record"? If everything is a record, or if you're unsure, evaluate carefully. You may really be a candidate for document management more than record management. Or Records In Place may be an easier step along your information management evolution.

Records In Place:

You can also let users declare records interactively through the context menu for Compliance Details. (This can also be a great use of a Ribbon-based Custom Action if you want to customize the UI).

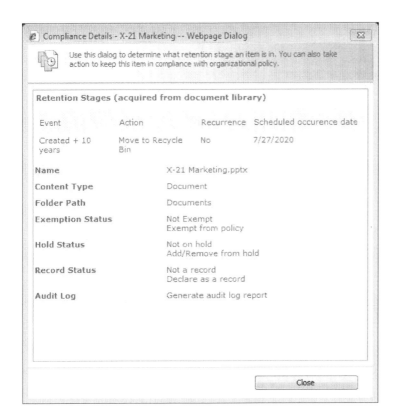

Figure 166 - Compliance Details

Information Lifecycle Management (ILM) Policy

As documents age, you can define a lot of things to happen automatically via Information Lifecycle Policies. Historically you could only define these on a per content type basis – but now you can also define this at a library or folder level. These settings are reached from the Ribbon for Library Settings.

Library Based Retention Schedule

By default, a library will enforce the retention schedule set on its content types. Alternatively you can stop enforcing content type schedules and instead define schedules on the library and its folders.

Source of retention for this library. **Library and Folders** (Change source or configure library schedule)

Content Type Policies

This table shows all the content types for this library, along with the policies and expiration schedules for each type. To modify the policy for a content type, click its name.

Content Type	Policy	Description	Retention Policy Defined
Document	None		No
Folder	None		No
Link to a Document	None		No
Document Set	None		No

*Note: Since this library is using library and folder retention, all documents will use those schedules. Content type retention policies are ignored.

Figure 167 - Location-based ILM Policies

Policies can be applied uniformly to all content, or can be excluded for files already flagged as a "Record". You can define stages and test for properties – usually based on document creation, modification or approval dates.

Figure 168 - ILM Stages

Most importantly, what can you do to these documents? A lot:

ILM Actions

- Move to Recycle Bin
- Permanently Delete
- Transfer to another site or Records Center
- Start Workflow
- Skip to Next Stage
- Declare Record
- Delete prior drafts
- Delete Prior versions

Finally – don't forget to generate a File Plan Report – it rolls up a summary of all the retention policies that govern a given library:

Documents: File Plan Report

Site:	Doc Center
URL:	http://msshome2010/DocCenter/Documents/Forms/AllItems.as
Description:	Share a document with the team by adding it to this document li
Report Generated	2010-08-05T15:54:37
Created By:	Chris McNulty
FolderCount:	1
Item Count:	20
Versioning:	Create major and minor (draft) versions
Require Content Approval:	No
Draft Item Security:	Any user who can read items can see drafts
Source of retention schedules:	Library and folders
Records Declaration:	Records cannot be edited or deleted. Any changes will require the record declaration to be revoked. The declaration of records can be performed by: All list contributors and administrators Undeclaring a record can be performed by: Only list administrators
Has Records:	Yes
Has Items on Hold:	No

Content Type	Policy Name	Policy Description
Document		
Document Set		
Folder		
Link to a Document		

Figure 169 - File Plan Report

By now, you should have a good insight into the power of SharePoint and how it can be customized to match your enterprise needs. SharePoint offers great power using tools available inside the web browser alone. Yet there are even more ways to tailor and enhance SharePoint with custom code. PowerShell brings the capabilities of coding and API functions to a command line oriented scripting language. Compiled C# code, especially Web Parts, written in Visual Studio 2010, allow for virtually infinite flexibility and complexity combined with rapid startup templates and integrated deployment tools. Finally InfoPath brings screen design and rich interactivity within the grasp of power users.

Let's start with PowerShell.

PowerShell

STSADM is dead. Long live STSADM! Well, not dead yet. But be put on notice – the arsenal of command line maintenance actions we've known for years is going away. Deprecated, not to be supported in the future. In its place – PowerShell, the command line scripting environment that not only duplicates STSADM commands but opens up access to API functions, program controls structures, and sophisticated decision logic.

PowerShell is an enhanced version of traditional scripting and command line approaches to systems management and administration. PowerShell is composed of extensible commands called "cmdlets". These cmdlets offer greater control (but less familiarity!) than STSADM.EXE.

By design, generic PowerShell is available from the Windows start menu. SharePoint itself supplies over 500 additional SharePoint specific cmdlets. These are available after you add them in using the cmdlet:

```
Add-PSSnapin Microsoft.Sharepoint.Powershell
```

Or, you can just start the SharePoint Management Shell from the Start menu on your SharePoint server. This launches a version of PowerShell with the SharePoint elements pre-loaded. Either way, you need to make sure you have SharePoint support installed for PowerShell.

Cmdlets

PowerShell is composed of specialized commands, and the SharePoint snap-in enable the 500+_ SharePoint specific commands. Any PowerShell cmdlet allows common command sequences to get more information, syntax, or examples. Here are the most common tools:

Parameter	Explanation
`[CMDLET] -?`	Shows help
`Get-Help [CMDLET] -examples`	Displays sample usage
`Get-Help [CMDLET] -full`	Shows syntax, examples, details

Pipe

The pipe is a way to channel the output of one command to the next command on the same line. Consider this entry, which extracts a list of all commands ("cmdlets") that begin with "SP":

```
Get-Command -Noun SP*
```

Next, let's dump that whole list of commands and other attributes to a Select command. This limits the selection to only the Name.

```
Get-Command - Noun SP* | Select Name
```

Finally, we can pass that limited list to the Out-File cmdlet, which saves that output to a text file:

```
Get-Command - Noun SP* | Select Name | Out-File Commands.txt
```

And one more trick. PowerShell itself includes a set of options call the PowerShell Integrated Scripting Environment (ISE). PowerShell ISE, included in Windows Server 2008 and later, includes a PowerShell cmdlet that receives data and displays it in a Windows dialog. So for our final "pipe game", we get all the site collections, and get all the subsites inside that, select just the URL, Name, Theme, and Site Icon, and pass that to a graphic component to display the result in a prettier interface.

```
Get-SPSite -limit all | Get-SPWeb -limit all | Select URL, name,
theme, SiteLogoURL | Out-GridView
```

The dialog is searchable, filterable, and sortable. Here's the output:

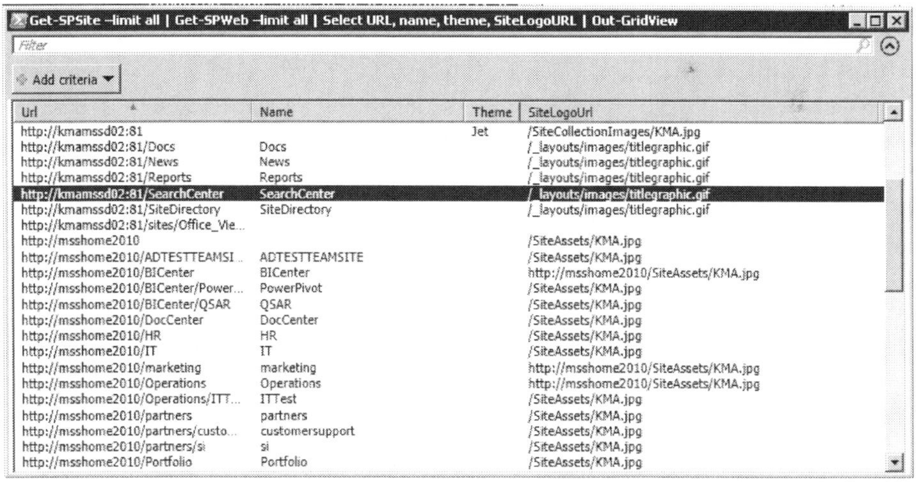

Figure 170 - Out-GridView Sample

You may want to see all the fields you could display in PowerShell. This is easy to explore. First, set a variable to represent the SharePoint site:

```
$web = Get-SPWeb http://yoursite
```

And then pipe that variable to the cmdlet Format-List to give you a full summary of all the retrievable properties for the site:

```
$web | Format-List
```

A portion of the output is shown below:

```
PS C:\Users\sp2010admin> $web = Get-SPWeb http://msshome2010
PS C:\Users\sp2010admin> $web | Format-List


DataRetrievalServicesSettings     : Microsoft.SharePoint.SPDataRetrievalSer
                                      vicesSettings
Lists                             : {Announcements, Cache Profiles, Calenda
                                      r, Content and Structure Reports...}
RootFolder                        :
Exists                            : True
Files                             : {default.aspx}
Folders                           : {Notes, ReusableContent, PublishedLinks
                                      , WebPages...}
Modules                           : {Default}
Webs                              : {AD Test Team Site, BI, Doc Center, HR.
                                      ..}
Features                          : {00bfea71-d8fe-4fec-8dad-01c19a6e4053,
                                      00bfea71-c796-4402-9f2f-0eb9a6e71b18, 0
                                      65c78be-5231-477e-a972-14177cc5b3c7, 00
                                      bfea71-5932-4f9c-ad71-1557e5751100...}
WorkflowTemplates                 : {Approval, Collect Feedback, Collect Si
                                      gnatures, Disposition Approval...}
WorkflowAssociations              : {}
Workflows                         : {}
PublicFolderRootUrl               :
EmailInsertsEnabled               : False
EventHandlersEnabled              : False
Alerts                            : {}
ListTemplates                     : {Record Library, Document Library, Form
                                      Library, Wiki Page Library...}
ViewStyles                        : {0, 6, 7, 8...}
DocTemplates                      : {None, Microsoft Word 97-2003 document,
                                      Microsoft Excel 97-2003 spreadsheet, M
                                      icrosoft PowerPoint 97-2003 presentatio
                                      n...}
IncludeSupportingFolders          : False
NoCrawl                           : False
CurrentUser                       : SHAREPOINT\system
Name                              :
TitleResource                     : Microsoft.SharePoint.SPUserResource
DescriptionResource               : Microsoft.SharePoint.SPUserResource
UserResources                     : {_CTDesc0x01010051F2D13925D01B419E8AABA
                                      376663AEA, _CTDesc0x010100C5060467EC7BD
                                      D4EB39DA242449F5BB0, _CTDesc0x010100DE6
                                      8B2622D106741ABF4C2E7FCDC17FC, _CTDesc0
                                      x0120D52000C48D894F398CF0439E9FC3D325BE
                                      43E3...}
IsMultilingual                    : False
OverwriteTranslationsOnChange     : False
SupportedUICultures               : {en-US}
Site                              : SPSite Url=http://msshome2010
ParentWeb                         :
```

Figure 171 - Site properties displayed with Format-List

Variables

I just used *$web* as a **variable**. Variables are "loosely typed" –
meaning, as a scripting language, you don't need to declare variables
before you start using them. If you want to say

```
$dumptruck = Get-SPSomething
```

congratulations, you know have a $dumptruck variable for whatever "something" you just picked up! (Just to be clear, Get-SPSomething isn't a real cmdlet.)

But PowerShell isn't limited to a single line – and that's where it gets a lot of its power. You can combine multiple lines into a text file, saved with the extension .ps1. In a multiple line PowerShell, you can start to use control structures to text and channel the flow of your script.

Control Structures

The most common is the if-then-else sequence. If you're used to C#, the structure of {} brackets will seem familiar to you. The basic if-then-else structure in PowerShell looks like this (there is no actual "then"):

```
if ( CONDITION )
{
    #Stuff we do if CONDITION is true
}
else
{
    #Do things if CONDITION isnt true
}
```

The next most common control technique in PowerShell is to get a set of things – a collection – and then walk through each item of the collection. In SharePoint, you'll do this all the time to get all the site collections inside a web app, and then all the subsites inside each site collection, and then all the libraries – you get the idea. The technique uses the **foreach** statement, which takes the form:

foreach (thing in collection.things)

In code, it looks like:

```
#get web application
$webapp = Get-SPWebApplication "http://MYWEBAPP/"
```

```
#getsites
foreach ($s in $webapp.sites)
{
    foreach ($SPweb in $s.AllWebs)
    {
        $SPdocLibs =
$SPWeb.GetListsOfType($SPBaseTypeDocumentLibrary)
        foreach ($docLib in $SPdocLibs)
        {

    }
    }
}
```

Comments

You've also noted the hash tag "#" which marks comments lines.

Launching a PowerShell Script

First, you may need to reconfigure your system to allow it to run
PowerShell scripts in the first place. For security PowerShell usually
requires us to sign or encode our scripts. This behavior is configured
with the cmdlet Set-ExecutionPolicy. The value can be inspected
using Get-ExecutionPolicy. To allow all scripts to run (not
recommended, although you are still reminded before you run
unsigned code):

```
Set-ExecutionPolicy Unrestricted
```

To require code signing for all scripts downloaded from remote
sources:

```
Set-ExecutionPolicy RemoteSigned
```

So you may want to launch a PowerShell script several different ways.
First, we'll start from inside the SharePoint Management Shell – a
PowerShell environment. PowerShell is fussy about full paths to files.
A quick workaround is to use the single dot shortcut for a parent
directory:

```
./myscript.ps1
```

VBScript
```
Set objShell = CreateObject("Wscript.Shell")
objShell.Run("powershell.exe -noexit c:\PS\script.ps1")
```

Batch File or Windows Task Scheduler
```
Powershell c:\PS\script.ps1
```

Windows Run
```
Powershell.exe -noexit c:\PS\script.ps1
```

TIP: *"Noexit" isn't a Sartre reference – it just means that the PowerShell windows should stay open after the script runs.*

Moving away from STSADM

I know it's hard – but get ready. Each time you find yourself reaching for a familiar Stsadm command, challenge yourself to look up and use the PowerShell equivalent. For example, instead of

```
Stsadm -o backup
```

Try:

```
PS> Backup-SPFarm
```

It's not hard, and you'll get to know PowerShell pretty quickly. The online help and samples are solid. Microsoft has a mapping of STSADM operations to PowerShell cmdlets at
http://technet.microsoft.com/en-us/library/ff621084.aspx

Sample PowerShell Scripts

Another way to learn is to write your own scripts. To give you a preview, here's a sample script to add 3000 items to a test list:

List Item Addition

```
[System.Reflection.Assembly]::LoadWithPartialName("Microsoft.Shar
ePoint")
##
$siteUrl = "http://yourhost.yourdomain.com"
$webName = ""
$spSite = new-object Microsoft.SharePoint.SPSite($siteurl)
$spWeb = $spSite.OpenWeb($webName)
$spList = $spWeb.Lists["YourList"]
##
for ($i=1; $i -lt 3000; $i++)
{
  $spitem = $spList.Items.Add()
  $spitem["Title"] = "Item"+$i
  $spitem["Number"] = $i
  $j = 1
  if ($i % 4 -eq 0){ $j = 2 }
  $spitem["Data"] = "datum"+$j
  $spitem.Update()
}
```

Visual Update

Here's a script to apply visual updates to all subsites on a migrated 2007 web application.

```
$webapp = Get-SPWebApplication http://sitename
foreach ($s in $webapp.sites)
{$s.VisualUpgradeWebs() }
```

Add MMS Term

Managed Metadata is also scriptable. This is an outline for the process of adding a term to an already created group and term set. For clarity, we've excluded the creation of the group and sets so we can focus on the CreateTerm method. It takes just two arguments – the term, and the code page (US English = 1033).

```
$str = "SAMPLE"
$site = new-object Microsoft.SharePoint.SPSite("http://MYSITE")
$session = new-object
Microsoft.SharePoint.Taxonomy.TaxonomySession($site)
$termstore = $session.TermStores["MYTERMSTORE"]

[...create group...]
[...create term set...]

$term = $termset.CreateTerm($str, 1033)
```

Create document library

This script invokes the SharePoint API to create a new document library and break security inheritance. In this technique, "101" is the integer value that tells SharePoint the new list is a document library.

```
#Load the Sharepoint .net Assembly
[System.Reflection.Assembly]::LoadWithPartialName("Microsoft.Shar
ePoint")

#set the url of the site collection to a variable
$siteurl = "http://msshome2010/"
$subsitename = "Marketing"
$newlibraryname = "NewLib"
$newlibrarydesc = "NewLib Description"

#create the new object passing the site collection URL, attach
subsite
$mysite=new-object Microsoft.SharePoint.SPSite($siteurl)
$subsite = $mysite.openweb($subsitename)

#make the new library - 101 is the generic for DocumentLibrary
template
$subsite.lists.add($newlibraryname, $newlibrarydesc, 101)

#open the new library and break inheritance
$mylib = $subsite.lists[$newlibraryname]
$mylib.BreakRoleInheritance($false)
```

This technique is the administrator's best friend. Here's another good PowerShell sample. This one walks through all, changing the setting from Strict to Permissive. The same pattern can be used to test for other conditions and set other properties. Some other techniques I'm using here:

- I'm explicitly registering the SharePoint Snap In at the outset, so this script can be run outside the SharePoint Management Shell.
- The logical structure of the script is simple. We take in a web application, than walk through all the site collections to walk through all the sub sites to walk through any libraries using the foreach statement.
- We invoke the SharePoint API to lookup the ID for Document Libraries, and use that to only retrieve a collection of document libraries.
- The script uses an if statement to see if we need to change a setting.
- The script "pipes" the output of some of the commands to a text file, using the out-File command and the –append parameter.
- SPWeb can have memory leaks in PowerShell. Although the memory is released when PowerShell is closed, it's good practice to dispose of the SPWeb object explicitly (not all SharePoint objects have .Dispose() methods, fyi.)

```
Add-PSSnapIn Microsoft.SharePoint.Powershell

#get web application
$webapp = Get-SPWebApplication "http://msshome2010/"

#getsites
foreach ($s in $webapp.sites)
{
    #Get Document Library
    $SPBaseTypeDocumentLibrary =
[Microsoft.SharePoint.SPBaseType]::DocumentLibrary
```

```
foreach ($SPweb in $s.AllWebs)
{
    $SPdocLibs =
$SPWeb.GetListsOfType($SPBaseTypeDocumentLibrary)
    foreach ($docLib in $SPdocLibs)
    {
        #Show properties of the doclib
        $doclib.GetType().FullName | out-File -Append LibOut.txt
        $doclib.ParentWebUrl | out-File -Append LibOut.txt
        $docLib.BrowserFileHandling | out-File -Append
LibOut.txt

        if ($docLib.BrowserFileHandling -ne "Permissive")
        {
            #If you need to change it from Strict to Permissive
            $docLib.BrowserFileHandling = "Permissive"
            $docLib.Update()
            Write-Host "Updated"
        }
        else
        {
            Write-Host "Permissive"
        }
    }
}
#cleanup
$SPWeb.Dispose()

}
```

That's it for PowerShell. For more information on PowerShell and even more cmdlets, two recommended resources are:

- Todd Klindt http://www.toddklindt.com
- Gary Lapointe http://blog.falchionconsulting.com

Your First SharePoint 2010 Web Part

Let's walk through a sequence to create a SharePoint 2010 web part. Custom development for SharePoint is a huge topic, and I don't pretend that a web part section in a small development chapter is exhaustive. However, it gives you an introduction to the elements and deployment process for a custom SharePoint web part.

This part will use the C# and the LINQ syntax to query information from a custom list, apply a filter, and display it in a custom part. This can be built and deployed in 15 minutes or less! LINQ stands for Language Integrated Query, and it provides a way to run T-SQL-style queries against data sources in code.

First, we set up a custom list called "Employees":

- Title (Text)
- JobTitle (Text)
- ProjectTitle (Text)
- DueDate (Date)

Put some test data in the list (I put full names in the Title field.)

Next, we're going to open up Visual Studio 2010 and create a new project. Visual Studio 2010 has templates out of the box for many innate SharePoint elements. We're going to create a new project for a Visual Web Part This template can be found in Visual C# | SharePoint | 2010, and will use .NET Framework 4.0. Also, as a Visual Web Part, the development will be simpler – but we can't put the solution into the 2010 "sandbox" for managed code. I've named this sample project CFMVWP2010.

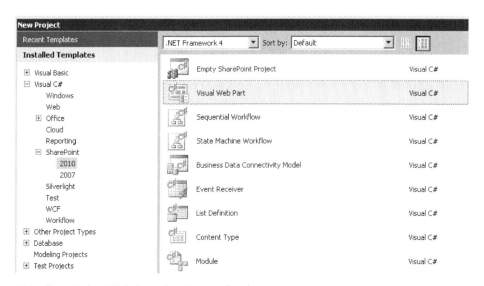

Creating a new project opens up another one-step wizard where you can specify the initial site to be used for debugging and deployment. Since we created a Visual Web Part, it can only be deployed as a farm solution. Other template types, such as the Empty SharePoint Projects, can be written as Sandboxed solutions from the outset.

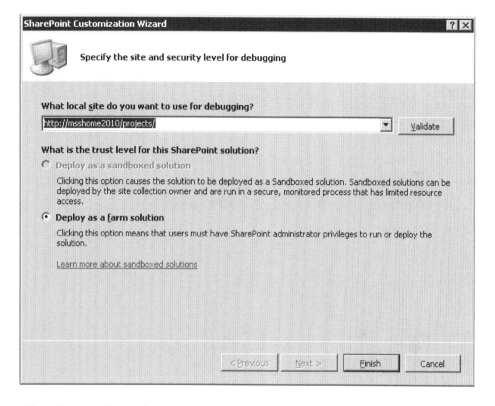

After that, we're going to use a command line tool to generate a full set of site entities. The tool is called SPMETAL.exe, and it's found in the SharePoint Hive. It can be called directly from the location of the source code if you have already included the BIN directory in the environment path. If not, you can add it at the command line with the following (assuming the default installation location for SharePoint.)

Open up a command prompt and navigate to the folder under the folder containing the solution in your visual Studio Projects folder. In this case, the folder is *C:\Users\[username]\Documents\Visual Studio 2010\Projects\CFMVWP2010\CFMVWP2010*.

```
set path=%path%;c:\program files\common files\microsoft
shared\web server extensions\14\bin
```

Staying in the same command prompt we can run the **spmetal** tool to
automatically generate a C# definition of all the entities and base
classes on our site. (If you didn't create the list first it couldn't be in
the entity list.) The command also takes parameters for the site
location, and the namespace.

```
spmetal.exe /web:http://msshome2010
/namespace:CFMVP2010.VisualWebPart1 /code:SPLinq.cs
```

After that, we need to add an IReference to SharePoint LINQ to our
project. Under the Solution Explorer, right mouse click on References
and Add Reference. Browse for a .NET Reference to
Microsoft.Sharepoint.Linq.

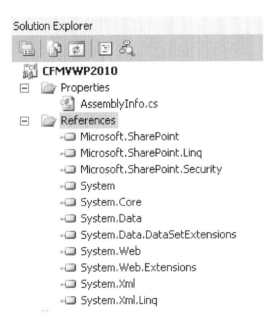

Next, we want to add the SPLinq.cs file generated by SPMetal to our
project (hint, it's an existing item, not a new item.)

After that, you'll need to add the following code to the .ASCX file for the VisualWebPart. This adds a SharePoint DataGrid "spGridView" and defines the grid to our four retrieved columns. (Which we haven't retrieved yet!)

```
<%@ Import
Namespace="Microsoft.SharePoint.WebControls" %>
<SharePoint:SPGridView id="spGridView" runat="server"
AutoGenerateColumns="false">
  <HeaderStyle HorizontalAlign="Left" ForeColor="Navy"
Font-Bold="true" />
  <Columns>
    <SharePoint:SPBoundField  DataField="Title"
HeaderText="Title"></SharePoint:SPBoundField>
    <SharePoint:SPBoundField DataField="JobTitle"
HeaderText="JobTitle"></SharePoint:SPBoundField>
    <SharePoint:SPBoundField DataField="ProjectTitle"
HeaderText="ProjectTitle"></SharePoint:SPBoundField>
    <SharePoint:SPBoundField DataField="DueDate"
HeaderText="DueDate"></SharePoint:SPBoundField>
  </Columns>
</SharePoint:SPGridView>
```

Oh, since we're using SharePoint and LINQ, we need to tell the program about it. Add these using lines to the ASCX code behinds – the VisualWebPartUserControl.asx.cs file (not just the ASCX file!)

```
using Microsoft.SharePoint.Linq;
using Microsoft.SharePoint;
using System.Linq;
```

And we're also going to add some code to the Page_ Load event of this code behind file. In order, we're:

- Connecting to our site in LINQ
- Creating a variable handle to the Employees list
- Defining a SQL-like query against our data list
- Sourcing and binding the data to our spGridView

Here's what we add to the Page_Load event:

```
var dc = new SPLinqDataContext(SPContext.Current.Web.Url);

            var Employees =
dc.GetList<EmployeesItem>("Employees");

            var empQuery = from emp in Employees
                           where emp.DueDate <
                           DateTime.Now.AddMonths(6)
                           select new
                           {
                               emp.Title,
                               emp.JobTitle,
                               ProjectTitle = emp.ProjectTitle,
                               DueDate =
emp.DueDate.Value.ToShortDateString()
                           };

            spGridView.DataSource = empQuery;
            spGridView.DataBind();
```

Assuming everything was added correctly it's time to compile and install the web part – Build and Deploy in Visual Studio 2010-speak ("VS2010"). When we created the project, you were asked to specify the target site for the deployment. (In case you need to change this, you can find that target in the Project Properties.)

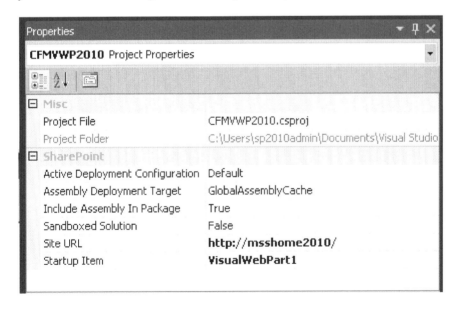

From the Visual Studio menu, click Build | Build Project to compile the solution. Then choose Build | Deploy Project to compile and install the solution on the target SharePoint site.

Almost there. Two final steps. First, under Site Actions, let's check the Site Collection Features and make sure our newly deployed feature is activated:

Name		Status
Advanced Web Analytics This feature comprises advanced Web Analytics reports, data-driven workflows, workflow for scheduling reports, the Web Analytics Web Part and customize reports functionality(for Enterprise SKU) at the site collection level.	Deactivate	Active
CFMVWP2010 Feature1 My Visual WebPart Feature	Deactivate	Active

Finally, we add the Web Part to a page, and we get a queried view of data from our list:

CFMCustomWP

Title	Job-Title	ProjectTitle	DueDate
Chris McNulty	Practice Lead	ACME	7/31/2010
Amy Talhouk	Project Manager	Beta Software	8/31/2010
Mike Gilronan	Partner	Candyco	6/30/2010
Alexey Abramkin	Consultant	Donovan Scores	7/31/2010
Vadim Mastrovsky	Practice Lead	Foxtrot Products	9/30/2010

TIP: *For new custom code, implement with the SPMonitoredScope block. In summary, this enables your code to generate logged counters for Developer Dashboard.*

Web Part Development

Managed Metadata is also completely addressable in custom code. The SharePoint API for Managed Metadata is exposed via the Microsoft.SharePoint.Taxonomy.dll, which can be browsed from Visual Studio 2010 IDE. Microsoft has published good reference code for the Taxonomy APIs. In the example below, the SocialTagManager interface returns a set of tagged URLs. When walking through the collection, the .count property gives us a direct statistic on how many times the term has been used. Elsewhere in the code, the aggregated data dictionary is bound to a DataGrid control and displayed in a Web Part. I've included this example to provide a general sense of how to approach metadata coding.

```
foreach (SocialTerm aTerm in socTerms)
    {
        string termName = aTerm.Term.Name;
        SocialTermStats.Add(termName, aTerm.Count);
        try
            {
            SocialUrl[] socURLs =
mySocialTagManager.GetAllUrls(aTerm.Term);
            foreach (SocialUrl aUrl in socURLs)
                {
                    string urlString = aUrl.Url.ToString();
                    if (!SocialUrlStats.ContainsKey(urlString))
                        {
                            SocialUrlStats.Add(urlString, termName);
                        }
                    else
                        {
                            SocialUrlStats[urlString] += ", " +
termName;
                        }

                }
            }
        catch (UserNotFoundException unfE)
            {
                //Handle exception if user not found.
            }
    }
```
(from http://code.msdn.microsoft.com/socialstatswebpart/)

During many initial presentations on MMS, users appreciated the tag cloud visually, but also sought hard data on how tags are being used. The MSDN solution is a good step in that direction. The default tag cloud is shown below:

2007 **2010** ACME baseball Blogs Calico Cat chart client demo Excel feline football fun h20 I like it InfoPath Intergalactic Fuels July lobsterbisque mekko microknowledge Mouse New York City Other Nassau Suffolk outerspace OWA PowerPivot

prairieschool recruiting rocketfuel **SharePoint** SPSBOS SQL water **X-21**

Screen Cleaner Z-22 Mouse Catcher

Figure 172 - Default Tag Cloud

The MSDN web part displays actual numbers of uses. Neat!

Tag Usage

Social Term	Uses
X-21 Screen Cleaner	6
2010	3
SharePoint	3
I like it	2
water	2
2007	1
PowerPivot	1
baseball	1
Cat	1
ACME	1
SharePointInternet	1
InfoPath	1

Figure 173 - MSDN Tag Statistics Web Part

InfoPath

InfoPath is a great forms designer, and power users can often start developing their own solutions quickly. Here are three quick tips to help add a little shine to your first InfoPath forms:

Adaptive forms

It's pretty simple to show or hide sections of an InfoPath form based on other form input. The trick is to add a "section" control from the standard toolbox.

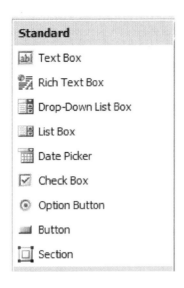

- Add an option button or check box control outside the section. (If you put the field inside the section, you won't be able to use the field to toggle the view once the section is hidden.)
- Drag the fields or layout tables you want to selectively show or hide into the section.
- Open the properties dialog for the section.
- Select the Display tab and click Conditional Formatting button.

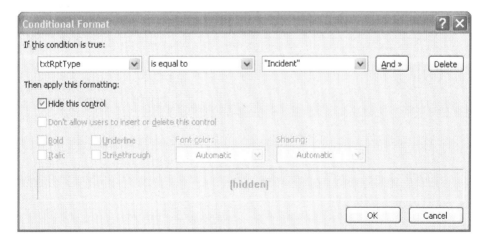

Figure 174 - Conditional Formatting

Set up the condition for when the section should be hidden, and check the **Hide this control** box.

Automatic Naming for Submitted forms

When users finish filling out forms, they need to figure out a unique name for the form. For commonly used forms, it's usually best to standardize the form naming.

- From the Menu bar, select Tools | Submit Options
- Click the Add button
- Create a New Connection to Submit Data

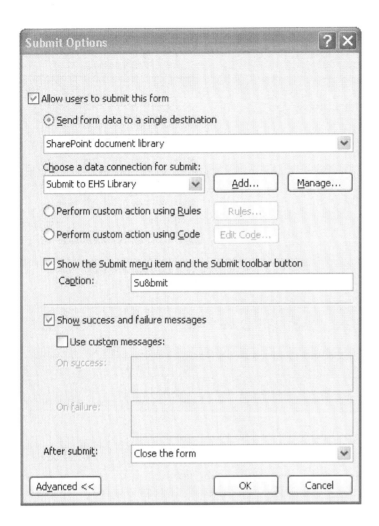

Figure 175 - Submit Options

- Specify the URL to the Forms Library
- Use the concat function to develop a unique file name format. Concat adds all the arguments into a single string. You probably want to use some combination of the submission time and the form fields to generate a meaningful, unique name.

Also, on the Submit Options screen, it's a good practice to close the form after submission – otherwise users are left in the form and may think they need to save (which asks them for a file name again, leading to confusion.)

SharePoint List Views as Secondary Data Sources

It's not uncommon for InfoPath forms to use dropdown lists that correspond to an existing SharePoint list. The problem for most lists is that they may contain extra information that needs to be filtered, and may require custom sorts. You can use a native SharePoint list connection, but the data elements will be retrieved in their default sort order (the auto incrementing ID field in order of data entry). Here, the trick is not to set up a connection to a SharePoint list, but to an XML "file". The trick is to use a URL to a SharePoint web service:

```
http://SITEURL/_vti_bin/owssvr.dll?Cmd=Display&List={ListGUID}&View={ViewGUID}&XMLDATA=TRUE&noredirect=true
```

Substitute the following parameters:

- **SITEURL**: put in the full URL to the site (and sub site if needed). Do not include the list name or ASPX page.
- **ListGUID**: GUID for the SharePoint List
- **ViewGUID**: GUID for the SharePoint List View

You can get the GUIDs for the list and view by opening up the view properties and inspecting the URL for the properties screen. You will see a section of the URL that reads, for example:

```
List=%7B7FA90930%2D2C35%2D4505%2DA077%2D6E381C0C6382%7D
```

You need to convert this into appropriate formats with brackets (%7B and %7D) and dashes (%2D):

```
{7FA90930-2C35-4505-A077-6E381C0C6382}
```

You can test the URL in a browser, which should return an XML page that resembles:

```
- <xml xmlns:s="uuid:BDC6E3F0-6DA3-11d1-A2A3-00AA00C14882"
xmlns:dt="uuid:C2F41010-65B3-11d1-A29F-00AA00C14882"
xmlns:rs="urn:schemas-microsoft-com:rowset"
xmlns:z="#RowsetSchema">
```

```
_ <s:Schema id="RowsetSchema">
_ <s:ElementType name="row" content="eltOnly"
rs:CommandTimeout="30">
_ <s:AttributeType name="ows_Attachments" rs:name="Attachments"
rs:number="1">
  <s:datatype dt:type="boolean" dt:maxLength="1" />
  </s:AttributeType>
_ <s:AttributeType name="ows_LinkTitle" rs:name="Product"
rs:number="2">
  <s:datatype dt:type="string" dt:maxLength="512" />
  </s:AttributeType>
_ <s:AttributeType name="ows_Company" rs:name="Company"
rs:number="3">
  <s:datatype dt:type="string" dt:maxLength="512" />
  </s:AttributeType>
  </s:ElementType>
  </s:Schema>
_ <rs:data>
  <z:row ows_Attachments="0" ows_LinkTitle="Another one"
ows_Company="Mine" ows_Therapeutic_x0020_Area="Oncology"
ows_Phase="I" ows_MarketPotential="Medium" ows_Status="Active"
/>
  <z:row ows_Attachments="1" ows_LinkTitle="Codename"
ows_Company="Classified" ows_Therapeutic_x0020_Area="Pain"
ows_Phase="II" ows_MarketPotential="High" ows_Status="Dormant"
ows_Corp_x0020_Overview="<div>To be developed</div>"
ows_More_x0020_Information="http://intranet/sample.doc,
http://intranet/sample.doc"
ows_AnnualRevenueEstimate="1000000.00000000" />
  <z:row ows_Attachments="0" ows_LinkTitle="Newest Product"
ows_Company="rrr" ows_Therapeutic_x0020_Area="Pain"
ows_Phase="III" ows_MarketPotential="Medium"
ows_Status="Dormant" ows_Corp_x0020_Overview="jjjj"
ows_AnnualRevenueEstimate="1000000.00000000" />
  </rs:data>
</xml>
```

Workflows

Workflows in SharePoint 2010 can be developed using three tools –
Visio, SharePoint Designer ("SPD"), and Visual Studio. Although you
can still use SPD to develop one-off workflows that are tightly bound
to a single list or library, you can also create reusable workflows that
can be attached to multiple lists or libraries.

In prior versions of SharePoint, the choice of SPD or Visual Studio was a hard fork in the road. Although SPD workflows can be easily created without coding skills, they can't be reused or invoke complex processing. Visual Studio allows for maximum complexity – but it's not a power user tool. But SPD2007 workflows were a dead-end road. If you started with SPD2007, and outstripped its innate functions, you have to start all over again in Visual Studio.

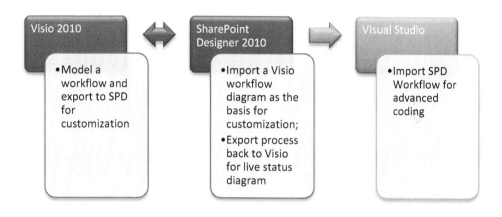

SharePoint 2010 broadens the workflow toolbench. You can, optimally, start in Visio 2010. A non-technical analyst can model a process flow as a workflow diagram to start. That workflow can be imported into SPD 2010 for further customization – for example, designing data entry forms, adding email addresses for notifications or lookups to other SharePoint lists. Finished SPD workflows can be republished to Visio Process Repositories (a document library) to give a live visual of the process flow.

You don't need to use Visio to start, but it may be a better design technique for more complicated processes. That said, SharePoint Designer is going to be the main tool for many SharePoint workflows. SharePoint Designer is delivered alongside the other Office 2010 application – except that SPD is a free download from Microsoft's web site[26]

When you launch Designer, you must first connect to a SharePoint site. Once connected, you can create a new workflow by clicking on Workflows in the left hand navigation. This will light up the New Workflows section of the Ribbon.

TIP: *The Ribbon is also where you can find the Visio import process.*

Figure 176 - New Workflow

List workflows are bound to a single list. Reusable workflows can be used anywhere in a site collection or to any content type; site workflows can be reattached to any list or library in the current site.

I've had a number of clients not understand workflow is in the first place – is it document publishing, is it approvals, or what is it exactly?

At a financial services firm, we created a series of workflows to manage new account setup. For this process, new account paperwork was continually bulk scanned into a temporary document library using the new account ID and date as a filename. This process happened "outside" SharePoint. But SharePoint workflows ran the rest of the show. From here:

- Pass the image to a reviewer to make sure the scan is complete or return the document for a rescanning request.

---

[26] http://sharepoint.microsoft.com/en-us/product/related-technologies/pages/sharepoint-designer.aspx

- Flag the document as 'Ready' so its shows up in an open application list used by a team of off-hours processing staffers.
- Allow any single processor to take control of the document and move it to their personal pending queue (a change to a custom status field and 'assigned to' value.) The processor would setup the new account in a mainframe system.
- If the account could be successfully opened, close the document, move it to an archive library, and send an alert to the customer relationship manager for the new account. If not, send notice back to the manager to get additional information or automatically return the application after seven days.

We also used Excel to create simple management reports and the status of the workloads and statistics on completed applications.

It may make sense to reference the actions you can take inside a Designer workflow to illustrate what you can – and can't – do in SPD workflow. As you'll note, the kind of actions vary based on whether or not you're running on SharePoint Server or SharePoint Foundation, and on the object type for the workflow (e.g. task, document).

General Actions
- Core Actions
  - Add a comment
  - Add Time to Date
  - Do Calculation
  - Log to History List
  - Pause for Duration
  - Pause until Date
  - Send an Email
  - Set Time Portion of Date/Time Field
  - Set Workflow Status
  - Set Workflow Variable

- o Stop Workflow
- List Actions
  - o Check In Item
  - o Check Out Item
  - o Copy List Item
  - o Create List Item
  - o Delete Item
  - o Discard Check Out Item
  - o Set Content Approval Status
  - o Update List Item
  - o Wait for Field Change in Current Item
- Task Actions
  - o Assign a Form to a Group
  - o Assign a To-do Item
  - o Collect Data from a User
- Utility Actions
  - o Extract Substring from End of String
  - o Extract Substring from Index of String
  - o Extract Substring from Start of String
  - o Extract Substring of String from Index with Length
  - o Find Interval Between Dates

SharePoint Server 2010

Start Approval Process, Declare Record, and Lookup Manager are only available on SharePoint Server 2010.

- Document Set Actions
  - o Start Document Set Approval Process
  - o Capture a version of the Document Set
  - o Send Document Set to Repository
  - o Set Content Approval Status of the Document Set
- Task Actions
  - o Start Approval Process
  - o Start Feedback Process

- o Start Custom Task Process
- List Actions
  - o Declare Record
  - o Undeclare Record
- Relational Actions
  - o Lookup Manager of a User

Task Actions

- End Task Process
- Set Content Approval Status (as author)
- Wait for Change in Task Process Item
- Wait for Deletion in Task Process Item
- Set Task Field
- Rescind Task
- Append Task
- Delegate Task
- Escalate Task
- Forward Task
- Insert Task
- Reassign Task
- Request a Change
- Send Task Email

Document content type

- Core
  - o Send Document to Repository
- Document Set Actions
- List Actions
  - o Delete Drafts
  - o Delete Previous Versions

Finally, you may notice a little button the Ribbon called an "Impersonation Step". An impersonation step runs in the security context of the user who first created, or most recently republished, the workflow. Impersonation steps allow you to modify item or document permissions based on workflow logic or document properties. Impersonation steps themselves can't be nested inside other steps.

Impersonation steps
- Inherit List Item Parent Permissions
- Remove List Item Permissions
- Replace List Item Permissions

Workflows can be made reusable at the outset, as we noted above. Publishing these workflows to the site collection saves them; and then can then be saved as a workflow Template in three Site Assets library. If you look at the Site Assets library, you will see the workflow saved as a WSP package – the same packing format used in Visual Studio. VS2010 provides in the box support to import Designer workflow WSPs into a new project. However, this is a one-way trip. One you edit the workflow in Visual Studio, it belongs to Visual Studio forever – you can't go back to Designer for that WSP again.

SharePoint gives you a diverse and full featured development platform for your solution. Whether you're making a simple InfoPath form or a full featured Visual Studio web part, you'll see you do almost anything with the system.

SharePoint 2010 adds social networking to its core workloads. During the past few years, the movement dubbed "Enterprise 2.0" has infiltrated the workplace. In brief, the peer communications advanced by Facebook and Linked In ("Web 2.0") have become an accepted form of business communication. As workforces evolve, information workers have come to expect these kinds of communications to be pervasive. Adopting social technology is not only a bo0on to productivity, but it implicitly helps with employee retention. It also aids information retention. Without enterprise social networks, workers often flee to public services like Facebook. Information is more easily secured when it doesn't leave the network.

Microsoft groups its social networking tools under the banner of "Communities" During the first year of SharePoint 2010's rollout, many observers described it as enterprise Facebook.   I think that's misleading, and suggests a more casual usage of the technology. SharePoint Social is more analogous to Linked In. It has a way to categorized profiles for people search and expertise finding. You can supply quick status updates and receive similar updates from people or metadata tags that you follow.   Comparing it to Facebook can scare off dubious business sponsors, and it's not accurate. There's no Farmville in SharePoint.

The centerpiece of SharePoint's social networking is the "My Site" How can something that's called "My" be social? Actually, social networking is pervasive through SharePoint. Although My Site is a personally convenient tool, social features show up through SharePoint's collaborative sites, including:

- People Search
- Ratings
- Tags
- Web Analytics

- Web Analytics Web Part
- Blogs
- Wikis

The most complex part of My Sites is establishing the User Profile Service, discussed above at page 117. Once UPS is running, My Sites are both really easy to keep running, and really hard to change – largely because of the architecture. Each My Site runs as an independent site collection, copied from a master template at time of creation. Making global changes to branding or features usually requires custom code and feature stapling, and is beyond the scope of this chapter. But there are some good tricks to use to enhance the My Site interface and people search.

My Site Tips and Tricks

My Links – Sharing and Customization

SharePoint 2007 had a simple way to add a link back to your main portal page from the home page of all My Sites. In 2010 there's a different way to get the same result – plus you're not limited to just one new link. And there's a new way to allow users to save and share their own personal links.

My Site Menu
On each user's My Site, you can add a link that always shows in the global navigation bar:

By default, SharePoint shows **My Newsfeed | My Content | My Profile** in the menu bar (above). To add My Links, go into SharePoint Central Administration.

- Select Application Management
- Mange Service Applications

- Select the User Profile Service
- Under the link for Personalization Site Links, add a link to the user quick links. By default, this link looks like: http://[**MySiteApp**]/_layouts/MyQuickLinks.aspx where **MySiteApp** is the host/domain name for the SharePoint My Site host web application.

Once you have a connection to the MyQuickLinks page, you can add, edit and share links. The dialog box shown below gives you control over the URL, title, groupings, and visibility of the links:

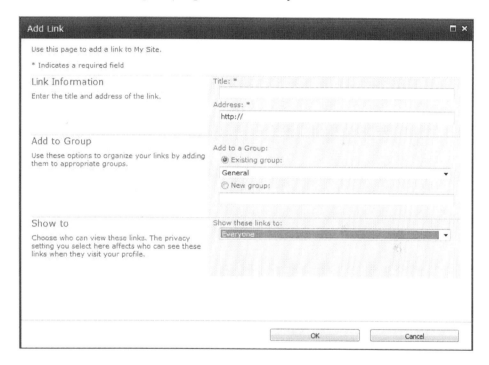

You can also use this page to add an MMS keyword tag to each link, based on the currently selected link and its **Group** (shown as "General" above and below.)

This adds a social tag to your My Site. Other users who follow you in their My Site stream will see the new link in their Newsfeed, and the tag is always available to you and your site visitors through your My Site profile page.

My Links Shared on My Site

Fine, you say, but if I'm sharing My Links with everyone, how do they see them? Well, the pages used for My Profile are common pages to all users of a given My Site application. Adding the appropriate web part to the right profile page will put your shared links out there for everyone to see (along with your tags and notes).

- Navigate to your My Site.
- Access the My Profile page
- Under the dropdown menu in the upper right hand corner of the page, select Sign In as Different User and login as a user with farm level administrative rights to the My Sites host application.
- If you have permissions, you should now see a Site Actions menu in the top left corner of the page. Select that and choose Edit Page.
- Pick the area of the page where you'd like to add a My Links part (the Middle Right zone is a common choice.) From there, click Add a Web Part.
- In the Ribbon dialog bar, select the Content Rollup category, and choose the My Links web part to add to your chosen zone.

That's it! Now when users visit your profile page, they'll see the links you're sharing – and you will see there's when you visit their page. You'll see the My Links section on the right side of the page below.

My Links, Shared on Portal Site

Finally, you can improve the accessibility of the links by adding the same web part to common enterprise portal pages. We've done this on the enterprise portal home page. In this context, each user sees only their links – not the shared links.

People Search Errors

No Users Found

Perhaps you can't find any users in your farm, even after the User Profile Service is provisioned and profile shave been imported and used. A quick look at the logs may show the error:

```
sps3://machinename  - Error in PortalCrawl Web Service
```

The problem is caused because the farm was been installed using the Farm Config Wizard, which uses the machine name for its default web application. This web application was not being used and so had no site collections created. The fix is to point the sps3:// url to a web application that did have a root site collection.

Duplicate Users Found

First, if you've ever run a SharePoint 2010 people search and found two listings for each name, it's an easy fix! You probably have duplicate entries in the definitions for the Content Source in the Search Service Application.

- In Central Admin, open up the Shared Services Application for Search.
- Under the left hand Quick Launch, click on Content Sources
- By default, click on the Local SharePoint sites source
- Under the list of target sites, you will probably find a duplicate URL that beings with the prefix "sps://". Remove the duplicate – just leave one that points to the host name of your principal internal site. Save this change (you need to make sure all crawls are stopped first!)
- Rerun at least an incremental crawl to remove the duplicate entries.

Profile Picture Editing

Now there's another Cumulative Update to love – the December 2011 CU for SharePoint 2010.   Somewhere along the way, administrators of the User Profile SSA lost the ability to update profile pictures for other users. That's been fixed in the December 2011 CU.

Keeping your customized SharePoint farm running at peak performance isn't hard – but it requires some ongoing care, as well as know how about user support and troubleshooting.

Patching

Servers need tending, and SharePoint is no exception. Microsoft has committed to releasing major service packs every 6-12 months, with aggregated Cumulative Updates every two months.

How best to learn about the updates? There are a couple of resources. First, Microsoft usually announces them on the SharePoint Team MSDN blog, http://blogs.msdn.com/b/sharepoint/ and consolidates the latest patch news at: http://technet.microsoft.com/en-us/sharepoint/ff800847.aspx

Also, I tabulate all the patch versions and build numbers on my blog at http://www.chrismcnulty.net/blog (look for Version-Build Numbers).

OK, so you've found a patch you want to install. Obviously, first you need to download them. Service Packs are usually directly available for download. For Cumulative Updates, you have to supply an email address, and you'll be sent a link to a password encrypted download file. Once you've extracted the files, you're ready to begin.

For SharePoint Server 2010, patches are usually installed in pairs, in sequence. The installation is performed via the patch executable file.

- SharePoint Foundation (first)
- SharePoint Server (second)

And at a high level, patching involves both installing the patch on relevant servers followed by deploying the patches on all servers. The deployment is usually run from the SharePoint Products and

Technologies Configuration Wizard, and updates databases, system settings and deployed code. Deployment also goes in sequence:

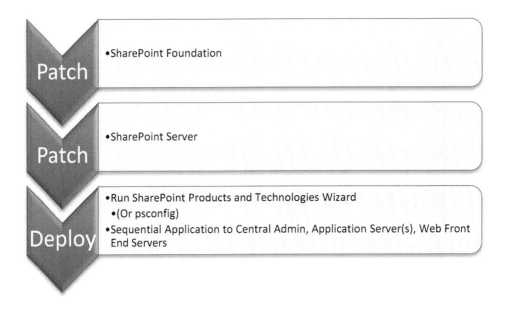

Here's the process:

- Run the SharePoint Foundation extracted file and accept the EULA.
- Allow the first hotfix to run to conclusion

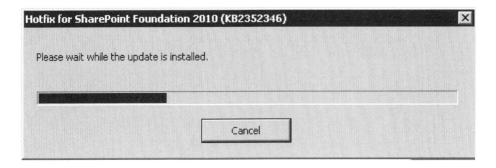

Figure 177 - Patching

- You should not need to reboot the server at the end of the Foundation patch installation.

- Run the SharePoint Server hotfix executable and allow the patch to run to conclusion.
- Reboot the server
- Login and run the SharePoint Products Configuration Wizard.

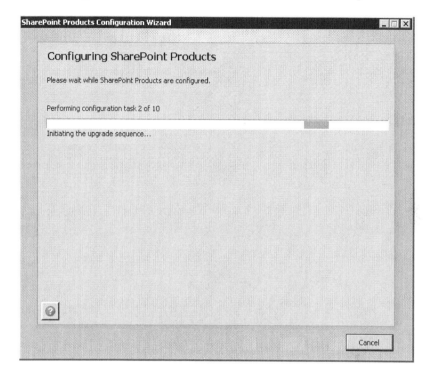

Figure 178 - The gray wizard, again

When the update completes, SharePoint Central Administration should launch, indicating that the system was successfully updated. You can check on the health of the update in Central Admin > Upgrade and Migration > Check Product and Patch Installation Status.

PSCONFIG for a stuck wizard

If you are running the "gray wizard" – the SharePoint Products and Technologies Configuration Wizard – occasionally you may see it get stuck during an upgrade, or, more commonly, a patch. There's a command line tool that can be used to "force" the patch upgrade process to complete.

```
psconfig.exe -cmd upgrade -inplace b2b -wait
```

"b2b" tells SharePoint it's an upgrade from build-to-build within the same version (2010). (There is a "v2v" option that can be used to force an upgrade from 2007 to 2010.) "Wait" tells the system to wait until the process is completed; there is also a "force" setting that cancels any other pending upgrade actions before starting the new upgrade request.

You can confirm the system update by checking the Servers in Farm screen in Central Admin. (This version number, "14.0.5123.5000" indicates the farm is running the August 2010 Cumulative Update.)

Farm Information

Configuration database version: 14.0.5123.5000

Configuration database server: KMAMSSD02

Configuration database name: SharePoint_Config

Server	SharePoint Products Installed
KMAMSSD02	Microsoft SharePoint Server 2010 Microsoft® Office Web Apps

You can also use PowerShell for this:

```
#Load the Sharepoint .net Assembly
[System.Reflection.Assembly]::LoadWithPartialName("Microsoft.Shar
ePoint")

(get-spfarm).buildversion
```

This will give you similar output at the command line:

```
PS C:\Users\sp2010admin> (get-spfarm).buildversion
Major  Minor  Build  Revision
-----  -----  -----  --------
14     0      5123   5000
```

When should you apply an update? In general, Microsoft performs extensive regression testing on Service Packs, and those should be deployed generally when released. CU's are more convenient aggregate packages than the dozens of separate fixes they contain. However, Microsoft's testing on them isn't as exhaustive as that for Service Packs. Microsoft will introduce new features, such as the storage quota reporting tool as part of a Service Pack. It's rare, though for a CU to contain new functions[27].

You should only deploy CU's if they fix a specific issue or if you are having other issues and the upgrade has been recommended by Microsoft or its partners. You don't have to plan to automatically deploy them every two months. In any event, always test Service Packs and CUs in a non-production area before a production rollout.

One detail about Service Pack 1 and Cumulative Updates. When you install SP1, you must also install the June 2011 CU (see http://support.microsoft.com/kb/2460045) because of known issues – some of the Service Pack actually relies on parts of that CU. My recommendation would be to test and move directly to the December 2011 CU, at least. Cumulative Updates for SharePoint were delivered in pairs (Foundation and Server) prior to August 2011. Afterwards, they were packaged as a single install. So it should be even simpler to add the December 2011 CU than the June 2011 CU.

Troubleshooting

Integrated Health Analyzer

SharePoint 2010 provides automated best practice analysis. When the Health Analyzer finds outstanding issues, it gives you a yellow or red

---

[27] The December 2011 SharePoint 2010 Cumulative Update added iPad support for many of the business intelligence functions in SSRS and PerformancePoint. See page 213 for more.

alert directly on the top line of Central Administration. If you inspect the rules, you'll see certain items flagged as "Red" – e.g. granting administrative permissions to service accounts. This is a bad practice for reasons too long to name here. However, if you've decided to live with it, **delete the alert and turn the rule off.** If you get used to seeing it atop the screen, you'll ignore it when it gives you a new alert – such as servers about to run out of disk space. To be fair, you should review the alerts and either resolve or disable all the yellow and red alerts as the Health Analyzer finds them. (And you can always turn the rule back on later.)

The SharePoint Health Analyzer has detected some critical issues that require your attention. View these issues.

Figure 179 - Red Alert

The health analyzer is installed automatically, and rescans your farm with a periodic timer service job. If you examine the list of open alerts in Central Administration, each contains links to get more information about the alert, and a link to "fix" the problem. However, not all the fixes are simple. For example, one common rule will alert if you about performance degradation if it sees that you are hosting databases on a server that's also running SharePoint. First, "click to fix" doesn't work unless SharePoint is automatically able to scan your network for available SQL servers with extra capacity, transfer the databases and update the configuration. (Sorry, it can't do that!) So there can't be a way to repair it automatically.   However, automatic repair is available for some rules when it makes sense.

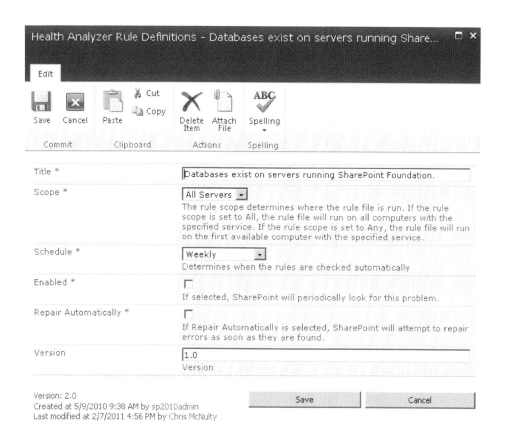

Figure 180 - Health Analyzer Rules

Second, some rules don't make sense in certain configurations. For example, the database rule is meaningless on a single server farm. For this situation, feel free to disable the rule.

Web Analytics

SharePoint also provides enhanced usage and web analytics as part of Site Settings. Analytics are available for single sites and for the whole site collection. Although there are more sophisticated systems available for tracking user and system activity (Quest Site Administrator, Axceler ControlPoint or AvePoint's DocAve), these tools are a good starting point when projects are budget constrained or there are no other tools available.

Traffic shows user activity. User reports, shown below, provide a high level trend about users, URLs, browsers, [page views and related statistics. The default date range is configurable, and statistics are recompiled by nightly timer service jobs.

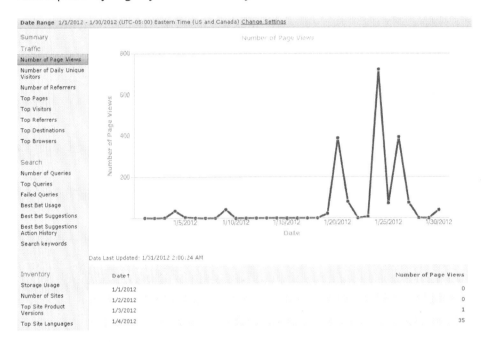

Figure 181 - Site Collection Analytics

Search statistics are also available, and, as noted elsewhere, reviewing the logs for frequently searched terms can be great input to determine if you need to adjust navigation of MMS classifications based on actual usage.

Inventory provides summary information about content growth trends, numbers of sites, and other data.

About the only difference between the site level and site collection level is the scope of the reports; site level Web Analytics are limited to a single site (which is sometimes more relevant) and excludes resource usage for storage (which you still might need).

Developer Dashboard

One of the most exciting new capabilities in SharePoint 2010 is the Developer Dashboard. The Developer Dashboard is essential to, wait for it, developers, obviously.

But it's also one of the most useful tools in the IT Pro toolbox too. Based on the Unified Log Services in 2010, Developer Dashboard automatically measures what happens, and how long, every time you load a page. Some of the classes of events include:

- HTTP Requests and times
- Database Queries and Times
- Web Part Events

For the non-developer, this gives you a good starting point to diagnose performance issues. The general rules for interpreting a Developer Dashboard trace:

- If IIS events on the left hand are running long, your IIS server may be low on memory.
- If a database query is taking a long time, check the SQL Server.
- Similarly, if there's a new web part on the page that takes a long time to render, there may be an issue in code.
- Finally, if the page is loading in a second or less according to the server (upper right hand corner) you may actually have a

network latency issue – the problem may lie between the server and the client.

How do you turn it on? Easy – you can either do it "old school" (STSADM.EXE) or "new school" (PowerShell):

With stsadm:

```
stsadm -o setproperty -pn developer-dashboard -pv OnDemand
```

In PowerShell:

```
(Get-SPFarm).PerformanceMonitor.DeveloperDashboardLevel =
"OnDemand"
```

Once you've done this, you'll get a little icon in the top right of each page to toggle the dashboard on and off.

Unified Logging Service

Despite your best efforts, users may eventually get the 2010 error screen:

Figure 182 - SharePoint Error

SharePoint errors always include a unique "correlation ID" to help identify related logged events in multiple areas. However, in a medium or large farm, the number of local log files to cross reference can become cumbersome.

However, in SharePoint 2010, the unified logging and monitoring service integrates information from a broad range of sources:

- Windows Event Logs
- Performance Monitors & Counters
- SharePoint Features and Web Parts
- Unified Logging Service (Diagnostics)

This process relies on the Usage and Health Shared Service Application, and by default, information is centralized in the WSS_Logging database. SharePoint uses timer jobs to aggregate information from all these systems across all the servers in your farm. The table structure of the database is complex; however, the database has prebuilt views for ULS, Analysis Service, Site Structure, etc. However, if you look at an out-of-the-box logging database, you will NOT see the NTEventLog and ULSTraceLog views shown here:

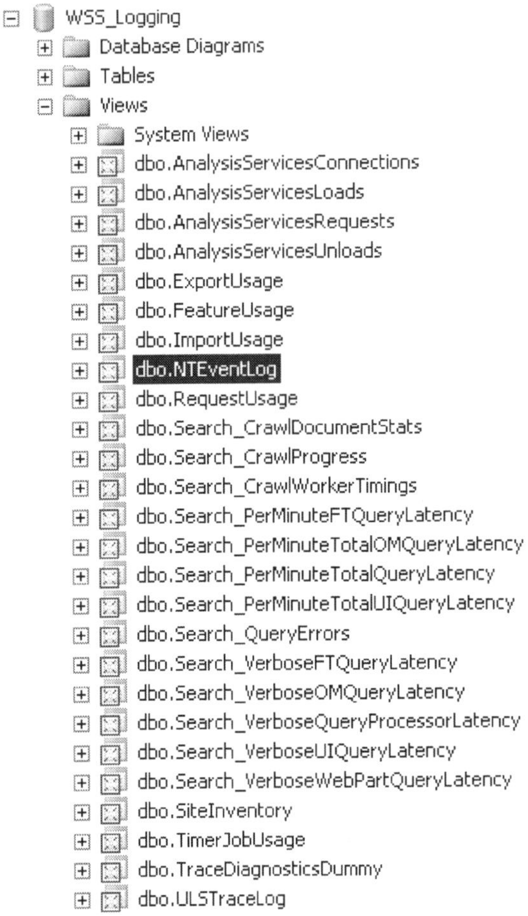

```
☐ 🗄 WSS_Logging
   ☐ 📁 Database Diagrams
   ☐ 📁 Tables
   ☐ 📁 Views
      ☐ 📁 System Views
      ☐ 📄 dbo.AnalysisServicesConnections
      ☐ 📄 dbo.AnalysisServicesLoads
      ☐ 📄 dbo.AnalysisServicesRequests
      ☐ 📄 dbo.AnalysisServicesUnloads
      ☐ 📄 dbo.ExportUsage
      ☐ 📄 dbo.FeatureUsage
      ☐ 📄 dbo.ImportUsage
      ☐ 📄 dbo.NTEventLog
      ☐ 📄 dbo.RequestUsage
      ☐ 📄 dbo.Search_CrawlDocumentStats
      ☐ 📄 dbo.Search_CrawlProgress
      ☐ 📄 dbo.Search_CrawlWorkerTimings
      ☐ 📄 dbo.Search_PerMinuteFTQueryLatency
      ☐ 📄 dbo.Search_PerMinuteTotalOMQueryLatency
      ☐ 📄 dbo.Search_PerMinuteTotalQueryLatency
      ☐ 📄 dbo.Search_PerMinuteTotalUIQueryLatency
      ☐ 📄 dbo.Search_QueryErrors
      ☐ 📄 dbo.Search_VerboseFTQueryLatency
      ☐ 📄 dbo.Search_VerboseOMQueryLatency
      ☐ 📄 dbo.Search_VerboseQueryProcessorLatency
      ☐ 📄 dbo.Search_VerboseUIQueryLatency
      ☐ 📄 dbo.Search_VerboseWebPartQueryLatency
      ☐ 📄 dbo.SiteInventory
      ☐ 📄 dbo.TimerJobUsage
      ☐ 📄 dbo.TraceDiagnosticsDummy
      ☐ 📄 dbo.ULSTraceLog
```

Figure 183 - WSS_Logging Views

How do you get them? By design, the Timer jobs for aggregating
event logs and ULS logs are disabled. In part, this is because the
potential for runaway database growth is significant if verbose logging
is used across a number of servers.

However, if you enabled the following two Timer jobs, the jobs will
create the "missing" SQL views:

- Diagnostic Data Provider: Trace Log
- Diagnostic Data Provider: Event Log

Once you have the correct data and views in the database, you can run a SQL query like the one below to find all the logged events that correspond to a given correlation ID:

```
SELECT * FROM [WSS_Logging].[dbo].[ULSTraceLog] WHERE
CorrelationID = '04377DAE-C2FD-4DBE-A57E-101B3005059E'
```

Watch the database sizes, but this can be a very effective technique when you need more information about a logged error.

User Access Control (UAC)

Under Windows 2008/2008R2, the first time you try to run the command line STSADM tool, you get an "Access Denied" message.

You will probably try some or all of these things to troubleshoot:

- confirm that you have local administrator access
- confirm you have farm admin rights
- confirm SQL permissions are at least dbo
- check the SharePoint version/patch number
- check the environment path variable and make sure you can find the right version of the executable in the 14 hive.

All good steps -- but that's not the fix. You'll want to disable User Account Control in Windows 2008. (It's the same interface that gave you those "A program needs your permission to continue" prompts in Windows Vista.)

In Windows Server 2008, navigate to Control Panel | Users | Turn User Account Control On or Off. Turn this function off and reboot.

Leaving UAC off is less secure, so for maximum security you may want to leave UAC on after you have finished using STSADM.

Get recently logged in users to display in a SharePoint list

This can be done by adding a new view to the logging table and then linking the view to an external list via BCS.

Troubleshoot Office Web App:

If Office Web Apps are available on a primary content web application, but not others, it's possible that that web application lacks the required SSA associations:

- Configure Service Application Associations in Central Administration | Application Management | Web Applications
- Make sure you select
  - o Word Viewing Service
  - o Excel Services Application
  - o PowerPoint Service Application

Administration

Auditing

Auditing is an essential function for governance. It creates visibility into user and system actions to ensure they remain within boundaries. And it also provides a level of reassurance to non-technical teams that SharePoint teams are only performing proper actions and content access. Enabling auditing consists of three steps:

In Central Admin | Security, configure Information Management Policy (http://kmamssd02:12345/_admin/Policyfeatures.aspx). Make sure Auditing is available.

Central Administration ▸ Information Management Policy Configuration
This list displays all of the available information management policy feature for use within lists, libraries, and content types.

Name	Description	Publisher	Availability
Labels	Generates labels that can be inserted in Microsoft Office documents to ensure that document properties or other important information are included when documents are printed. Labels can also be used to search for documents.	Microsoft	Available
Barcodes	Generates unique identifiers that can be inserted in Microsoft Office documents. Barcodes can also be used to search for documents	Microsoft	Available
Auditing	Audits user actions on documents and list items to the Audit Log.	Microsoft	Available
Retention	Automatic scheduling of content for processing, and performing a retention action on content that has reached its due date.	Microsoft	Available

Figure 184 - Information Management Policy

At the Site Collection Audit Settings screen (in Site Collection Administration) select the events you want to audit on libraries and documents, etc.

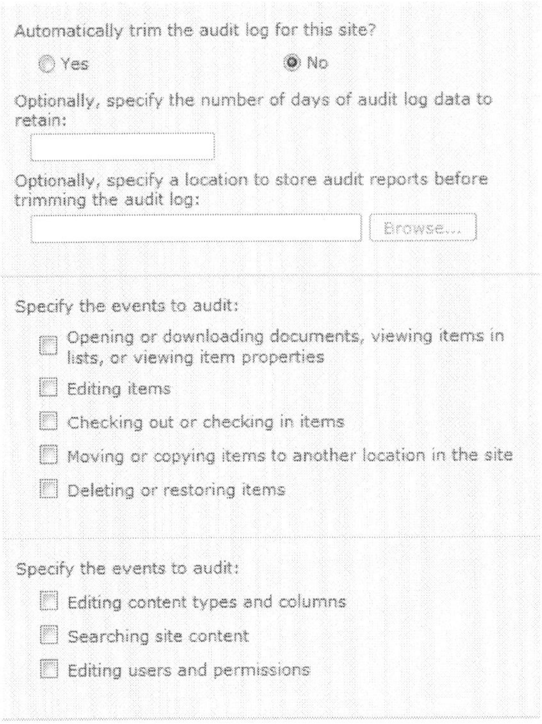

Automatically trim the audit log for this site?

◯ Yes   ⦿ No

Optionally, specify the number of days of audit log data to retain:

[   ]

Optionally, specify a location to store audit reports before trimming the audit log:

[   ] [Browse...]

Specify the events to audit:

☐ Opening or downloading documents, viewing items in lists, or viewing item properties

☐ Editing items

☐ Checking out or checking in items

☐ Moving or copying items to another location in the site

☐ Deleting or restoring items

Specify the events to audit:

☐ Editing content types and columns

☐ Searching site content

☐ Editing users and permissions

Figure 185 - Audit Configuration

At the Site Collection Settings screen, select View Auditing Reports to run audit reports.

Storage Management

Service Pack 1 adds an interface to visualize how much space is being used by your libraries, folders, and files.   Site Actions | Site Collection Administration | Storage Metrics opens up the Storage Manager. You can also add /_layouts/storman.aspx to the end of a site URL.

Type	Name	Total Size↓	% of Parent		% of Site Quota		Last Modified
📁	Shared Documents	63.6 MB	63.14 %	▬▬▬	25.45 %	▬▬	11/2/2011 1:47 PM
📁	Personal Documents	38.6 MB	38.31 %	▬▬	15.45 %	▬	11/1/2011 10:40 AM
📁	_catalogs	1.3 MB	1.24 %	┃	0.50 %	┃	11/2/2011 4:20 PM
📁	Mobile Documents	227.8 KB	0.22 %	┃	0.09 %	┃	11/2/2011 1:33 PM
📁	Lists	107.6 KB	0.10 %	┃	0.04 %	┃	11/1/2011 8:23 AM
📁	Form Templates	78.8 KB	0.08 %	┃	0.03 %	┃	10/25/2011 9:30 AM
📁	Customized Reports	70.4 KB	0.07 %	┃	0.03 %	┃	10/28/2011 8:03 AM

Figure 186 - SP1 Storage Manager

Storage Manager graphs the percentage of storage space used by files and folders as compared to their parent, and to the site quota. You can navigate among libraries, folders, and contents. It's especially helpful in managing storage usage and site collections with relatively small storage quotas, such as My Sites.

Office 365 Administration

SharePoint Online, as a shared service, restricts access to some SharePoint administrative capabilities. You can't get access to Central Administration or the command line. But you can gain access to many of the same features once you login to the Office 365 portal with an administrative account.

Figure 187 - Office 365 Administration

One of the most important features of this page is user administration. The left hand navigation link for Management | Users allows you to browse the list of users to configure settings. Each user has four screens:

- **Details** – Directory Information
- **Settings** – Controls Administrative Permissions and Locations
- **Licenses** – Checkboxes for the user's eligible Office 365 services. This is where you "turn on" SharePoint for an account
- **More** – Exchange and Lync Settings

The main portal page leads to a SharePoint Online Management page (shown below):

administration center

Manage site collections
A SharePoint site collection is a group of related Web sites organized into a hierarchy. A site collection often shares common features, such as permissions, content types, and consistent navigation, which can be managed together.

Configure InfoPath Forms Services
InfoPath Forms Services enables users to open and fill out InfoPath forms in a browser without requiring Microsoft InfoPath installed on their computer.

Configure InfoPath Forms Services Web service proxy
The InfoPath Forms Services Web service proxy enables communication between InfoPath Forms and Web services.

Manage User Profiles
The User Profile service provides a central location where administrators can configure user information, including user profiles, organization profiles, and My Site settings.

Manage Business Data Connectivity
Business Connectivity Services bridges the gap between SharePoint sites and other web services, databases, and external business applications. It enables SharePoint to create read and write connections to external data in lists, and to display external information in Web Parts.

Manage Term Store
A Term Store contains a set of related keywords (called managed terms) organized into a hierarchy of information, such as a well-defined product category or materials list, that you can then use to control the entry of list values. A Term Store helps improve the consistency, reliability, and discoverability of information within a site collection.

Manage Secure Store Service
The Secure Store contains credentials such as account names and passwords, which are required to connect to external business applications. The Secure Store provides a method of mapping the credentials, and associating them to an identity or group of identities.

Figure 188 - Office 365 SharePoint Administration Center

The links on this page correspond to functions you can administer in SharePoint Central Administration SSAs or InfoPath Settings for an on-premises installation. These work almost identically to the same interfaces for on-premises SharePoint.

- Configure InfoPath Forms Services
- Configure InfoPath Forms Services Web service proxy
- Manage User Profiles
- Manage Business Data Connectivity
- Manage Term Store
- Manage Secure Store Service

However the first setting of the page, **Manage Site Collections**, leads to a screen not previously used in traditional SharePoint for Site Collection administration. This screen allows an administrator to create new site collections. More importantly, since SharePoint Online restricts the amount of storage and resources, this screen lets you distribute the allocation of storage and processing resources (like the sandbox) among your site collections.

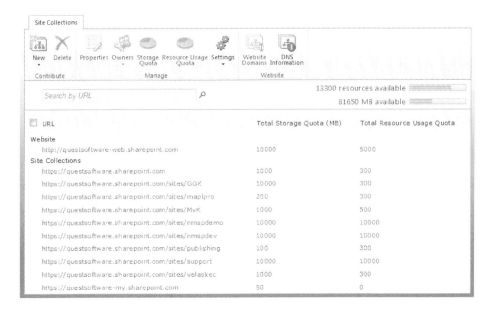

Figure 189 - Office 365 Site Collection Administration

All of this happens as an analog to Central Administration. But if you're used to the default Site Settings screen, you'll see the one used in Office 365 is almost identical.

Support

SharePoint, like any other enterprise application, should be supported in concert with other similar enterprise systems. Make use of the help desk, incident management, and configuration systems that are already in use. Listen to, and empower, your first tier help desk to deliver as much support as they can. Service Level Agreements (SLAs) for response and resolution should match other enterprise systems, such as Exchange or CRM. Remember, a good help desk can be your eyes and ears, and they are perceived as the face of your IT organization.

No matter how well designed and implemented, and no matter how well governed and trained, users will still need support. Here's a recap of some the most common user support questions and how they can be addressed.

Users Receive "Cannot Connect to Configuration Database" Web Page

Usually, this means the SharePoint farm account is locked out, probably from someone "guessing" at the password to get access to something. Unlock the account. In the long run, don't use the farm account for interactive administration, and don't tell people its password. Use separate accounts, as noted earlier, for IIS pools, farm/database access, search, and interactive farm administration (four accounts)

Another possibility is that SQL Server is down – reset the SQL Server.

No one can upload anything but site is up

This usually means that the databases can't write any data. Immediately, it means that the data disk volume is full, usually. After you clean up immediate disk space, check for some likely runaway consumers of disk space. SQL transaction logs sometimes get big. If so, truncate logs and move to simple recovery, or use backup settings and database maintenance to shrink logs periodically.

This can also happen if disk based SQL or SharePoint backups have grown large. Runaway backups are also bad because they can stop you from making new backups. In this case, move the backups to a different disk partition – not the same as the database. You may also want to retain fewer days on disk, or, ideally, put backup files on removable media such as tape.

In a virtualized environment, the host file system may be full. (Another reason not to put SQL on virtual disks!) Shrink some expandable disks or add storage.

Finally, the content databases themselves may have become overgrown. The best answer here is to use content retention policies, archiving and deletion to reduce total content size. Finally, you can consider using RBS/EBS to move file content to alternate storage.

I can't find a document I think I should see; someone can't see a file I just uploaded

This user issue has three common causes. First, check permissions – users may not have the same rights to the document. Second, check to see if there are any ILM document policies or content organizer rules that might have moved the file to a new location.

Finally, if the document has required properties that are missing, it stays checked out on its first upload until those fields are supplied. Checked out documents can only be seen by admins and authors, so checking in the document with all necessary fields will solve the issue.

Repeated requests to re-enter Windows credentials

Users **hate** this one when it happens. It's usually because the URL is in a different DNS zone than the user. Sometimes, clients are connecting to a SharePoint farm from untrusted domains. These users would still like to access the site as if they were in a Windows authentication automatic access zone. This is also true for related Office applications – they don't want to be prompted for login each time they open a Word document! In order to support this, in Internet Explorer:

- Tools | Internet Options | Security
  - Select the Intranet zone
    - Click the sites button and choose Advanced
    - Add the SharePoint web site
  - Custom settings
    - Advanced
    - Scroll to bottom of list
    - Under User Authentication, select Logon | Automatic logon on in Intranet

       ⊙ Logon
           ○ Anonymous logon
           ◉ Automatic logon only in Intranet zone
           ○ Automatic logon with current user name and password
           ○ Prompt for user name and password

Or you could add the site to the IE Trusted Sites list. Once these steps are completed, the "save password" option in user login screens will be effective for saving passwords.

"My workflow didn't start"

There are two simple things to check here. First, recycle the time service job in Central Administration, which may clear a range of "stuck" jobs. Next, make sure the user isn't using a system account. Declarative (auto-start) workflows don't run for system accounts, by design, so run those workflows from a regular user account.

"I'm not seeing the right search results"

Every time I've heard this, I think (silently) "how do you know?" Well, first, make sure that search crawls are running and complete by checking crawl logs. Restart a full crawl if crawls finish OK. Finally, take a look at authoritative results and Best Bets to see if there are other elements being given precedence next to your favored bit of content.

"I need a file back that I deleted"

Fortunately there are a lot of things to suggest here. The simplest is to ask the user to recover their file from the Recycle Bin. If that doesn't work, there are a lot of innate choices   Granular backup and restore allows you to get just a piece of SharePoint back without restoring the whole farm. You can also restore from an unattached content database and use PowerShell to move content from there to a new location. Many third-party ISVs provide a detailed index of prior backups and make it easy to zero in on the one containing the content desired.

Other Tips

Finally, here's a grab bag of other miscellaneous troubleshooting tips. They've been used many, many times out in the field to rescue critical SharePoint situations.

Bad web parts on page

If you have custom web parts on a page, and the page starts erroring out, how can you get back to the page to figure which part is causing the problem so it can be hidden or removed? Simple.   Navigate to the page URL, and add the parameter

```
?Contents=1
```

to the end of the URL. This will open up a configuration screen where you can list all the parts on the page, and selectively close or delete those that are reporting errors.

HyperV & DiskPart

Many times, you may be running SharePoint in a virtualized system on Microsoft's virtualization platform, HyperV. If you ever need to make a virtual disk bigger, the guest system may not see all the added space at the outset. Here's what to do inside the virtualized system.

- From the **Run** menu type "diskpart.exe" to enter the command line utility to resize disk partitions
- The command **list volume** will show you all the available volumes.
- Select your volume; **select volume 1** corresponds to the "D" volume.
- Extend the volume with the **extend** command.

If all goes well, the partition will be immediately extended under the Disk Management snap in.

Save site as template

To save any site as a template, just go to Site Actions | Site Settings | Save Site as template. This saves the site as a standard .WSP package in the Site Collection Solutions Gallery (/_catalogs/solutions/Forms/AllItems.aspx). You can save content along with the site, but that will add to the size of the template. You might need to increase the default size of 20MB to allow for larger templates. There a simple command line setting for this:

```
stsadm -o setproperty -propertyname max-template-document-size -propertyvalue size_in_bytes
```

Security Applied via AD Groups and SharePoint Groups

SharePoint makes it very easy for power users to add and maintain user security on sites, libraries, folders and documents. However, end users don't usually understand the contents of groups – so most of the time they assign rights to individual user accounts. This creates a huge administrative burden when you need to add a new accounting user with permissions "just like Cheryl" – you need to find all those hand tooled permissions and add a new user for each of those. Far better to use an Active Directory group (e.g. AD\SharePoint-AccountingUsers) and assign permissions to that group. That way, each new user need only be added to one place, rather than dozens.

There will always be one-off permissions, and tools like Axceler Control Point, Quest or AvePoint can help with user security administration, but this technique will get rid of 80% of the burden.

Recovery Practice

Who wants to discover their backups are empty in an emergency? SharePoint gives us even more tools, such as granular recovery and unattached database restore – but in a pinch, you may not realize where these backups live (or worse, discover they were never enabled.) Run a test backup and restore operation at least quarterly.

Customization

Every SharePoint system benefits from a little extra attention and customization. These are the most common techniques.

Navigation

As previously noted, a site collection contains a top-level navigation bar – "Global Navigation". Global navigation is maintained inside **Site Settings | Look and Feel | Navigation**.

By default, the global navigation bar can automatically add links to subsites as they are created. Global navigation can also contain links to other site collections, or any other manually selected links, even to off-site content (e.g. www.bing.com).

Figure 190 - Navigation

Suppose you have four site collections on your intranet:

- http://intranet (root)
- http://intranet/sites/HR
- http://intranet/sites/IT
- http://intranet/sites/PMO

Each of those site collections has an independent set of global navigation bars. You might want them to look different, but you also may want them to be consistent. All site collections in the farm can use the same top level navigation but it will be up to you to create the same menu bar across all those site collections. If you add a subsite to the intranet, it will be automatically added to the global navigation bar at the root site collection, but you'll need to add it manually to each other site collection.

Similarly, each site has its own left hand navigation quick launch. This is maintained from the same place, and is referred to as "Current Navigation". Lists and libraries, as created, are automatically added to the current quick launch for each site. Each quick launch can be similarly edited to remove unwanted elements or add other links. Current navigation isn't shared across sites, by definition.

PowerPoint Branding

2010 adds the ability to redefine a theme from the browser – you can select different colors and fonts for many standard page elements. In addition, there's a quick and dirty way to use PowerPoint to create a SharePoint interface theme. There are more sophisticated techniques, but this is a good one for users to try.

- Open PowerPoint
- Create a presentation with intended colors, fonts, backgrounds, etc. Save that file as an Office Theme (.thmx) file.
- Go to the Site Collection root and open up Site Settings.
- Open the Theme gallery and upload the theme file.
- Go to Target and apply theme in Site Settings.

Master Page Changes

Here's an example of why you might deploy a custom master page. A client needed to widely distribute the ability to create subsites, but needed to suppress the appearance of the Site Settings item from the Site Actions menu. This is an easy change to make in the site master page.

In the master page, there is a section with the ID **SiteActionsMenuMain**. Inside that section there is a setting called SharePoint:MenuItemTemplate with an ID of MenuItem_Settings. By default, the security trimming on this item is:

```
PermissionsString="EnumeratePermissions,ManageWeb,ManageSubwebs,AddAn
dCustomizePages,ApplyThemeAndBorder,ManageAlerts,ManageLists,ViewUsag
eData"
```

There is a related setting that tells SharePoint to show the section if the user has "Any" of these permission levels. So if you edit that setting to:

```
PermissionsString="ManageWeb"
```

Only users with full control of the site will see the Site Settings item in Site Actions. Note that this doesn't remove their permission to get to the page using http://hostname/site/_layouts/settings.aspx - just the link to it.

Mobile support

Once access is established, SharePoint intrinsically allows a light bandwidth, simple view of the elements on a web page by adding the parameter "?mobile=1" to the site URL. So this URL, http://www.chrismcnulty.net

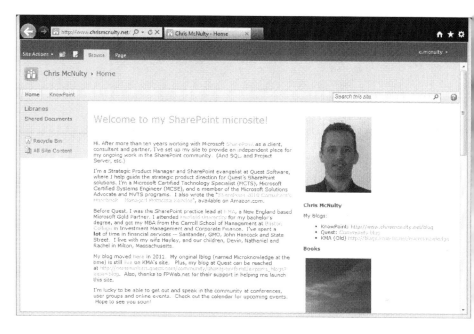

becomes http://www.chrismcnulty.net/?Mobile=1 :

Collaboration Best Practices

Figure 191 - Multiuser graphic collaboration in windows, preschool

SharePoint as a document storage system is well understood. However, most enterprises are looking for more. The first step beyond using SharePoint as a browser-based file locker is to enable effective collaboration. That's easier said than done.

But SharePoint has fantastic innate capabilities. Understand these, share skills, show examples, and let the collaboration energies build. Here are some best practices to help align usage with SharePoint's best capabilities.

(Here's the summary – email bad, links are good!)

Locations

To start, where should we collaborate? The first bit of guidance is to align the information architecture to your organization's working patterns. It's easy to conceive a hierarchy that matches geographies and departments. However, increasingly, people work across geographic and hierarchical divisions. They work in teams. Cross functional teams need collaboration areas that match their teams.

Is it OK to keep draft documents for a marketing project on the "Marketing Site"? Sure. How about keeping them in a team site for that project? Sure again. There's an appropriate place for each technique. What matters most is that the pattern is clear, consistent and governed. If navigation is ambiguous and creation patterns are unclear, it's hard to predict where a document library will live – so people give up looking and either stay offline, or create another duplicate repository. Remember, it's called SharePoint, (singular!) not ShareFuzzySetOfOverlappingLibrariesAndSites!

Also, My Site is **NOT** "Our Site". In general, shared team sites offer a single place to collaborate. Don't collaborate on My Sites, and monitor the growth rates to make sure that that paradigm doesn't become established. It's better to keep the content in one place and allow people to use different links and clients to access it, rather than copying it to multiple locations and clients.

Also, go beyond the firewall! Use an extranet to extend your collaboration to partners and external users, instead of email.

Social

SharePoint's social support also allows document sharing. Although social governance is also a topic for the governance chapter, there are some good adoption and governance rules that have generally worked well.

- Keep the My Site user quotas high. Encourage users to use their private document library as a replacement for their Windows desktop of local file storage. Keeping personal documents in SharePoint allows for versioning, tagging and search, while guaranteeing backup and stability. Plus, if users use SharePoint Workspace for offline access, they get the dual benefits of local document access combined with easy laptop replacement. Since everything is stored on SharePoint (think "private cloud") switching to a new laptop is much easier. With local file encryption, a lost laptop presents much less inconvenience – just get a new system and go. Plus, keeping your documents in SharePoint makes it easier to use them from other devices – home systems, tablets, or smartphones.
- My Site is not "our" site. Don't run collaborative teams from a My Site – based location.
- Don't keep master copies of essential corporate documents in My Site. You should be able to delete or archive a My Site when an employee leaves without significant disruption.
- Many users struggle with what they're "supposed to" put in their Shared Documents library. The best guidance is to keep the dozen or so documents that people always ask you to email to them. If "you" are seen as the finder of content, it's faster to direct people to your site than to litter the emails streams with multiple contending versions of a document.

Usage

Here's the easiest tip – you can still use the Feedback Workflow introduced in SharePoint 2007. It's a great way to send a document around for comments, and get back an integrated summary of everyone's comments. SharePoint handles all the messages and reminders for you. And it keeps the content in SharePoint, instead of email. Again, keep the documents out of email!

Sometimes two people need to edit a document together at the same time. Multiuser editing, or, "multiauthoring", is intrinsically supported as part of Office Web Applications.

- Use tags and metadata for Categories, not folders.
- Use document versioning for versions, instead of renaming successive copies.

Office Web Applications

SharePoint 2010 provides a server version of Office applications – Office Web Access, or "OWA". In part, this enables simultaneous multiuser editing of Office documents. The table below shows which applications – browser or Office client – can be used to "multi-author", and how user edits are contained or locked while other users are in the same document. Multi-authoring requires that the documents are saved in a SharePoint document library.

Multiuser Application	OWA	Office 2010 Client	Locking
Excel	√		Cell
Word		√	Paragraph/section
PowerPoint		√	Slide
OneNote	√	√	n/a

Multiuser editing is pretty simple. For Microsoft Word 2010, users need to open up the document from a library without checking it out. (Remember – check out means **exclusive** access to the document!)

Once two users are in a document, they each get visual indications that multiple users are in the document. The first is in the status bar at the bottom of the screen. This button shows how many users are sharing the document at the moment.

Inside Word, you'll be able to see sections change colors and "lock" as edits are being made – identifying who's doing what.

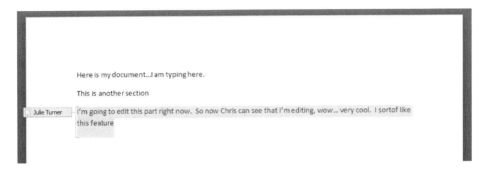

Here is my document...I am typing here.

This is another section

Julie Turner | I'm going to edit this part right now. So now Chris can see that I'm editing, wow... very cool. I sortof like this feature

Figure 192 - Multiauthoring in Word 2010

Finally, the Save and Refresh button 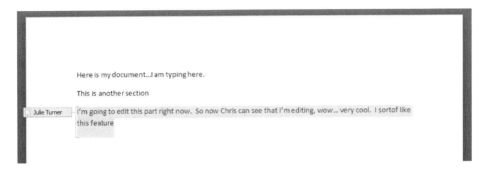 lets you save a new interim version and updates your copy with the most recent real-time updates. If you are working on a large document, each click will generate another version and use more storage – so try not to refresh every 10 seconds!

Client	Rich Client	Office Web Applications	Locking
Word 2010	Yes	No	Paragraph
Excel	No	Yes	Cell
PowerPoint	Yes	No	Slide
One Note	Yes	Yes	Full collaboration

TIP: *There's a document library setting under versioning to "Require Checkout" before a document can be edited. This setting is* **incompatible** *with multi user authoring. Document checkouts are exclusive, so if you force the first user to check a document out to edit it, no one else can edit it during the checkout. Finally, any library with documents for multiuser authoring should* **always** *use versioning; without it, there's no way to trace back the source of potential competing edits.*

Share PowerPoint files via Broadcast Sites

If all you need is watching a common PowerPoint file during a phone call, SharePoint supports connections via a customized site collection template, called a PowerPoint Broadcast Site. To create a PowerPoint broadcast site by using Central Administration:

- You need to be a Farm Administrator
- In Central Admin | Application Management, select Create Site Collection
- Specify the following settings"
  - Web Application that will host the site collection
  - Title
  - Description (Optional)
  - URL
- Template Selection - On the Enterprise tab select PowerPoint Broadcast Site.

As with all site collections, you need to specify a primary Site Collection Administrator, and can optionally add secondary administrators and quotas.

Once that's done, the PowerPoint 2010 Backstage view incudes a link for Broadcast Slide Show under Save and Send.

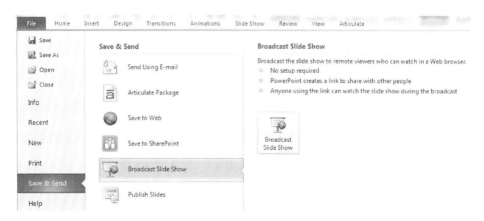

When users select this button, they can broadcast using the URL of the PowerPoint Broadcast site. The site generates a custom URL so users can watch the presentation from their browsers.

Working Remotely

Everyone needs to work on documents from SharePoint offline sometimes. You don't need to email the docs to your Yahoo account, and you don't need to drag the to your laptop hard drive. Bad things happen! Very bad things! First the document moves outside the scope of SharePoint's management. Second, if you make changes, odds are those changes don't make their way back to the original.

Fortunately, Office 2010 includes SharePoint Workspace ("SPW"). SPW lets you synchronize documents to your laptop for offline access, and lets you resync changes automatically as you are connected. This is the best way to work on files during long airplane flights or when Internet or VPN connectivity is unavailable.

Messaging

Finally, every time someone emails a document from a SharePoint library, God kills a tree! Don't email documents if you can avoid it – instead, email a link instead!

Governance

The noted 20th Century philosopher Peter Parker[28] once said "with great power comes great responsibility". SharePoint 2010 is powerful, but comes with the responsibility to wield it carefully. How long should you keep an employee's My Site after they leave the company? I know the answer is "it depends". But if you've worked with your user stakeholders to have clear statements about what kinds of documents belong on My Sites, it will be clearer. You don't want to retain sites forever assuming they're needed if they're not. Conversely, if you

---

[28] A/k/a SpiderMan.

purge the sites six months after people leave, you could run afoul of compliance requirements. Engaging users about their needs is a great way to spotlight the business value of information technology.

SharePoint 2010 provides more opportunities and more importance for reengaging users and sponsors about governance issues than before. Consultants are often challenged if asked to hold a business focused conversation with sponsors outside the traditional SharePoint IT core. Eventually, most SharePoint implementations grow beyond the common starting point – web-based document collaboration. Regardless of whether the next wave functions are forms-based workflow, enterprise project management, or financial business intelligence, for example, SharePoint technologists need to speak to business users about solving business problems.

Talking to users and sponsors about document collaboration "rules" is a good starting point for many, and serves as a natural stepping stone to discussions of business processes and decision making.

Governance Defined

Microsoft provides a succinct summary on TechNet:

*"Governance is the set of policies, roles, responsibilities, and processes that **guide, direct, and control** how an organization's business divisions and IT teams cooperate to achieve business goals."*[29] *[Emphasis added].*

There's a convention in writing about governance to cite a commonly used definition. Most IT management frameworks have their origins in common high level principles. Some examples of these frameworks include

---

[29] Microsoft publishes a lot of SharePoint governance material at http://technet.microsoft.com/en-us/sharepoint/ff800826.aspx

- ITIL – Information Technology Infrastructure Library
  (http://www.itil-officialsite.com/home/home.aspx)
- COBIT -- **C**ontrol **OB**jectives for **I**nformation and related
  Technology (http://www.isaca.org/Knowledge-
  Center/COBIT/Pages/Overview.aspx)
- CMMI – Capability Maturity Model Integration
  (http://www.sei.cmu.edu/cmmi/)
- MOF – Microsoft Operation Framework
  (http://technet.microsoft.com/en-us/library/cc506049.aspx)

And there are others.   SharePoint governance can itself be gridlocked
or overwhelmed if there's not a simple shared understanding about
what governance means.

A Tale of Two SharePoints

Although each individual governance plan will be unique, the basic
principles should be recognizable across most SharePoint enterprises.
It may help to consider the experiences at two similar US
multinationals.

OneCo: Guidance
One large financial services organization implemented SharePoint
2003 as its enterprise intranet and document collaboration solution.
(Let's call it "OneCo".) Some of the hallmarks of OneCo's plan for
"running" SharePoint:

- Enterprise-level global steering committees
- Business sponsors engaged as project sponsors
- Simple reproducible training offerings for site owners
- Predictable service levels and SLAs for uptime, recovery and
  incident resolution
- Clear self-service process for requesting new sites, with
  documented timelines and expectations for production and
  test usage

- Defined cost chargeback model that encouraged migration and customization
- Documented change control procedures for reviewing, communicating and applying significant modification to production environments
- Alignment with other enterprise systems for help desk support and incident/problem management

TwoCo: Control

For OneCo, this was a good start at an acceptable governance program. But this framework was woefully inadequate at a different (but similar) financial services firm ("TwoCo"). The two firms could not have been more different in their use of SharePoint. Hallmarks of the TwoCo governance plan included:

- Mandatory requirements for required training and certifications before site creation requests would be processed
- SLAs for how many months lead time were required for site creation
- Strict policies about what was forbidden in team sites (e.g. versioning, blogs, wikis)

When representatives of these two firms met, their governance discussion was fascinating. OneCo expressed almost of its governance plan in terms of guidance; TwoCo was focused on control. They had almost no common stories to share. Questions from OneCo included:

- How do we get even more people to use SharePoint?
- What other business processes can we automate ion SharePoint?

And questions from TwoCo included:

- Why isn't more of your governance plan documented?
- Should there be a formal user certification and training plan?

- And (my favorite) what else should we turn off in SharePoint so we don't get in trouble?

Understandably, each of these firms faced different challenges as their SharePoint environments matured. It's very simple to suggest that OneCo had it "right", but that's an oversimplification. In time, their concerns shifted to managing performance and capacity as the environment grew rapidly. In addition, the loosely enforced guidelines around non-production systems led to more than a few recovery requests for critical documents that were accidentally deleted from "test" systems. Some policies were clearly defined, but others were only documented as part of kickoff presentations, or not at all.

TwoCo faced challenges from their business users about speed-to-market for getting new sites – but almost no complaints about system performance or uptime. And every policy they had was clearly documented.

Governance Documents
I've also seen more than a few organizations describe their SharePoint governance as detailed and sophisticated. When asked, they commonly pull out a lengthy Microsoft Word document that details every aspect of their technical infrastructure – database names, service accounts, web applications, and web.config customization – as it existed when the environment was built a year earlier. Sometimes, this file is described as the "governance document".

Guidance, control, documentation – these are all aspects of governance. But they fail to tell the full story. Consider the yin/yang relationship of adoption and governance.

It's hard to get widespread adoption without some level of governance – procedures, training or guidance on how to use the system. In many organizations, ungoverned SharePoint can take off like a flock of startled birds – an explosion of sites, application and content, taking off in all directions with no discernible common direction or purpose. Unmanaged chaos is a bane to user productivity and sustained usage. But it also can open the door to legal or compliance exposure. Documents may be deleted or retained with no clear conformance to established retention timelines. User activity may open up even broader ranges of messages and communication to subpoena, or create potential liabilities when there are no frameworks for "proper" use.

Without actual usage, governance becomes theoretical. It's hard to motivate stakeholders. But trust the ability of governance to foster user confidence and spur high adoption. Governance is not a "chicken-and-egg" debate with adoption, where it doesn't matter which comes first. It's true that adoption furthers the need for governance. But without governance, it's hard to get the adoption you need in the first place. So governance isn't a luxury tax imposed after the fact on the most successful SharePoint projects – it's an essential, ongoing program in almost all SharePoint installations from day one.

Governance provides the balance between runaway users and users running away. When users run away from SharePoint, their content still goes somewhere. It's clearly harder to manage a maelstrom of overlapping SharePoint sites than a world where key content might be in SharePoint, file shares, email, cloud systems, local laptops or other platforms.

Understanding Resistance

Governance sometime gets a bad reputation in SharePoint. There are a few reasons. One is the word itself. It's become de rigueur to talk about governance for technical issues -- web sites, for messaging, for social solutions. In addition, economic and regulatory factors, such as options pricing, Sarbanes-Oxley, and the recent global recession have led to extensive discussion about reforming corporate management and boards of directors – a/k/a governance. The problem with the word is that although its meaning is loosely shared among practitioners, it can be confusing or alienating for folks who don't work with it on a regular basis.

The second issue is the "bad cop" scenario. In this, governance is seen exclusively as a controlling force, reining in users who are just trying to do their jobs.   This is a narrow interpretation of governance, and can reflect a damaged technical culture that needs to nurture its trusted relationships. In these situations, users try to see how much they can get going before someone stops them; or they get resigned to being shut down eventually, so they never even start using the system

Where and How Much Governance

In many publications you can usually find the Governance Pyramid:

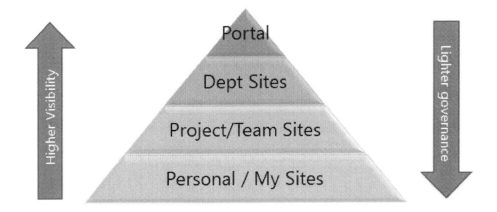

Figure 193 - Governance Pyramid

The Pyramid expresses a simple concept – the most prominent and trafficked portions of your SharePoint world usually require the most governance. Single user SharePoint systems are unlikely to need much in the way of governance. User guidance, control and direction are pretty simple when you have only one person to cover!

We could also express the amount of required governance as an arbitrary formula for G:

$$G = \frac{\sqrt{\frac{C}{100}} * \max(\log(u), 1)}{100 * t_d}$$

Where

- C is the volume of content expressed in GB
- U is the number of users in the environment
- t_d is the % of tolerable unscheduled system downtime

Again, it's an arbitrary formula. I'm not really advocating that we calculate a value in "govs" of how much governance is appropriate for a given SharePoint environment. But it does tell us that an 8000 user environment with 600GB of content and a high degree of business criticality (99.99% uptime) with a G score of 956.1 probably requires more care in its governance than a 40 user environment with 30 GB of data and a 99.9% uptime requirement. [G score of 8.7].

Key Factors
It's overly quantitative to calculate this value for all environments. But we do advocate the consideration of several factors in determining the how much governance is appropriate:

- Environmental size and complexity
- Usage
- Business criticality

The key point is that larger sites with more users and business impact need more attention than smaller ones.

Analogy of the shopping mall

Supreme Court Justice Potter Stewart famously remarked in the 1960s of a particularly hard to define legal concept "I know it when I see it."

So let's consider an example of a highly adopted, well governed community-oriented endeavor. Ladies and gentlemen, I give you the American shopping mall.

Most Americans have strongly "adopted" the local shopping mall. For example, the Roosevelt Field Mall in Garden City, New York, at 2 million square feet, has over 20 million shoppers annually.[30] Why are malls like this so highly used? Believe it or not, governance is a central factor.

Without governance, few would dare set foot in the mall. There would be no guidance about how to enter the building. Suppliers and merchants would be fearful about letting unsold merchandise remain on premises after hours. Even the food court might descend into a chaotic hellscape of health risks, dirty tables, and stolen tables.

At first blush, it may not seem that the shopping mall has "governance". There's no steering committee, no shopper training. However, the mall is governed by a blend of laws, rules, regulations, and social conventions. Some of the topics include daily operations, like cleaning, signage, or transaction security. Some are training-oriented, like new hire orientation. And some are more long range, like the local ordinances and lease contracts for adding a wing to the mall.

Here are just some of the "rules" of the shopping mall.

- Hours of operation are clearly posted.
- Rules are posted and enforced by on premises staff.
- Unsold merchandise is stored safely and securely in places where visitors lack access.

---

[30] Source, Simon, at
http://www.simon.com/Mall/LeasingSheet/62024_RooseveltField.pdf

- Stores are able to generate reports on daily sales and credit transactions as needed.
- Heat, light, plumbing and sanitation utilities are almost continuously available.
- Central customer service desks and frequent maps provide guidance to shoppers, as do staff on sales floors.
- New hires are given training by the mall as well as their own stores.
- The design and location of the mall makes it as simple as possible to arrive, park, browse and find products and services, and complete purchases. This happens with little **explicit** guidance – it runs by social conventions, signage, and learned behaviors.

Let's draw a few analogies between browsing for sweaters and browsing the intranet.

Mall Example	SharePoint example
Unsold goods are locked up overnight.	User are kept out of privileged sites without authorization
Secure credit card transaction histories	Reports on documents with unique (uninherited) permissions
Open 10am-10pm 364 days a year!	Highly available (>99.9% availability
Frequent "You are Here" Signs	Consistent global links to video how-to library
You can find the perfect sweater	You can find the perfect PowerPoint doc

Operations

Technically, speaking, a SharePoint site can "operate", and be managed, regardless of governance or adoption. But in practice, governance establishes a rationale and a framework of policies and procedures that empowers both operational management and usage.

Many of the tools and techniques of any process are echoed in governance – communication, documentation, collaboration, and workflow. SharePoint itself offers a great platform for these core activities.

Governance *per se* doesn't mean "backing up the SharePoint farm". Governance begins with awareness that users need deleted file recovery, and a policy decision that may be based on cost analysis, audit report and logs. Once the policy determines that there needs to be operational support for single file recovery, good governance also creates the procedure for requesting recoveries and user education about the process. Over time, a governance program will evaluate how well the process works and determine if and when self-service recovery is needed, for example.

Governance is distinct from, and yet bound to adoption and operational management. Many of the same tools and techniques used as part of sound systems management are echoed again in governance. But governance and administration is not the same thing. If we reflect back on our earlier definition, governance is expressed as cooperative roles, policies and procedures to achieve business goals. Although, ultimately, all IT operations s exist to serve business goals, there are other aspects of SharePoint management that most immediately serve technical needs. In a survey of the five pillars, we can see a blend of these business and technical goals. For instance, auditing exists predominantly to support business processes and decision making. The reliability pillar, on the other hand, supports immediate technical objectives to further the business policies that guide the SharePoint platform. It's an oversimplification, but probably a useful one, to think of governance as focused on business goals, whereas operations stress technical criteria.

Organization culture is another crucial consideration. Culture should reflect preferred modes of action and interactions in any group. SharePoint governance should never stand in opposition to culture – rather, it reflects, and even enhances any team's mission.

Maturity levels

Sadie van Buren, an author and community leader, has published an extensive and well received SharePoint maturity model, available to the community at www.spmaturity.com. The van Buren model considers multiple aspects of SharePoint maturity, such as collaboration, search, infrastructure, publication and staffing. Each of these is mapped to a CMMI-derived five stage model:

- 100 – Initial (Ad hoc processes)
- 200 – Managed (Process partially standardized and implemented)
- 300 – Defined (Process defined and observed
- 400 – Predictable (Process fully established, monitored and measured)
- 500 – Optimizing (Mature, self-regulated process)

Each of the major stages has its own set of elements and definitions – for example what constitutes 200-level collaboration or 500-level staffing. Finally, each of the elements is composited into a hybrid maturity score.

In the van Buren model, governance is only referenced at the 300 and 400 levels. Therefore, I'd like to propose a complementary approach to assessing governance maturity.

- 100 – Initial: No governance at all
- 200 – Managed: Ad hoc training available, usage rules and guidance are similarly variable. Business needs are presumed by technical stakeholders who act as sole governors of usage, on behalf of enterprise business units.
- 300 – Defined: Business goals are clear. Policies, roles, guidance and procedures are documented but not uniformly shared or used. Governance stakeholders are known but meet and communicate irregularly.
- 400 – Predictable: business goals are commonly known and documented. Stakeholders meet and/or communicate regularly. Governance standards are well shared, reviewed, followed, in some cases enforced. Governance success is measured by repeatable quantitative and qualitative criteria.
- 500 – Optimizing: Governance standards exist and are reviewed and adjusted over time; intelligent automation of governance practices like security request and site retirement. Governance becomes self-sustaining. The principal goal of the governance stakeholders is to review results, resolve exceptions, and implement new tools and techniques for SharePoint governance.

As is commonly the case, be realistic in your assessment about current governance maturity levels in your organization. Leaping from 200 to 500 is seldom accomplished in a short time. Progress, not perfection!

It's better to move up one level in a six or twelve month time period successfully, than it is to allow overaggressive maturity plans to fail.

Establishing a SharePoint Governance Program

By now, we've established a broad definition of governance. We described its major pillars and its relationship to technical operations and management. It should come as no surprise that we view governance as a cycle of continuous improvement, rather than a single implementation.

Rome wasn't built in a day. Or, to continue our shopping mall analogy, neither was The Mall of America in Minneapolis, Minnesota (the largest mall in the United States). Nor can any effective SharePoint governance program be implemented in a one-time, one day burst of activity.

Core Process

Governance typically cycles through multiple core processes. Although each of these activities warrants its own white paper, we'll introduce the major elements.

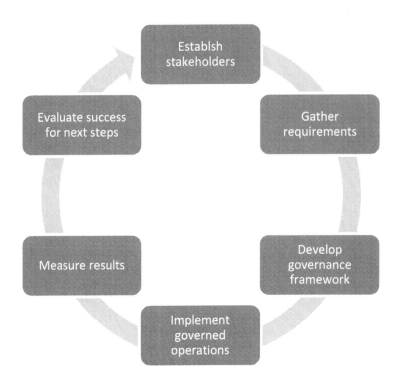

Establish stakeholders

Although SharePoint often begins as an IT initiative, SharePoint is really business software for business users. Just as successful SharePoint implementation projects need to engage a cross section of business owners, it's important to make sure that governance gives voice to business goals, operations teams, technology management and users. Stakeholders may be fluid through the years, but continuous stakeholder engagement should remain constant beyond the original implementation project.

Keeping business participants engaged can be a challenge for any steering committee. It helps to make sure meetings and communications are crisp and focused.

Gather requirements

Governance begins with an understanding of business goals. Over time, it also transits to include tactical needs and system capabilities and constraints. Shepherding this process is complicated. Working with business and technical disciplines requires education, tact, and really careful translation to assure that all governance decisions are made in consideration of commonly understood goals.

Develop governance framework

Policies and procedures are the key outputs of this activity. Turning governance requirements into effective, enforceable policies and procedures is a complex process. The governance pyramid, discussed above, can help prioritize areas and sections of your farm that require the most attention. Policies and procedures should be documented as much as possible.

Implement governed operations

This is another huge endeavor as well. Training and communications are parts of this process. Procedures should be automated to the extent practical. Matching the tactical execution to the governance strategy requires perception and cultural awareness. Practical governance works across multiple user scales – from individuals through an entire user ecosystem. It also may vary from broad usage guidelines to tightly controlled and restricted policies. Parts of implementation may involve additional software tools or custom development. It may also lead to new technical training and operating practices.

Measure results

Sustained governance programs require some degree of evaluation. In 200/300 level governance, much of this evaluation is based on qualitative or narrative feedback, but as higher levels of maturity are reached, statistical evidence can be gathered such as monthly site requests compared to actual site creations.

Evaluate success for next steps

All governance programs require ongoing emulation to determine if they are effective in channeling SharePoint to help achieve business goals. Again, it's not going to be perfect at first, but if stakeholders are able to make honest appraisals of their success, they can determine next steps. One of those next steps may be identifying additional stakeholders. In that case, continue back to the top of this list!

How your structure these activities is going to be particular to your organization – although, as noted above, SharePoint itself should play a large role in supporting effective collaboration.   Your collaboration about governance is going to surface interesting questions that rarely come up at the beginning of a deployment. Here are two I've heard:

- "Our sales force is going through a lot of turnover – can we minimize the risk of information leakage from offline access to our product literature in SharePoint Workspace?"
- "Our security team usually deploys patches to servers. Our DBAs recently built their own SharePoint system to learn more, and we just hired a new SharePoint engineer. Who should install SP1?"

Here are the answers that came up from each company's governance process:

- We should look at all their rights to determine what makes sense – SharePoint Workspace is only one piece of the puzzle.
- It depends, but SharePoint patching is different from other Microsoft updates. Let's figure out a plan for communications and deployment that fits with other systems.

 These answers clearly don't work in all organizations, and they may evolve over time. Dialog and evolution are essential elements of sustaining your governance program.

Key Elements

Finally, the major elements of your governance plan must include the following defined elements.

Roles and responsibilities

There should be a clear list of the named stakeholders who are involved in determining and approving the overall governance plan. Specific, named people.

Business goals

There must be at least a mid-level set of business goals. My mid-level, we are prescribing a level of detail that's more specific than a mission statement – i.e., maximizing stockholder value is good to know, but probably too broad to help shape SharePoint governance. "Enabling international sales team to collaborate from remote locations and across national boundaries" is a better business goal to shape governance.

Policies and procedures

Policies and processes comprise the heart of a governance program. For less mature organization these may be generally known and expressed casually. Many organizations will embody these in documents and web pages, rather than shared anecdotes and advice. This material is also often reviewed in training as part of new employee onboarding and in-service programs. The most advanced firms embed policies and procedures into automated, self-guided processes for actions like requesting a new SharePoint site.

Current state

Although this is almost never prepared by a governance team directly, it's one if the important inputs to governance. As noted above, current configurations and operational reports are critical to resolving user support needs, or ensuring system uptime and user satisfaction.

SharePoint Designer

SharePoint Designer has been a free download since 2008. It's a powerful tool in the hands of users with Design permissions on a site. It can also wreak havoc on an installation if those users start modifying master pages, adding web parts to odd areas, or other untoward behaviors.

Monthly Web Analytics Review – Usage, Storage, Search

Web Analytics in SharePoint 2010 are stronger than before. At least once a month, take a look at site usage trends and storage use to anticipate capacity constraints before they happen. It's also helpful to look at the query logs to see the most popular searches. Often, this gives you a clue to things and links that should be highlighted directly on the home page of the site.

Content Governance

I use the online photo site Flickr a good bit. Tags and metadata are essential to how Flickr runs, and they should be essential to your SharePoint 2010 implementation. When I'm asked to present on the IT Platform and Management in SharePoint, I usually spend a few minutes covering governance topics. Frequently, we spend so much time going over the nuances of upgrade and the Developer Dashboard that we get very little time to expand on governance concepts for Enterprise Content Management and Metadata. So, here are some good ECM concepts to consider in your governance plan.

Who controls the ILM Lifecycle?

Prior to SharePoint 2010, some of the limitations in information lifecycle management made it unlikely to gain widespread usage. Each variation in rules usually required a new Content Type, which quickly grew unwieldy. However, in 2010, the flexibility around Records Management and property-based rules make ILM much more appropriate. And it also increases the likelihood that a document isn't going to stay where a user left it. It may begin in a Drop-off Library, move to a Document Center and retire to an archive site collection or a Records Center after a few years. This can lead to some user driven "requirements" like "the system should never move my documents".

It's important to have business sponsorship for ILM rules, and enlist those sponsors when adopting lifecycle policies. Often it helps to remind users that although URLs may change, document IDs don't.

There is a season, turn, turn, turn...

Archiving documents is not a bad thing. One of the frequent knocks on search, especially in SharePoint 2007, is that it found too many documents. At a minimum, moving obsolete documents to a different site makes it easier to weed them out through search refinements and or custom search scopes. Realistically, a search for Holiday List should probably only turn up two or three – the current year, last year, and next year. The 1998 holiday list, maybe not. Getting users to contribute new content is great, but let's help them out by clearing out older items for them. You may not need to delete them, but reorganizing them makes sense.

Let the system version your documents

SharePoint's been doing versioning for a while now. It may seem obvious, but make sure that most users know this if you enable versioning on your libraries. With comments and version tracking, there's almost no reason to see this in a library:

- 2011MarketingBudget
- 2011MarketingBudget Old
- 2011MarketingBudget.v4

Which one is right? Remind your users it's OK to add a new document as a version to older document when saving – it's a great governance guideline.

Only one save per document please. Please?

I hate finding the same document in six different places on a SharePoint farm. The role of project sites, department sites and My Site needs to be clear to people. Discourage publication of the same document to multiple sites – instead, ask people to save each document to only one place. Get consensus around the business purpose of your SharePoint sites and help make this clear to your users.

Not all feedback is good.

We spend a lot of time focusing on the new ratings functions, and the easy "I like it" button that we forget the inverse implications. What about 1 star ratings? I may learn that my new white paper is poorly received. In an open culture that can learn from that kind of feedback to refine future content and winnow out less successful material, it can be great. However, in some cultures, the potential for negative feedback leads to less sharing (at best) and reprisals (at worst). Out of the box, there's nothing to stop you from creating an "I hate it" keyword. And someone will try.

Understanding your corporate social mores is important. At a SharePoint Saturday event, a panelist mentioned his attempt to introduce document ratings with the US Army. He was told that no one who ever wanted to get promoted would tag a general's document with less than five stars.

I'm optimistic enough to believe that openness and transparency is usually a good thing. At the same time, your governance statements to end users need to emphasize the important of honesty and professionalism in tagging other users' content.

Use ECM, MMS, Clients, and Training to Keep Content in SharePoint, reduce duplicates, and sustain searching/ browsing

That's a whole lot for a heading! But it summarizes the goal of keeping your relevant content **in** SharePoint. How so? It's easy with in-the-box Enterprise Content Management. You just need to be willing to introduce these ideas to your users as part of ongoing governance. Each of these steps can help:

- Use workflows to collect feedback instead of emailing document out of SharePoint (which invariably come back as duplicates, or make the copy left behind obsolete)
- Use the Workspace client to let users keep documents on their laptop without taking them outside the SharePoint frontier,
- Use content management as content ages to move less relevant material from primary sites into archive areas.
- Restrict the default search scopes to EXCLUDE archives (although scope expansion should be one click away)
- Train users to keep collaborative documents in collaboration areas and personal documents in My Site. Try not to intentionally upload multiple copies!
- Use MMS tags and content types to help guide Content Organizer rules to get new files to the "right" place.

A tip

The noted 20th century historian Crane Brinton spent much of his career comparing and contrasting historical revolutionary movements. In Anatomy of a Revolution, he noted that the organizational structure of the revolutionary moment becomes the form of government for the new regime itself. If you have an openly selected legislative body running your revolution, you're more likely to get the U.S. Congress at the end, for example, than if you organize the revolution around a single strongman and a military tribunal.

What does this mean for SharePoint governance? Well, practice what you preach. The governance committee needs to live by its own policies and procedures. For example, I consulted with an organization whose governance policy mandated that all documents and projects should be stored in SharePoint for effective collaboration. However, the governance team just collaborates with email. They had a hard time establishing their policies because they set a weak example, and struggled to understand the practical implications of using their own policies.

SharePoint governance is expected to remain a critical focus throughout the SharePoint world in the coming years as the user population, content size, and functional options all grow. Proper SharePoint governance is an aid to broad adoption and technical management. Without governance, SharePoint becomes unusable and unmanageable. Although the need for governance is paramount, a lack of clear understanding about the meaning of governance can stall these efforts. Finally, governance needs to be approached as an ongoing process. It has its own maturity levels. Structuring SharePoint governance for continuous evolution is the best way to ensure sustained SharePoint adoption, success, and user satisfaction.

Adoption

Adoption is another one of those really popular SharePoint buzzwords. We talk about it all the time – but it may obscure the point. The real goal of any SharePoint system should not be mere "adoption" – you can force that by making the portal home page the default for all user browsers. What really matters is user satisfaction – the ongoing use and efficacy of SharePoint to support business goals.

SharePoint 2010 can be compared to a functional "firehose", having grown from a simple tool for team documents and dashboards in 2001, to the rich multifunctional environment of SharePoint 2010. (BI! Workflow! Social computing! Data integration! Etc.) And if you can't push on a rope, as they say, you really can't push a firehose – users need to pull it in.

There are two broad classes of adoption stakeholders. Technical stakeholders seek to justify and sustain their investment of time and resources in the platform. For them, adoption is a "push" – put solutions out there and look for end users to pick them up. Business stakeholders have a different perspective. They seek results from the system, and hope that they can pull enough value from the technology to attract other users and sustain a network effect of productivity.

Keep in mind one definition of adoption – "To choose as standard or required"[31]. If adoption is a choice, not a mandate, it's about reaching mass approval, not just the satisfaction of those who mandate usage. Adoption is a conscious selection by users.

There are many signifiers and enablers to successful SharePoint adoption. Sustained, reliable uptimes are essential to capturing user confidence in the platform. Happy users with minimal complaints about support are another hallmark of well adopted systems. Another fantastic indicator of a culture that sustains adoption is measurable return on investment. If business users can point to quantitative measures of success, it helps spread the word and win over mindshare among those not yet using SharePoint. Finally, speed to market is essential. If it takes too long to get a new project or process implemented on SharePoint, users start to lose interest and look for alternatives.

There are also known roadblocks to adoption. A poorly planned architecture, with bad interface design and too man y irrelevant documents obscures all the valuable content users need from the platform. Bad governance – either too much or too little – can either drive users away or make usage patterns so chaotic that usage becomes difficult. Ironically, many users also cite the speed-to-market of SharePoint solutions as a roadblock as well. It can lead to a

---

[31] www.thefreedictionary.com

boil-the-ocean climate where SharePoint gets positioned as the answer to all business needs, and the pace of change outstrips users' ability to learn and adapt. Finally, disconnects between IT and the business can lead to the "Field of Dreams" problem. "If you **build** it they will come" only works if you stop to ask what "they" need. Uneducated guesses about user requirements turn SharePoint rollouts into social experiments instead of nimble business tools.

Good adoption practices

At KMA, we once used "Bring Your Child To Work Day" to solicit some usability feedback about our intranet from the preschool set – with both humorous and insightful results![32]. Today, we'll walk through some additional guidance – not from the playground, but from the consulting field. First, let's start with the "do's" – how to launch an effective intranet.

---

[32] See "Youngest Focus Group in SharePoint History Designs Your Intranet" at http://blogs.kma-llc.net/microknowledge/2010/04/youngest-focus-group-in-sharepoint-history-solves-your-intranet-design-needs.html

Figure 194 - A successful launch - Apollo 11 (NASA)

There's a lot you can do to help nudge adoption along. Here are some helpful techniques, honed through field work and conference surveys.

Applications - if you buy it, they will come

Use what's already out there. The SharePoint ecosystem is full of prebuilt solutions, most of which are free or low cost. For example, Microsoft's open source site, www.codeplex.com, is loaded with prebuilt solutions such as security reporting or Silverlight rich media controls. In SharePoint 2007, Microsoft provided 40 free application templates for common needs like IT Help Desk or Event Planning. Although Microsoft didn't rework these templates for 2010, the community has developed 2010-based version of the so-called "Fab 40". You can download these from http://www.techsolutions.net/SharePointSolutions.aspx

In addition, Quest Software has released a free community forum web part at www.quest.com, and Bamboo Solutions also offers a free time and weather web part at www.bamboosolutions.com. These tools help you get real web tools out to your users quickly. And there's no shortage of product releases from a broad range of ISVs to enhance SharePoint with prebuilt components.

Some successful applications for SharePoint intranets have included:

- Lunch Application – The way to the heart may be through the stomach. On many successful intranets, food is critical. (Not just during software development!) For example, one of my clients provides free lunch daily. When they moved to a SharePoint intranet, we set up an application to let all staff preorder and customize any sandwich requests. The app is considered so important it's become an explicit part of their internal SLA. They have an emotional bond to SharePoint! Other clients have used similar systems – some with InfoPath, some with custom forms, some with standard lists – to let people order breakfast, lunch, or catering from their desk or mobile device.
- Dynamic Content on Home Page – Offering a fresh cycle of new information on the home page is thought to be equally or more important to clean attractive design.
- Birthday List – another example of fun, unique and essential information that bonds users with the site
- Today @ ACME – this was a custom home page web part the summarized all the meeting room calendars for a single day, and it was also posted to a "clean web page" for ease of bookmarking on tablets and smartphones. This created a "cool factor" of the SharePoint intranet that spurred usage beyond expectations.

Assessment

- Surveys – SharePoint has its own survey tool. Use it to measure success with users and determine future needs.

- Help Desk – End user facing support staff are the first line eyes and ears of IT. They are a great source of information about how a new platform is being received, and can also be powerful advocates for – or against – change as they work with multiple user populations.
- As noted above, Sadie van Buren has published a guide to a standard SharePoint Maturity model at www.spmaturity.com. Measuring your organizational progress year over year helps spotlight areas than need relatively more attention.

Training

- Lunch and Learn – This widely used technique to attract people to events designed to foster usage-oriented learning.
- Formal Training – multiple opinions exist. Internal training is seen as being more tailored to particular corporate needs; external trainers are often more available and easier to schedule. In addition, it helps to distinguish training on the platform itself from training on customized solutions. Consultants or internal development teams are the only ones who can explain and teach users about how to use their customized solutions. But it's inefficient to expect them to also train users about general SharePoint use. Training specialists almost always can deliver standardized training on how to use SharePoint more efficiently than consultants or developers.

Marketing

- Branding/Naming – In particular when companies are launching or relaunching a SharePoint based project, it helps to brand the project with the name of the site (e.g. "I'm using 'BaseCamp'" instead of "I'm using "SharePoint".
- Marketing & Segmentation – It's important to understand that the adoption message needs to be distinguished not only for different groups of business users (power users/casual users) but also different IT constituents (developers/server

teams/analysts & PMs). For example, .NET developers and Java developers are likely to have different needs and questions about moving to the use of SharePoint.

Project Design

Set a good example! If you want an effective intranet, use a new intranet to run the project, and teach your business stakeholders how to use it to communicate. And be discerning in your use of newer Web paradigms (Facebook etc.) to engage that conversation. Why not use a vanilla SharePoint 2010 Communities site to encourage more collaborative approaches - instead of big meetings and emails?

Move quickly with rapid prototypes and sustained momentum. SharePoint lends itself to quick iterations - make sure you plan frequent small deliverables and reviews instead of waiting until everything's cooked.   Think multicourse meals!

- Departmental Approach – build success at a lower level first before tackling enterprise wide adoption. The first department is almost always IT – it's a friendly pilot, and unlikely to go awry. However, the most important group to get right is the second department, where not all the natives are friendly and first impressions of SharePoint are likely to spread through the firm. Choose that second phase group wisely – they should be influential but scaled so their goals are achievable in reasonable timeframes.
- Steering Committee (Cross-Functional) – it helps when the project is accountable to a frequently meeting team of empowered business stakeholders drawn from multiple departments, not just IT and HR.
- Move Fast – quick early successes count more than long, late successes

Support

Users need to know they can get help if they need it. Some suggestions include:

- SharePoint -> SharePoint – use a SharePoint site itself to supply support to users
- Prepare Support Teams – make sure Help Desks and customization teams are available and trained in advance to minimize the risk of failing to meet rising expectations.
- Self Service Support/Communities – some companies reports tremendous success using discussions, blogs, and wikis to help users help each other
- Team Leaders Support/Decentralized – Another approach is to decentralize support to power users or team captains in each logical group of users
- Tech Sheets – Quick one page tips or FAQs can be written and distributed to users and helps desk via email, web sites, print distribution or knowledge bases.

Launch Events

Figure out an effective marketing and launch plan. The right approach depends on your culture –it may be a series of "lunch and learn" meetings or a launch "party". It could be a site scavenger hunt, or a branded coffee cup or t shirt. It's important to understand that to launch the intranet site you need more than just an email announcement.

Many users schedule a "big event" (usually a breakfast event in the morning, sometimes a lunch, rarely an evening happy hour) the day the site "launches". In conjunction, these events often offer:

- Training
- Contests and prizes, often with a scavenger hunt
- Public awards

- Giveaways – branded coffee cups, mouse pads or wallet cards with tips and helpful information

Remember that your user population is more diverse than you may have expected. Different generations adopt technology differently. There are varying comfort levels with web technology (corporate sites vs. social networking) and platforms (PC or laptop or smartphone). Also, remember that global audiences can also be distinguished not only by different preferences for platforms or tools, but even bandwidth and site performance expectations.

Miscellaneous
- SLAs – some companies offer internal discounts or higher service levels for divisions that move to SharePoint away from more costly legacy technology
- Home Page – If the home page is enough of a gateway to needed information, some enterprises lock in the SharePoint intranet as their home page. Performance and site design can become more critical is you're forcing users to the site.
- Mandate – In some companies, adoption is as simple as corporate policy or tying individual compensation/reviews to usage.
- Viral Communications/Social Communities – hard to plan, but very effective if you can use it, especially if SharePoint based

X and Y
In the 1960s, Douglas Macgregor at the MIT Sloan School characterized individual behavior into Theory Y and Theory X. Theory Y users are self-directed, and are influence most effectively by tools like incentives, SLAs, and peer influence. On the other hand, Theory X users are externally motivated, and respond well to mandates and home page lock ins. Theory Y users like to believe they have a clear choice between a legacy platform and SharePoint, and select SharePoint by individual choice. Theory X users may need to have

their old intranet shutdown before they move to SharePoint. Either way, you have both personality types in your organization. The proper mix of techniques will account for the blend of these in your user population.

Bad adoption practices

Surprise – there's also a lot you can do to doom your SharePoint intranet project! [All names have been changed to protect the innocent!] And, for the record, failure rate percentages are completely subjective.

Figure 195 - Less than complete success

We can't fairly call these "worst" practices, but here are some bad things to avoid.

Run it as an IT project without business engagement.

The "business" hates being told what to do. Building a SharePoint site that presumes to guess at the real needs is great way to get an abandoned site. "We never asked for it, so I don't see why we should use it just because IT says so" is usually the end result. *Likelihood of project death - 90-100%.*

Migrate legacy file shares as-is

This is one of my favorites. Usually, some senior person complains they can never find anything on the "H drive". Since SharePoint offers a searchable web interface, it has to be better, right? Sure - except if you just dump all that content in without thinking, all you get is a SharePoint site with top level folders called "bobtest", "newtest", "newtest 2", and "sales1997". Same problem, in a new shiny package. *Likelihood of project death – 50%.*

Deploy hundreds of content types

Just because you can have lots of content types doesn't mean you should. Without proper training, you will only confuse people, at least, until someone else goes in and simplifies it. SharePoint is powerful, often complex. Entering at the pinnacle of complexity management is a surefire way to alienate early adopters. We've seen this multiple times, and the result is almost always the same. *Likelihood of project death – 75% (until someone new comes in to clean up the complexity.)*

Do no marketing, training or launch events.

This one is pretty simple – how do you define success? If success equals a well-used, highly-adopted site, then this virtually guarantees failure. Simply sending around an email announcing your new site doesn't cut it. People learn differently, and many folks need multiple "touches" before they feel comfortable. *Death rate – 75%*

Keep the home page out of box, unbranded, and static.
This one is debatable. If users have never seen SharePoint before, things will still look new to their eyes, so it may not be a showstopper. It tends to be more of an issue when there is internal "competition" among different solutions to your intranet needs. Also, initial projects may be constrained by experience and or/budget, so sometimes it's a necessary tradeoff. However, if nothing ever changes on the home page it's hard to establish it as a useful destination. *Project failure rate – <25%*

Assume that search will solve all data access questions.
This one seldom kills the project outright. But "I can't find anything" is one of the most common intranet complaints. Keeping pages clean and free of navigation signposts, while expecting users to know what search terms will reveal recent, relevant information is asking way too much. Users don't know what they're looking for, most of the time. *Project failure rate - <25%, buts can grow over time.*

Too much, or too little governance.
Sometimes multiple users establish multiple sites for same pools of data. As a result, no one knows where they should go, search yields numerous incompatible results, navigation is inconsistent and performance is degraded. On the other side, we've seen enterprises make it too hard to get started – in the interest of governance, they establish a 30 day waiting period, establish stringent pre-education requirements, and curtail functionality to the point that SharePoint is only a web-fronted file share – without versioned libraries, customization, apps, forms, data, blogs, wikis. Ugh. Either way, you're not balancing manageability and usability. *Project failure rate – about 50%.*

Some conclusions on adoption

As I've said, adoption and governance are closely linked. Sustained adoption requires a level of ongoing governance oversight and review. As a start, here are five things to do after your first few months on a new SharePoint rollout.

Check the search logs

Search logs are a target rich environment for information architects. No two clients will use a site the same way - but many of them use search when they can't find something. Understanding the mostly frequently searched terms and documents tells you about things not easily found. If the number one searched for document is the corporate holiday schedule, shouldn't that be prominent on your home page?

Similarly, the rest of the search history gives you a great dataset for how to build a better navigation structure, and rich tag sets. It's another way to listen to your users and give them what they want, in terms they can intuitively understand.

My Site usage

If you're rolling out My Sites, check to see how many users have updated their profiles. If you're somewhere around 30-60% you're off to a good start. However, it's common for user profiles to languish, and, if so, you may need to strengthen the message with some ongoing training.

Content growth trends

SharePoint planning usually forecasts some level of storage growth – 10-20%. Take a look at how your major content pools have grown to see if those numbers are on track. Site Collection Web Analytics provide a high-level trend chart. You should watch for high growth (suggests great adoption) as well as flat growth

Repeat rollout training

This is simple. Whatever training you helped during kickoff week should be repeated. Some users may have been unavailable. Other users may have forgotten, or are new to the company. Repeating the training not only helps users but demonstrated a level of commitment to the platform that sustains user confidence.

Re-evaluate roadmap

Be honest about what works and what doesn't. Not every solution will be perfectly used, and SharePoint is no exception. Don't be afraid to propose changes in operations and support as you gather additional information about usage and satisfaction.

Seven Deadly Sins for the SharePoint Professional

We've covered a lot of ground in this book. In closing, I'd look to revisit seven deadly sins – seven things that no SharePoint professional should allow.

Public domain, from photo-mine.net - William Howard Case, April 8, 1910.

No SQL maintenance plans

All gardens need weeding. SQL databases need tending too. Left on their own, content databases and config databases will generate runaway transaction logs. Combined with overzealous local backup retention plans, you'll quickly fill up your storage. Take a little time to understand Full Recovery vs. Simple Recovery in SQL. Or, more importantly, use a maintenance plan to backup and truncate your logs – it's not that hard.

Default names for every database

The default database name for a SharePoint content database is "WSS_Content", and if you take the defaults, all subsequent databases will take the default format **WSS_Content_[really-long-GUID]**. But down the road, during backup, restore or SQL maintenance operations you'll be constantly jumping into Central Admin to figure out which sites use "WSS_Content_abdc1234-1111-2222-878adf0e". Much better to name the databases according to a person- friendly standard – "WSS-Content-HRPortal", etc. Even if it's obvious to you, it may not be obvious to your DBA or anyone else.

No patching

Given my crazed obsession with SharePoint version numbers (see my blog!) this is not a stretch. Microsoft has made it as easy as possible to stay in sync with the latest patches, Service Packs and Cumulative Updates. Do you need to update your systems every two months? Probably not. Should you still be running the over five year old RTM version of SharePoint 2007? Definitely not.

One environment for everything

Don't build a development environment. Don't build a test environment. Just make all changes live, in production. What could ever go wrong? My favorite exchange between a consultant and a client on this topic:

Client: "We don't have a development environment, we just make our changes live."

Consultant: "No, you don't have a production environment."

One account for everything

If you don't pay attention, you may be tempted to use one master account for the SQL service, for the installation, for the farm account, for search, for content access, and for the IIS pools. Then, when you administer the site, it's always easy to work around security restrictions by handing out those account credentials to a wide group of people. Next thing you know, someone forgets the password and locks out the account. The great news is that you don't need to build a monitoring system for this alert, because everyone and I mean everyone, will get the dreaded web page that reads:

`Cannot connect to configuration database.`

So don't give out the admin accounts, and, especially, don't reuse the farm account.

Single server install with SQL Express

If you don't pay close attention on the original installation sequence, you may pick a "standalone" single server installation. You're starting with only one server for now, right? Unfortunately, you'll wind up with a server that can't be expanded, running SQL Express Edition. And limited to 4GB of content database size. Well, at least you'll avoid the next problem:

Runaway content database size

Microsoft recommends that SharePoint content databases stay below 100GB (200GB if it's the only content DB in a SharePoint 2010 site collection). But SharePoint doesn't stop you from adding more – it's a recommendation for optimal user performance. However, I've seen too many installations that grew grew grew to 250GB, 500GB or more. Plan your content database sizes in advance of critical sizes. You can add databases and site collections to create more manageable units, or use Remote Blog Storage (RBS) to pull those file of attachments out of the databases and into external storage, reducing file sizes.

Chris McNulty is a Strategic Product Manager and Evangelist for SharePoint Solutions at Quest Software. Chris is a Microsoft Certified Technology Specialist (MCTS), Microsoft Certified Systems Engineer (MCSE), and a member of the Microsoft Solutions Advocate and MVTSP programs. A frequent speaker at events around the US, Chris is the author of the "SharePoint 2010 Consultant's Handbook – Managed Metadata Service" and writes the popular KnowPoint blog at www.chrismcnulty.net/blog. Prior to Quest, Chris led the SharePoint consulting practice at KMA, a New England based Microsoft Gold Partner. He holds an MBA from the Carroll School of Management at Boston College in Investment Management and has over twenty years' experience in financial services technology with John Hancock, State Street, GMO and Santander. He lives with his wife Hayley, and his children in Milton, Massachusetts.

- **KnowPoint Blog** http://www.chrismcnulty.net/blog
- **KMA Blog** http://blogs.kma-llc.net/microknowledge
- **Quest:** http://www.sharepointforall.com
- **Twitter**: http://twitter.com/cmcnulty2000
- **LinkedIn**: http://www.linkedin.com/in/cmcnulty

About KMA

Knowledge Management Associates, LLC, is a full-service IT consulting firm established in 1995, and based in Waltham, Massachusetts. As a Microsoft Gold Partner, KMA focuses on solutions for SharePoint, SQL, .NET and Microsoft Office across a broad range of industries. Key specialties include:

- Collaboration: Portals, Communities, Internet and Content Management
- Insight: Enterprise Search and Business Intelligence
- Productivity: Forms and Office Client Customization

For more information, visit http://www.kma-llc.net

About Quest

Quest creates simple-to-use, innovative IT management software that saves time and money across physical, virtual and cloud environments. Established in 1987, Quest is a global software company offering a broad and deep selection of products that target common IT challenges.   More than 100,000 worldwide customers enjoy the simplicity of working with a single vendor who can solve so many IT management pains. Quest solutions cover databases, monitoring, data protection, user workspace management, Windows server management, and identity/access management.

Quest solutions for SharePoint simplify migration, administration, recovery, security and auditing, access management, and customization and development. Quest has the products, support and experience you need to make your SharePoint environment more efficient and manageable.   Visit Quest online at http://www.quest.com.

More information from Microsoft

- Microsoft – http://sharepoint.microsoft.com
- SharePoint Product Team – http://blogs.msdn.com/sharepoint
- TechNet – http://technet.microsoft.com/sharepoint
- MSDN – http://msdn.microsoft.com/sharepoint

Sources and Acknowledgments

Much of the material here is based on concepts originally presented at Microsoft's Ignite 2010 sessions, and at SharePoint Conference 2009. David Frette has done a lot of work on performance testing term store load times; his web site at http://davidfrette.wordpress.com/ was a great source of information on how to use PowerShell against MMS. MSDN's Code Gallery contains a full version of the Taxonomy Web Part at http://code.msdn.microsoft.com/socialstatswebpart/.   Sadie Van Buren has contributed extensively to my presentation style and content, especially on Business Intelligence. Also, my section on SharePoint governance, and the SharePoint community as a whole, owe a lot to Sadie and her SharePoint Maturity Model at www.spmaturity.com.

13481281R00213

Made in the USA
Charleston, SC
13 July 2012